# LOTUS
## ALL THE CARS
# Anthony Pritchard

**Aston Publications**

Lotus: All the Cars
by Anthony Pritchard

Published in 1990 by
Aston Publications Limited
Bourne End House, Harvest Hill
Bourne End, Bucks, SL8 5JJ

ISBN 0 946627 62 2

Designed by Chris Hand

Printed in Hong Kong

Sole distributors to the UK book trade
Springfield Books Limited
Norman Road, Denby Dale
Huddersfield
West Yorkshire, HD8 8TH

Sole distributors in the United States
Motorbooks International
729 Prospect Avenue, Osceola
Wisconsin 54020
United States

# Contents

# Author's Note

I was first introduced to Colin Chapman at the Crystal Palace in 1954, when he was racing the MG-powered Mark 8 sports-racing cars and struggling to achieve real success. As a young enthusiast, I was already a Chapman and Lotus supporter; that meeting sealed my enthusiasm for both and I have felt that way ever since. I also met a number of Chapman's earliest supporters, including Tony McCusker, a school teacher and AC enthusiast, whom I encountered at an AC Owners' Club driving test meeting in 1954. AC was – and has always remained – one of my special interests.

Colin Chapman was one of the most intelligent design engineers ever to involve himself in motor sport, but he was also fiercely ambitious, possessed remarkable business acumen and was a dedicated motor sport enthusiast. There was, of course, a dark side to his character that alienated many friends and associates over the years, but only became public knowledge, as opposed to paddock gossip, because of the de Lorean enquiry.

Chapman was great, not only because of what he achieved, but because he achieved so much and for much of his career in motor sport on such limited finances. It was only in later years, with the advent of tobacco sponsorship in motor racing (of which Lotus and John Player were pioneers), that the purse strings eased.

Much Lotus design work was conceived by Chapman and his ideas were interpreted by Lotus design staff; but all Lotus designs during Chapman's lifetime bore his distinctive stamp. This book is intended, for the first time, to put together and illustrated account of all Lotus models from the first specials to today's production cars built by Lotus Cars, now a subsidiary of General Motors, and the latest Formula 1 cars built by the still independent Team Lotus.

Obviously some of the early photographs are now rather 'hackneyed', because of the difficulty of finding new illlustrations of the early cars, but many of the later photographs are completely new.

# Introduction

Although this book is primarily about Lotus cars and not about the company, it is necessary to give a brief run-down of the organization of Lotus to fully appreciate the way that the cars developed.

Lotus Engineering Company was formed on 1 January, 1952, as a partnership between Colin Chapman and Michael Allen. Following the destruction of the Mark 6 prototype in 1952, the partnership was dissolved and its place was taken by Lotus Engineering Company, initially the trading name of Colin Chapman, but by February 1953 this had become a limited company known as Lotus Engineering Company Limited with Colin Chapman and Hazel Williams (later Chapman) as directors. In 1954 Colin Chapman formed Team Lotus as the racing organization, originally run by enthusiasts on an amateur basis, but rapidly formulated into a professional team.

During these years Lotus was based in premises at Tottenham Lane, Hornsey, on land owned by Colin Chapman's father. Lotus Cars Limited, which was to become responsible for the production of the Elite, and Lotus Components Limited, which would construct the competition cars, together with the Lotus Seven, were formed in 1959 to constitute the Lotus Group of Companies when in June of that year Lotus moved to a new purpose-built factory at Cheshunt in Hertfordshire.

Lotus' expansion was such that in 1967 the Company again moved to new premises on the former airfield at Hethel in Norfolk. In September 1968 Lotus was floated as a public company. The result was that Group Lotus Car Companies Limited became a holding company with effect from 6 January, 1969, and with subsidiaries including Lotus Cars, Lotus Cars (Service), Lotus Cars (Sales) and Lotus Components. Team Lotus was retained by Chapman, becoming in due course Team Lotus International

Jim Clark and Chapman had a very close relationship that enabled Lotus to become the most successful Grand Prix entrant. Clark's death in an insignificant Formula 2 was a blow from which Chapman never fully recovered.

Colin Chapman at the Brazilian Grand Prix in 1973 with
Ronnie Peterson and Peter Warr. *(Nigel Snowdon)*

Limited, and has always remained under family
control. At the beginning of 1971 the name of
Lotus Components Limited was changed to
Lotus Racing Limited and this company
concentrated in the main on the manufacture of
competition cars. Lotus Racing was headed by
Mike Warner, who had been an original
employee, left to set up his own company and
rejoined the Lotus Group in 1968.

Lotus' financial fortunes were often very
shaky and towards the end of 1970 Warner was
informed that he would have to cut back on staff
and reduce his company's overheads. In April
1971 Warner resigned from Lotus Racing,
existing orders were fulfilled and thereafter the
production of Lotus racing cars for sale to the
public ceased.

In 1977 Team Lotus acquired Ketteringham
Hall, not only as a base for Team Lotus, but also
as a Research and Development Centre. This
was a very large and dilapidated country house,
which was totally refurbished, having served as
Group Headquarters for US 8th Air Force
during the war and subsequently as a boarding
school. In 1977 the Lotus Group entered into an
arrangement with American Express, who
became the Group's principal bankers and took
an option to buy up to 10 per cent of the share
capital. The following year Lotus became
involved in the design and development of the
De Lorean car, which was not only to be
financially lucrative, but also resulted in
financial scandal and delays in development of
Lotus' road cars.

Lotus has always distributed cars to the
United States through distributors, but in 1975
Lotus Cars of America was organized. It proved
a financial disaster and this arrangement with
one American distributor only was terminated
in 1979. The company then entered into an
agreement with Rolls-Royce for the distribution
of cars by them in the United States; once again
financial disaster followed, no cars were
exported to the United States in 1981 and 1982
and it was not till late 1982 that a new Lotus
distribution company, Lotus Performance Cars
LP, was set up.

Colin Chapman suffered a fatal heart attack
on 16 December, 1982, and this resulted in
major problems in the organization of both the
Lotus Group and Team Lotus. In 1981 it had
been announced that Lotus Cars and Toyota
Motors would be co-operating on a long-term
basis in engineering, manufacturing and other
areas. Toyota took a shareholding in Lotus.
Following Chapman's death Lotus was under
pressure because of the withdrawal of the
American Express finance, David Wickens of
British Car Auctions became Chairman and it
seemed likely that Toyota would take over the
company. However, this did not happen and in
1986 General Motors bought out the shareholders
of the public company.

Team Lotus International Limited continues
to run from Ketteringham Hall as a private
company, with the shares held by Hazel Chapman
and the Chapman family. At this point it would
be convenient to indicate the different names
under which Team Lotus has competed in
Formula 1:

| | |
|---|---|
| Gold Leaf Team Lotus | 1968–1971 |
| John Player Team Lotus | 1972–1978 |
| Martini Team Lotus | 1979 |
| Essex Team Lotus | 1980 |
| John Player Team Lotus | 1981–1986 |
| Camel Team Lotus | 1987–1990 |

In addition occasional entries were made
under the name World Wide Racing in 1981 and
1982, when for political reasons Team Lotus did
not wish to make and entry in their own name.

A number of other teams have also been
allowed to use the Team Lotus name when
running a works team on behalf of the works,
including Ron Harris and Ian Walker.

# Mark 1

## *Trials Special, 1948*

Based on a 1930 Austin 7 saloon with fabric bodywork and originally registered PK 3493, this was Colin Chapman's first Lotus. The original chassis was retained with the main members boxed and the rear axle turned upside down (so that the suspension links were now at the top, thus flattening the springs and eliminating oversteer). The overhauled 747cc engine had a higher than standard compression ratio, double valve springs, a specially made inlet manifold and Ford downdraught carburettor. The new body featured a stressed framework with three bulkheads and was constructed from alloy bonded plywood; there was room for two passengers (or ballast) in the back. The wings were attached by wood screws and rawlplugs so that in the rough and tumble of a trial they would simply detach and would hopefully remain undamaged. The car, named the 'Lotus' as Chapman wanted to avoid the usual 'Austin Special', was characterized by a radiator cowling made from copper sheet and rather aping that of Rolls-Royce, and was re-registered OX 9292.

After competing in two trials early in 1948, Chapman modified the Lotus by fitting Ford disc wheels at the rear and by adopting independent front suspension; the front beam axle was split and pivoted in the centre. Competition appearances were limited because of Chapman's preoccupation with his University degree finals. Although it was used competitively only once more, Chapman did not dispose of the Mark 1 until late 1950.

The original Lotus Mark 1 trials special built in 1948.

# Mark 2

*Trials and Racing Special, 1949*

After graduating, Chapman joined the Royal Air Force, and it was during this period that the Mark 2 was conceived as a Trials car, which steadily progressed through 1949. The chassis was again the Austin 7, with Ford front axle, Austin 7 rear axle, Ford 1172cc side-valve engine only very lightly modified and the Austin 7 4-speed gearbox. The body was broadly similar to that of the Mark 1 but more compact and with a neat nose cowling behind which the headlamps swivelled with the wheels.

Throughout 1950 Chapman competed with the Mark 2 mainly in Trials, but also competing in two Speed Trials, two race meetings, two rallies and Great Auclum hill climb. In October 1950 Chapman sold the Mark 2 to Mike Lawson, in whose hands it enjoyed a very successful Trials record.

Colin Chapman with the Mark 2 competing in the Maidstone and Mid-Kent MC Speed Trial at Gravesend Aerodrome on 7 May, 1950. Chapman took second place in his class. The Mark 2 was used in virtually every form of competition. *(Guy Griffiths)*

The Mark 2 was sold to Mike Lawson, who used it in the main in its original role, as a trials car. Here Lawson is seen competing in the Lancia CC Bramley Rally in March 1951. *(Guy Griffiths)*

# Mark 3

*750 Formula Cars, 1951–2*

For 1951 Colin Chapman determined to build a car to comply with the 750 Formula of the 750 Motor Club, for Austin 7-based cars. Early in the construction of his new car he met Michael and Nigel Allen, who had excellent workshop facilities, and they put together a plan whereby they would build three of these cars, with Chapman's to be finished first and the other two later in 1951. In fact, only Chapman's original Mark 3 was completed. The Austin 7 chassis had the wheelbase shortened to 81 inches with an extension to the rear which mounted the shock absorber struts and an Austin 7 fuel tank. This tank was partially cut away to clear the rear axle casing. At the front Chapman used a Ford 8 split axle with a transverse spring above it, providing independent front suspension. At the rear the Austin 7 axle was used, with the rear springs set flat. The engine was originally a two-bearing unit, but very early on, because of big-end problems, a three-bearing engine was substituted. This engine was slightly over-bored. There were larger inlet valves and smaller than standard exhaust valves, a Scintilla Vertex magneto was fitted, driven from the dynamo. The most important change made by Chapman was that he 'de-siamezed' the usual two-port Austin block by opening up the inlet ports and building up special manifolds from welded sheet steel with a vertical strip in the centre of the manifold extending into the ports. A Stromberg twin-choke downdraught carburettor was fitted. The result was as if the Austin had a twin-carburettor induction system. Transmission was by an Austin 7 'Nippy' gearbox. A very stark two-seater body was fitted, with cycle wings and the headlamps let into the bodywork above the nose air intake.

During the 1951 season Chapman scored a remarkable run of successes with the Mark 3, which was also driven during the year by Michael and Nigel Allen. So successful was the Mark 3 that the 750 Motor Club banned Chapman's modification to the porting by prohibiting the dividing of the siamezed inlet ports.

Although by the end of the 1951 season, Chapman had moved on to the development of the Mark 6, a second 750 Formula car designated the Mark 3B was completed for Adam Currie. This car was basically very similar to Chapman's own car, but the bodywork was to a rather more professional standard and instead of their being a 'schnorkel' pipe over the carburettor, there was a bulge round this. This car was also distinguished by its very smart black paintwork. Currie scored a number of successes during 1952, but then emigrated.

Chapman at the wheel of the Austin-powered 750 Formula Mark 3 at The Eight Clubs meeting at Silverstone in June 1951. The car ran on three cylinders and even in this form built up an enormous lead before the crankshaft broke. *(Guy Griffiths)*

# Mark 4

*Trials Car, 1952*

After Chapman received an order from Mike Lawson for a new trials car, to be designated the Mark 4, he entered into a partnership agreement with Michael Allen, and from 1 January, 1952, they traded as the Lotus Engineering Company.

The Mark 4 again incorporated a boxed Austin 7 chassis, with a somewhat roomier body than that fitted to the Mark 2. Although the car followed the design of the Mark 2 in many details, the front transverse spring and axle pivoted at a central point, giving a front lock similar to that of a tractor, and ideal for use on the more difficult sections of a trials course. Once again the 1172cc Ford side-valve engine was used, with a Ford 8 gearbox and, at the rear, the familiar Austin 7 axle. Chapman incorporated in the design hinging cycle-type front wings which could be tilted inwards so as to reduce the width of the car when the driver was faced with a very narrow section. Although the car was originally designed so that Lawson could use it on the road as well as for trials, as trials became more and more specialist, so

The Mark 4 was built for Mike Lawson specifically as a trials car. Lawson is seen competing in the 1953 London MC Autocross. In its original form the Mark 4 had featured twin headlamps mounted behind a cowling.

modifications were made to the car. The original single carburettor was soon changed for a twin-choke carburettor and Lawson quickly abandoned the novel front suspension arrangement in favour of a conventional Ford axle. Lawson used the car regularly in competitions until the end of 1954, when the specialized and changing conditions of trials forced him to move on.

# Mark 5

*Designation intended for a 750 Formula car to be capable of 100 mph, but never built.*

# Mark 6

*Sports Car, 1952–5*

For Chapman the design and construction of the Mark 6 was a major step forward, and one made with Michael Allen, who was working for the newly formed Lotus Engineering Company on a full-time basis. The Lotus Engineering Company was the partnership of Chapman and Allen, which occupied premises in Tottenham Lane, Hornsey, part of property owned by Colin Chapman's father.

The new car was intended for production and featured a multi-tubular space-frame chassis, weighing 55 lb without fittings and 90 lb with the mounting brackets and stressed panels. At the front Chapman had retained swing-axle suspension, located by radius rods and with inclined coil spring/damper units. At the rear Chapman used a Ford rigid axle, located by a Panhard rod and torque tube and suspended on coil spring/damper units. With the Mark 6 Lotus started a long liaison with Williams & Pritchard, bodybuilders of Edmonton, who not only built the body of the Mark 6 but took responsibility for the stressed components incorporated in the chassis.

Chapman had decided that the power unit for the new Mark 6 should be the 1508cc Ford Consul engine, but no one could supply him with one, so he went round Ford dealers buying spare parts until he had sufficient components to build up his own engine. The stroke was shortened so as to bring the engine within the 1500cc category and it was fitted with twin SU carburettors. There was a Ford 3-speed gearbox which incorporated close-ratio gears manufactured by Buckler, who were themselves long-standing constructors of sports cars supplied in component and kit form to enthusiasts.

This first Mark 6 was entered at the MG Car Club race meeting at Silverstone on 5 July, 1952, where two second places were taken. It

Hazel Williams (later Chapman) with the first Mark 6 before the start of the Ladies' race at the Aston Martin OC meeting at Silverstone in July 1952. Chapman is centre behind the car with Nigel Allen (apparently disinterested!) to his left. Hazel finished third. *(Guy Griffiths)*

Perhaps the most successful of all Mark 6 drivers was Peter Gammon who scored a whole string of successes in 1954 with his MG-powered car. Here he is seen at Goodwood at the BARC meeting at the end of March 1954. *(LAT)*

ran in a number of other events, but after the Boreham meeting in August it was wrecked in a road accident while Nigel Allen was at the wheel, when another car pulled out in front of him from a side turning. Chapman and Allen were unable to continue racing for financial reasons and at the end of the year Allen withdrew from the Lotus business. Chapman decided that he would re-form Lotus Engineering as a limited company, with himself and his fiancée, Hazel Williams, as Directors and he laid down the components to build eight production Mark 6 cars.

One of the first cars was built by Mike Costin, who became a member of the Lotus organization, and his car, registered 1161 H and powered by a Ford side-valve engine reduced in capacity to 1099cc, performed remarkably throughout the year. Other cars were built up from components by Nigel Allen, P. A. Desoutter, whose car was raced in 1172 Formula events organized by the 750 Motor Club for side-valve Ford-powered cars, Peter Gammon (racing an MG TD, who did not in

Brighton furrier Mike Anthony, who competed as a member of Team Lotus, at the wheel of his MG-powered Mark 6 at Prescott hill climb in May 1954. He won the 1500cc Sports Car class and set a new class record. *(T. C. March)*

fact have his Mark 6 completed for racing until 1954, when it was powered by his engine from the TD) and Fred Hill, who raced with great success a car known as the 'Empire Special' and powered by a 746cc supercharged MG engine.

Lotus progress was such that by 1954 the Mark 6 was in full production and while Chapman himself had moved on to the new Mark 8 car, the Mark 6 was being raced with considerable success. Brighton furrier Mike Anthony,whose car was also powered by the 1496cc MG XPAG engine, raced his car as part of Team Lotus, Chapman's newly formed amateur racing team, and both he and Gammon enjoyed substantial success. Gammon defeated Chapman with the Mark 8 on several occasions, took third place in the British Empire Trophy Race at Oulton Park in early 1954, and in the 1500cc Sports Car race at the British Grand Prix Meeting at Silverstone in July he finished second to Chapman with the Mark 8 and defeated the works Porsche of Hans Herrmann.

Quite a variety of engines were used to power these cars in addition to Fords and MGs, and among the more interesting variants were Bill Perkins's with a 2-litre BMW engine, Fred Marriott, who raced a car with a Coventry Climax FWA 1098cc engine, and John Harris, who had a similar car but with a de Dion rear axle.

The Mark 6 dominated the 1172 Formula of the 750 Motor Club for two years and in 1956 John Lawry won the 1200cc class of the Autosport Production Sports Car Championship with his Mark 6. Production of the Mark 6 ceased at the end of 1955 by when approximately 100 cars had been completed.

### Specification (1953):
ENGINE: Ford side-valve 4-cylinder 1099cc (61.5 x 92.5mm) developing 40 bhp at 6000 rpm.
GEARBOX: Ford 3-speed.
CHASSIS: multi-tubular space-frame.
FRONT SUSPENSION: swing-axles and coil spring/damper units.
REAR SUSPENSION: Ford rigid axle suspended on coil spring/damper units.
WHEELBASE: 7ft 3.5in.
FRONT TRACK: 4ft 1in.
REAR TRACK: 3ft 9in.
WEIGHT: 8.5 cwt (kerb weight).

Peter Gammon with his MG-powered Mark 6 on his way to third place in the 1500cc Sports Car race at the Grand Prix meeting at Silverstone in 1954. *(T. C. March)*

# Mark 7 (unofficial designation)

## *Sports-Racing Car, 1952–3*

The first Mark 7 was the result of the Clairmonte brothers asking Chapman whether he would design for them a Formula 2 car. The brothers possessed a 2-litre ERA engine which they intended running in unsupercharged form and the design created by Chapman to house this engine was a space-frame, with at the front double wishbone suspension and at the rear a de Dion axle.

Apparently, and it may be apocryphal, because no one knows any longer, the ERA engine was effectively destroyed during testing,

so when the new single-seater was ready for delivery, the Clairmontes merely took delivery of the body-chassis unit. Eventually the car was completed by the Clairmontes as a sports car with two-seater bodywork, cycle wings and, in place of the original ERA unit, a Lea-Francis 1960cc engine which may or may not have been Connaught-modified but was near enough to Connaught standard. Painted black, it was raced extensively by them in Club events during 1953–4 and achieved more than a fair measure of success. So far as Chapman was concerned, it never was a Lotus, just an outside commission, and so he gave it no designation as such, just as no numbering was allotted to his work for BRM and Vanwall.

The Clairmonte Special in the paddock at the MG CC meeting at Silverstone in July 1953. The author remembers its high standard of finish and that it was both very quick and exceptionally noisy. *(Guy Griffiths)*

# Seven

*Production Sports Car, 1957–73*

So far as Colin Chapman was concerned, the original Seven had been deleted from the numbering sequence once it became the Clairmonte Special, and he was free to use the number again for the long-planned replacement to the Mark 6. While Chapman was planning the Elite as an advanced and sophisticated GT, the Seven, as a basic, rudimentary, sports car, was to both complement and contrast with the Elite in the range. In all there were four basic models of the Seven built between 1957 and 1973, when the design rights were sold to Caterham Cars, who have continued to build derivations of the original design as the Caterham Seven.

## Series 1

From the Mark 6, Lotus chassis had progressively evolved so that the space-frame used for the Seven was a direct descendant of that used for the Mark 6, but was also a simplified version of the Eleven with fewer tubes but additional stiffening provided by riveting the undertray transmission tunnel, body sides and rear body panel to the frame. Frame construction was mainly from 1in and 3/4in round and square-section tubing and the chassis were built for Lotus by Arch Motors. At the front, suspension was basically the same as for the 12 Formula 2 car and the Elite, by double wishbones and coil spring/damper units, while at the rear there was rigid axle (normally the Standard Ten) located by trailing arms and suspended on coil spring/damper units. There was Burman worm-and-nut steering (later replaced by Elite rack-and-pinion) and 8in drum brakes were fitted front and rear. As can be seen from the photographs, the body of the Seven manufactured in alloy by Williams & Pritchard, could hardly have been simpler or starker, and was evolved from that of the Mark 6, but was less curved at the rear, with the engine cover held in place by four clips and with Dzus fasteners used to hold in place the nose section and instrument panel.

Initially production commenced at Hornsey, but was transferred to Cheshunt with the opening of the new factory in 1959. No precise production figures for the Series 1 are available,

D. C. Frost with his Lotus Seven Series 1 at a combined Jaguar and Lotus Club meeting at Brands Hatch in April 1964. The Seven carried on the concept and spirit of the Mark 6 in production form. *(Guy Griffiths)*

but according to Ortenburger (*Legend of the Lotus Seven*, 1981), the best guess is 242. The Series 1 was built in the following forms (the prices quoted are for the cars in kit form):

**Seven F:** The basic car with Ford 100E side-valve 1172cc 40 bhp engine and Ford 3-speed gearbox. The price was £587.

**Seven 7:** The export version as above, but engine fitted with twin SU carburettors, four-branch exhaust and raised compression ratio. A tachometer and spare tyre (not on the home version) were included as standard.

**Super Seven (Seven C):** Initially Climax-powered cars were sold only to favoured customers, but because of demand this model became generally available. The production version was fitted with the Coventry Climax FWA 1097cc engine in 75 bhp form and a BMC 4-speed gearbox. Wire wheels replaced the pressed steel of the more basic models. At £700 it was a steal.

**Seven A:** The basic model but with BMC 948cc push-rod overhead valve engine and 4-speed gearbox substituted. The price was £611.

**Seven A America:** Conceived for the United States market, this model was as for the Series A, except that it incorporated glass-fibre wings, hood, fabric doors, carpets, tachometer, fan and spare tyre in the price of $US 2897.

## Series 2

In June 1960 Lotus introduced the Series 2 car, which, in concept, differed little, apart from what was claimed to be a redesigned chassis, but in reality was a simpler (and weaker) variant of its predecessor. Chassis breakages were frequent, especially when more powerful engines were fitted for competition work. Production of the Series 2 between 1960 and 1968 amounted to approximately 1350 cars. The various models were as follows:

**Seven F:** The familiar formula of the Ford 100E 1172cc sidevalve engine and 3-speed gearbox. The price in 1961 was a rockbottom £399.

**Seven A:** The BMC-powered version with 948cc or 1098cc A-series engine with either single or twin SU carburettors, a four-branch exhaust, power output between 37 and 55 bhp and a BMC 4-speed gearbox as used in the Austin-Healey Sprite.

**Seven A America:** As Seven A above, but the United States export version with minor changes.

**Basic Seven:** Introduced in 1961, this version was powered by the 997cc Ford Anglia push-rod 105E engine, fitted with either twin SU carburettors or a single Weber, and had a power output of 50 bhp. Transmission was by a 4-speed Ford Anglia gearbox. The price in kit form was £499.

**Super Seven:** Also introduced in 1961, this version featured the 1340cc push-rod ohv engine, as used in the Ford Classic, modified by the fitting of a Cosworth head, twin Weber carburettors and a four-branch exhaust. The power output was 85 bhp and a Ford Classic 4-speed gearbox was fitted. The price was £599.

**SCCA Cosworth:** A very limited production version with the 1340cc Ford 109E engine built for Sports Car Club of America competitions.

**Super Seven 1500:** Introduced in 1962, this model used the Ford Cortina 116E engine with five-bearing crankshaft, single Weber carburettor and a power output of 66 bhp. A Ford Cortina gearbox and front Girling disc brakes were included in the specification. The price of £585 included a tonneau cover and fabric doors.

**Cosworth Super Seven 1500:** A version with Cortina 116E engine modified by Cosworth (twin Webers, high-lift camshaft, four-branch exhaust, 95 bhp).

**7/20:** Cheshunt-built 'special' based on crashed Series 1 in 1962, for owner Keith Hamblin. Modified by project engineer Hugh Haskell with the approval of Colin Chapman, the space-frame closely resembled that of the Eleven. There was independent rear suspension, Girling disc brakes (inboard at the rear) and the engine was a Cosworth-modified Ford 105E Anglia 997cc developing 87 bhp at 7200 rpm. The car was

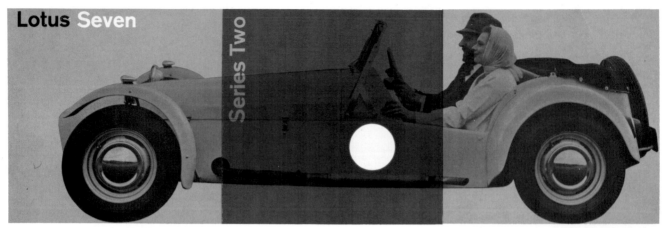

Sales catalogue for the Seven Series 2 issued by Lotus Components Ltd. This catalogue is circa 1964.

The Seven Series 3 was a purely interim car built only between 1968 and 1970. It was this model in improved form that re-entered production as the Caterham Seven.

A.C.B.Chapman, B.Sc

very successful in the hands of a number of drivers (including Colin Chapman, who drove it in the 1962 750 Motor Club Six Hours relay race at Silverstone), and four further examples were built, all based on the Series 2 car.

### 'Three-Seven': See 37, Page 93

*Series 3*

Evolved by Lotus Components, the Series 3 built from 1968 to 1970 was an only slightly modified version of the Series 2, incorporating the wider-track Ford Escort rear axle, disc brakes at the front, Triumph Herald rack-and-pinion steering, new dashboard, larger 8-gal fuel tank, seat belts and, later during the production run, a strengthened rear chassis. Later Series 2 cars and Series 3 cars were marketed solely through Caterham Car Sales. Total production amounted to about 350 cars and the Series 3 was marketed in the following forms:

**Economy:** Ford 225E Escort GT 1300cc engine developing 68 bhp and Ford Cortina 116E 4-speed gearbox.

**Standard:** Ford 225E engine in 1600cc form, with cross-flow cylinder head, four-branch exhaust system and twin-choke Weber carburettor developing 84 bhp. Gearbox as above. The price was £775.

**Seven SS (Super Seven Twin Cam):** Lotus 1600cc twin-cam engine in 90 bhp form or could be powered by a Holbay-modified engine with two twin-choke Weber carburettors and developing 125 bhp. The price for the basic model was £1250.

**Seven S:** Displayed at the 1969 Racing Car Show and built by Lotus Components, this was a very up-market version of the Series 3, fully and luxuriously upholstered and finished, with Holbay-modified 1600cc Ford engine developing 120 bhp at 6200 rpm. The price quoted in assembled form was £1600 and a number were made at Hethel to order.

**Seven X:** Built for private owner Tim Goss in early 1970, this chassis featured a chassis similar to that used on the Series 4 with independent rear suspension, outboard disc brakes and Holbay-tuned Ford 1600cc engine. It won the 1970 Clubman's Championship.

The glass-fibre-bodied Seven Series 4 built between 1970 and 1973 was aimed at a very different market from its predecessors and was not a commercial success.

## Series 4 (Lotus 60)

All previous Sevens had been intended for competition at Club level as well as road use, but the Series 4 was conceived as a much less sporting car intended to compete with less worthy rivals in the then current vogue for fun cars.

The Series 4 featured a new, more traditional, ladder-type, chassis constructed from round- and square-section tubing and with sheet steel front suspension bay, scuttle and side panelling. The front suspension, derived from that of the Lotus Europa, was by double wishbones and coil spring/damper units, while at the rear there was the familiar Ford Escort axle suspended on coil spring/damper units and located by leading and trailing arms on an A-bracket. Once again there was rack-and-pinion steering and (slightly smaller, 8.5in) disc brakes at the front.

For this model Lotus adopted thoroughly nasty glass-fibre bodywork of angular lines and moulded in four sections. A front-hinged bonnet (on which the headlamps were mounted) was fitted. The combination of the less rigid chassis of the Series 4 and the separate body resulted in excessive chassis flexing and did little for the handling. Between 1970 and 1973 about 1000 of these cars were built in the same forms as the Series 3, but the twin-cam was no longer known as the 'Super Seven'. On the introduction of the Series 4 in 1970 the Standard 1600cc model was priced at £895 and the Twin Cam at £995.

Another two dealers, in addition to Caterham Car Sales, were appointed to sell the Series 4, but the model was doomed to failure. Sales never reached the expected level, Lotus Components became Lotus Racing, Lotus Racing closed, Lotus Cars took over production, and the imposition of Value Added Tax (which applied to kit cars whereas Purchase Tax applied only to completed cars) was the final straw.

Production ceased early in 1973 and in May of that year Caterham Car Sales purchased all the available jigs, moulds and parts from Lotus Cars and continued production of the Series 4 as the Caterham Seven for about a year. In 1974 Caterham threw out the Series 4 and started production of the Caterham Super Seven, an updated version of the Series 3, which was preferred by enthusiasts and this remains in production today.

# Mark 8

*Sports-Racing Car, 1954*

For 1954 Chapman conceived the Mark 8 sports-racing car and it proved to be, as he had planned, a major advance in design and for his small company. In many respects the chassis represented a development of the Mark 6. There was, however, a new fully triangulated space-frame constructed in 1¼in. 20- and 18-gauge tubing. In essence it consisted of two sections, either side of a central bulkhead. The front section was triangular in plan and the rear section triangular in side elevation. At the front a triangular frame of sheet steel with the base set across the top chassis members and the top pierced by the upper chassis members located the front swing-axle suspension and took the front suspension loads. The front engine mounting consisted of a tubular pyramid of four ⅝in wall steel tubes. Another secondary mounting at the rear took out rear suspension loads. This chassis has been described as the 'most nearly perfect sports car chassis yet made' by Michael Costin and David Phipps (*Racing and Sports Car Chassis Design*, B. T. Batsford, 1961), but it was decidedly lacking in practicality. Before the

engine could be removed from the chassis even the cylinder head had to be detached, and removal of the engine took 12 hours and 24 were required to re-install it. As mentioned, at the front the familiar Chapman swing-axle suspension with coil spring/damper units was retained, whilst at the rear there was a de Dion axle, with a transverse coil spring and Armstrong piston-type dampers.

The power unit on the first car was a 1467cc unit built up from MG and Morris components, with a Laystall-Lucas light alloy cylinder head, twin SU carburettors and a claimed power output of 85 bhp at 6200 rpm. Transmission was by a 4-speed MG gearbox. Lockheed hydraulic brakes with Al-fin drums were mounted outboard at the front and inboard at the rear.

The body was the work of Frank Costin, at that time still an aerodynamicist with the de Havilland Aircraft Company, and resulted from a great deal of aerodynamic research. It was built by Williams & Pritchard, who built most Lotus bodies in the 1950s. There was a very low nose-line, twin tail-fins, fairings over the rear wheels, a full-length undertray with ducts for the rear brakes and there were no headlamps in the wings; these were folded away into the engine bay, and to erect them it was necessary to

Colin Chapman with the Mark 8-MG on his way to a win at Silverstone in the 1500cc Sports car race on the day of the British Grand Prix. Apart from the skinny tyres, the car shows signs of an already long season's racing with a dent in the right front wing, tatty paintwork and it badly needs a wash. *(T. C. March)*

remove the engine cover secured by Dzus fasteners. A metal tonneau fitted over the passenger seat and there was a small perspex screen around the cockpit. On the first car, raced by Chapman and registered SAR 5, only the front section of the body was removable and the remainder was riveted to the sheet alloy support. On the small number of production cars that were built accessibility was greatly improved.

The Mark 8 first appeared at the British Empire Trophy at Oulton Park in April 1984, when it was still unpainted. It crashed on the way to the circuit, was extensively rebuilt and, after practising in a special session, Chapman started at the back of the grid, but retired in his heat because of a blown cylinder head gasket. After another failure at Goodwood on Easter Monday, Chapman won the 1500 class of the Sports Car race at Silverstone in May and then entered the car in the Eifelrennen at the Nürburgring. Because of Chapman's inexperience, the car was driven by Erwin Bauer, who finished fourth. Chapman crashed at the inaugural meeting at Aintree at the end of May, but the car was ready to race again by the Whitsun Goodwood meeting just over a week later. He won the 1500 class of the Sports Car race. He subsequently scored a win at the Crystal Palace, finished second to Peter Gammon with the Mark 6-MG at Brands Hatch, and won the 1500cc Sports Car race at Silverstone, defeating the works Porsche 550 of Hans Herrmann.

Another win followed in the 1500cc Sports Car race at Fairwood near Swansea, but the engine put a rod through the crankcase in the Unlimited Sports Car race. Even so, by the following weekend Chapman, over-ambitious as always, was ready to compete again at the Nürburgring and planned to return to England to compete in two British events on the August Bank Holiday Monday. At the German race there were two new Mark 8s for private owners Dan Margulies and Nigel Allen. All three cars retired and Chapman was eliminated by a broken de Dion tube. On the Monday Chapman finished fourth in his heat at Brands Hatch, drove to the Crystal Palace, and retired on the second lap of the race there. He returned to Brands Hatch, where he then drove Nigel Allen's Mark 8 in the final of the Sports Car race, but again retired with engine trouble.

Later in the season Chapman finished third in the Sports Car race at Castle Combe behind Salvadori (Maserati) and Scott-Brown (Lister-Bristol) and he crashed in the Tourist Trophy on the Dundrod circuit, where he was co-driving with Mike Costin. Subsequently he was sixth and first 1500cc finisher in a sports car race at the Crystal Palace, took second place to McAlpine's Connaught at Aintree and collided with Scott-Brown's Lister at Snetterton.

Private owners who took delivery of Mark 8s in addition to those mentioned above were John Coombs, who transferred the engine from his Connaught to the Lotus and took fourth place in the 1500cc Sports Car race at Silverstone in July as well as a number of other successes; Dickie Steed (who was the first to fit a Coventry Climax FWA engine into a Lotus), Brian Naylor and Tip Cunane. In addition a few cars were exported to the United States.

John Bolster road-tested the works Mark 8 for *Autosport* in November and recorded a maximum speed of 121.5 mph, 0–60 mph in eight seconds, 0–100 mph in 23.8 seconds and the standing quarter-mile in 15.5 seconds. Fuel consumption was estimated at 30 miles per gallon.

The only really successful Mark 8 was Chapman's Team Lotus car, and this was rapidly superseded by new cars for 1955. At the start of 1954 Chapman had set up Team Lotus as an independent amateur-supported racing team to separate it from the commercial activities of Lotus Engineering Limited. It was not until the end of 1954 that Colin Chapman and Mike Costin gave up full-time work to concentrate on the company.

## Specification:

ENGINE: MG/Morris 1467cc.
GEARBOX: MG 4-speed.
CHASSIS: multi-tubular space-frame.
FRONT SUSPENSION: swing-axles and coil spring/damper units.
REAR SUSPENSION: de Dion axle, transverse coil spring and piston-type dampers.
WHEELBASE: 7ft 3.5in.
FRONT TRACK: 4ft 0.5in.
REAR TRACK: 3ft 11.5in.
OVERALL LENGTH: 13ft 8in.
WEIGHT: 10.25 cwt.

# Mark 9

## Sports-Racing Car, 1955

For 1955 Chapman and his team produced an improved version of the Mark 8, with a chassis of lower weight, generally more compact because of the use of smaller-section tubing and with a revised de Dion rear layout incorporating stronger hubs. Costin had revised the bodywork, which was now shorter, but with higher tail-fins, reshaped nose to improve airflow to the radiator and the front brakes and with hinge-down doors on both sides. Perhaps the most important change, from the point of view of the practicability of racing the cars, was improved access, with the whole of the upper half of the front bodywork removable giving access to the engine, front suspension and the rear of the instrument panel. At the rear a panel could be moved from the tail to give access to the final drive and inboard-mounted brakes. The perspex screen was now lower, wrapped more fully round the driver, and with a 6-gal fuel tank mounted in the tail of the car. For Endurance racing auxiliary tanks of different sizes could be installed on the passenger side of the bodywork.

At the beginning of the season, Lotus built two cars for the use of Team Lotus, 9 EHX, an MG-powered car usually driven by Colin Chapman, and XPE 6, usually powered by the

Coventry Climax FWA 1098cc engine and driven by Peter Jopp. Both works cars used MG J2 'crash' gearboxes.

It was the Climax version that was supplied to private purchasers and these were fitted with an MG gearbox with synchromesh on the upper ratios. Lotus was compelled by purchase tax (not applicable to cars sold in component form) and a lack of factory space to sell most of the cars in component form. The quoted price however for a complete Climax-powered car was £1150 plus purchase tax. Once Le Mans was over, Lotus offered the Climax-powered car as the 'Le Mans' and there was also the option of the 'Club' with Ford 1172cc engine, gearbox and back axle and drum brakes with modified brake linkage. At the beginning of the season, works cars had 11in brakes with Elektron drums, but later in the year Girling 9in. disc brakes were adopted, inboard at the rear, and it was possible for private purchasers to have disc brakes as an extra.

The first two cars were delivered to the United States in time for the Sebring 12 Hours race in March and were fitted with Coventry Climax engines and the 1954-type 9in. brakes. Both cars ran extremely well, leading the 1100cc class, but one car, driven by Samuelson, went off the road and holed the sump, whilst the second car, driven by Miller/ Rabe, was disqualified after receiving a push-start in the pits.

Early in the season Chapman had a run of

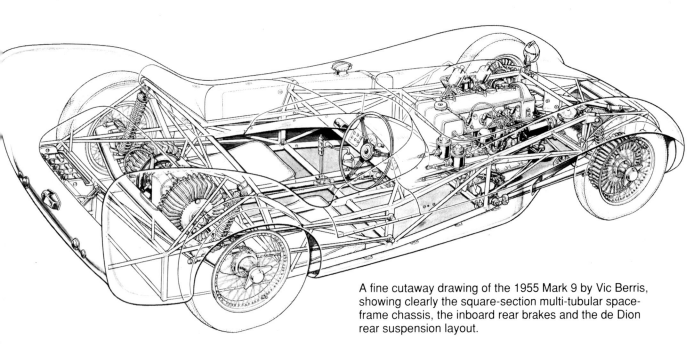

A fine cutaway drawing of the 1955 Mark 9 by Vic Berris, showing clearly the square-section multi-tubular space-frame chassis, the inboard rear brakes and the de Dion rear suspension layout.

The Mark 9-Climax 1098cc car entered at Le Mans in 1955 for Chapman/Flockhart and seen here with Chapman at the wheel. It was disqualified after Chapman reversed back on to the circuit without waiting for permission from the marshals after an off-course excursion. *(Geoffrey Goddard)*

back luck with the MG-powered Mark 9, retiring at Oulton Park, Goodwood and Silverstone. By the Whitsun weekend good fortune had returned to the team and he won races at both Snetterton and Goodwood, whilst Jopp, who had still not received the works Climax-powered car, won a race at Brands Hatch.

In 1955 Team Lotus made an entry at Le Mans and the Climax-powered works car was driven by Colin Chapman and Ron Flockhart, who had been brought into the team because of his experience. This car differed from the ordinary run of Mark 9s in that it was of rather a more substantial construction than the production cars, with heavier 22-gauge aluminium panelling, and featured conventional headlamps under perspex covers. Despite problems in practice caused by oil leaking into the clutch, Chapman led the 1100cc class until he lost time because of the slipping clutch, and just after six hours from the start he slid off into the sand at Arnage. Quickly he reversed out and rejoined the race, but the Lotus was disqualified because Chapman had not waited for a signal from the marshals before rejoining the track. What had happened quite simply was an over-reaction to the horrors of the earlier disaster involving Levegh's Mercedes-Benz. During the remainder of the

year a whole string of successes were scored in British races. After Chapman had finished in a dead-heat for second place at Brands Hatch with Bueb's Cooper in July, Chapman with the MG-powered car won the 1500cc class of the Sports car race at the British Grand Prix meeting at Aintree. He won again at the Crystal Palace on August Bank Holiday Saturday, finished third at Brands Hatch on the Monday because of a minor engine problem and then retired at Snetterton two weeks later with a broken half-shaft.

Both Team Lotus entries, MG and Climax-powered, retired in the Goodwood 9 Hours race, and in the *Daily Herald* International Trophy at Oulton Park Cliff Allison crashed badly with the 1100cc car and Chapman was plagued by problems with the MG-powered Mark 9. Subsequently Chapman won the 1500cc Sports car race at Aintree with the Mark 9-MG. In the Tourist Trophy the 1500cc car driven by Peter Jopp-Mike Anthony was involved in the multi-car accident that brought the use of the Dundrod circuit to an end, whilst Chapman/Allison, delayed by a broken oil pipe, finished second in the 1100cc class and 11th overall. A few minor successes followed before the end of the season.

The 'one-off' Mark 9 with Ghia coupé body that first appeared in 1956. It has frequently – and erroneously – been described as an Eleven. It competed in a number of Italian hill climbs.

Now that Lotus Engineering Ltd had become a member of the Society of Motor Manufacturers and Traders (accepted only as makers of accessories initially) the company was able to exhibit at the Earls Court Show and there was on the Lotus stand a very specially prepared and finished Mark 9 without body panels. Subsequently this car was completed by Ghia with a very stylish open body and exhibited in Geneva in 1956. In all about 40 Mark 9s were built.

*Autosport* was still very much in favour with Lotus and John Bolster was allowed to test both the MG and the Climax-powered cars. The performance figures were as follows: MG-powered Mark 9: maximum speed 128.6 mph. 0–60 mph: 8.6 sec. 0–100 mph. 22.4 sec. Standing quarter mile: 15.4 sec. Fuel consumption: racing, 20 mpg; road, 30 mpg (approx.).

Climax-powered Mark 9: maximum speed 127.7 mph. 0–60 mph: 7.8 sec. 0–100 mph: 23.6 sec. Standing quarter mile: 15.8 sec. Fuel consumption: as for the MG-powered car.

John Bolster commented: 'The Lotus, particularly in its Climax-engined form, has phenomenally high cornering-power. I was extremely happy to take it very fast through the curves of a road circuit and there are no peculiarities to learn. I would, however, require a good deal more practice before I was certain that the ultimate limit was being attained. The whole cornering process is so effortless, with no rolling, bouncing or tyre scream to give an air of

urgency to the proceedings, that only experience gives warning that one is going from the improbable to the impossible. I know a particular corner which I habitually negotiate just on 100 mph in the better class of sports car. The Lotus Climax took it first try at better than 110 mph. You see what I mean!'

Already, however, Chapman was planning a new model for 1956 and those owners who had been unfortunate enough to buy Mark 9s soon found that their cars had been superseded.

However, in Ford-engined form, the cars continued to achieve success in 750 Motor Club racing and another success achieved in 1956, albeit at a minor level, was the win by Peter Lumsden with his Climax-powered car in the Brooklands Trophy for performances during the year at BARC Members' meetings at Goodwood.

**Specification (production):**
ENGINE: Coventry Climax FWA 1098cc.
GEARBOX: MG 4-speed.
CHASSIS: multi-tubular space-frame.
FRONT SUSPENSION: swing-axles and coil spring/damper units.
REAR SUSPENSION: de Dion axle and coil spring/damper units.
WHEELBASE: 7ft 3.5in.
FRONT TRACK: 4ft 0.5in.
REAR TRACK: 3ft 11.5in.
OVERALL LENGTH: 11ft 8in.
WEIGHT: 8.25 cwt.

# Mark 10

## *Sports-Racing Car, 1955*

During 1954 Mike Anthony in particular had been pressing Colin Chapman to produce a version of the Mark 8 that would take the Bristol 2-litre engine and gearbox. Chapman was keen on the idea and so the development of the Mark 10 in fact preceded that of the Mark 9. The new Mark 10 was in effect a modified Mark 8, with an enlarged engine bay to accommodate the bigger engine, but with a similar rear axle layout to that of the Mark 9, lowered transmission line using a Salisbury hypoid bevel final drive and, to counterbalance the greater weight of the 2-litre engine, the fuel tank positioned behind the rear axle, together with the fuel pumps and battery. The valances over the rear wheels were deleted and this coupled with the bulge in the bonnet distinguished the Mark 10 from other Lotus models. The bonnet was only 2.5in higher than that of the Mark 9. This was the first Lotus to be fitted with disc brakes as a standard and Dunlop discs were used front and rear. All-up weight was 11 cwt. Lotus Engineering quoted a price of £925 without engine and gearbox.

Cars to be powered by Bristol engines were supplied to Mike Anthony, Peter Scott-Russell, Cliff Davis and Dr Vaughan Havard. In addition Mike Young acquired a Mark 10 chassis to fit a Connaught 2-litre engine, George Nixon's car was powered by a Turner 1500cc engine and a Mark 10 was ordered by James Dean to be powered by an Offenhauser engine, but he was killed in a road accident with his Porsche before it was delivered.

The principal opposition in the 2000cc class was the Lister-Bristol. The Lister was undoubtedly the better balanced car and handled better than the Mark 10, and Lister possessed one major advantage, Archie Scott-Brown, a driver of exceptional ability. The Mark 10 drivers were never able to beat him, although they could usually cope with the other, private Listers.

Anthony turned up with his car, still unpainted, at the Goodwood meeting on Easter Monday and took third place. Anthony's car was fitted with the engine canted in the chassis, converted to dry sump lubrication and fitted with sidedraught carburettors. Anthony finished second to Scott-Brown at Ibsley, won at Goodwood on Whit Monday and finished second at Brands Hatch on August Bank Holiday Monday. Peter Scott-Russell took a class second

Cliff Davis with his unpainted Mark 10 Bristol about to be lapped by Archie Scott-Brown (Lister-Maserati) at the British Grand Prix Meeting at Silverstone in 1956. *(T. C. March)*

at Snetterton in August and in the Goodwood 9 Hours race that month Davis/Bicknell finished 12th overall and second in class. Scott-Russell won the 2000cc class of the *Daily Herald* International Trophy at Oulton Park and finished second in the 2000cc class at Aintree the following weekend. At the Boxing Day Brands Hatch meeting C. M. Lund won the Unlimited Sports Car race with Anthony's Mark 10 with Scott-Brown, who on this occasion was driving a Jaguar C-type, second. During 1956 Scott-Russell continued to race his car until it was burnt out at Silverstone. Dimitri Kasterine acquired Anthony's car, which he raced in the black and white colours of the Six Miles Stable and Cliff Davis raced his Mark 10 through 1957.

**Specification:**
ENGINE: Bristol 1971cc.
GEARBOX: Bristol 4-speed.
CHASSIS: multi-tubular space-frame.
FRONT SUSPENSION: swing-axles and coil spring/damper units.
REAR SUSPENSION: de Dion axle and coil spring/damper units.
WHEELBASE: 7ft 3.5in.
FRONT TRACK: 4ft 0.5in.
REAR TRACK: 3ft 11.5in.
OVERALL LENGTH: 13ft 8in.
WEIGHT: 11 cwt.

Peter Scott-Russell with his Mark 10 leads the Jaguar D-type of Ron Flockhart and the Maserati 300S of Benoit Musy in the 1956 British Empire Trophy at Oulton Park. *(T. C. March)*

# Eleven (also known as 11)

*Sports-Racing Car, 1956–8*

*Series 1*
*(Note: this designation was applied*
*retrospectively to distinguish the early cars*
*from the later Series 2.)*

The 1956 sports-racing car was known simply as the 'Eleven' or '11' as Chapman had decided to drop the 'Mark' in reference to all new models to prevent complications in the future. The Eleven was a logical development of the Mark 9, but had been changed in most respects. There was a new space-frame constructed in 1in and ¾in 18- and 20-gauge tubing. The swing-axle front suspension now featured a lower pivot-point, which much reduced the understeering tendencies of the Mark 9, and at the rear there was a much lighter de Dion axle through which the articulated half-shafts passed and which was located by twin radius arms on either side. Other features were new rack and pinion steering, Girling disc brakes front and rear, a lighter and completely ducted radiator and the fuel tank had been moved from the tail to the left-hand side of the chassis. In standard form it had a capacity of 9.5 gals, but for endurance racing an additional 11-gal tank could be fitted on the right.

In appearance the Eleven was dramatically smoother and more compact that the Mark 9, with both bonnet and tail sweeping down more steeply and the tail fins replaced by higher rear wings. Both front and rear wings partially enclosed the wheels, headlamps of a conventional kind were mounted behind perspex covers, both front and rear sections of the bodywork pivoted on the ends of the frame to improve accessibility, bottom-hinged doors were fitted both sides and the interior was properly trimmed. The majority of cars were characterized by a very prominent headrest, metal tonneau over the passenger side and a wrap-round perspex screen round the driver. For international racing, a full-width screen was fitted and the headrest deleted.

When the Eleven was announced, it was stated that it would be available with either a Coventry Climax or a Ford engine, but during the year Lotus Engineering settled on three individual models with distinct specifications on paper, although there was often a lot of overlapping of detail between the different models when they were raced. These three models were:

## Le Mans

Intended purely for competition work, this car was powered by the Coventry Climax FWA 1098cc engine inclined ten degrees to the left in the chassis, which permitted a carburation arrangement with horizontal induction tracks. The gearbox used an Austin A30 casing with special Lotus close-ratio gears, although the MGA gearbox was later substituted. The 9.5in Girling disc brakes were mounted outboard at the front and inboard at the rear. Certain of these cars raced by the works and by favoured private owners were powered by the Climax FWB 1460cc engine developing 142 bhp at 6750 rpm.

The 'Le Mans 75' was priced at £1337, the 'Le Mans 85' with Stage 2 FWA engine at £1387 and if the FWB was installed the price increased by approximately £250.

## Club

This model retained the Coventry Climax engine and Lotus gearbox, but a live rear axle located by parallel trailing arms was substituted for the de Dion axle of the Le Mans and there were drum brakes. The Club was normally sold with full-width screen, wipers and hood and was priced at £1083.

## Sports

Powered by the Ford 1172cc side-valve engine and Ford 3-speed gearbox, and otherwise similar to the Club, the Sports was priced at £872. It was primarily intended for road use, but not many were sold, and its main claim to fame were its performances in the *Autosport* Production Sports Car Championship. Graham Hill drove one of these cars, in fact one of the 1956 Le Mans cars in Sports form, in that year's *Autosport* Championship, and the following year it was raced in the Championship by Ian Walker. When Walker raced the car, it was fitted with Willment inlet over exhaust cylinder head, and Walker won overall victory in that year's *Autosport* Championship.

In the 1500cc heat of the British Empire Trophy at Oulton Park in April 1956 Denis Taylor (Cooper-Climax) heads Mike Hawthorn (with the Team Lotus Eleven normally driven by Reg Bicknell), Les Leston (Cooper-Climax) and Bicknell (Eleven). *(T. C. March)*

These cars were immensely successful in 1956, especially when raced by Team Lotus, were much in demand by private owners and overall were much more successful than the rival Cooper-Climax. At the beginning of the season the works Coopers and the Team Lotus cars were very closely matched, but ascendancy moved very much in Lotus's favour as the season progressed.

The Team Lotus entries were usually driven by Colin Chapman and Reg Bicknell (formerly a driver of his own Revis Formula 3 and Sports cars whose Lotus remained unpainted all season). Amongst the most successful private entrants were Ivor Bueb's Ecurie Demi-Litre, whose car was usually driven by Mike Hawthorn, Tommy Sopwith's Équipe Endeavour and John Coombs's entry, which were driven by a number of different drivers during the year.

The first two Elevens were shipped to the United States to run in the Sebring 12 Hours race and one with an FWB engine had been entered by Briggs Cunningham and was to be co-driven by Colin Chapman. This car non-started after a practice crash, so Chapman co-drove the 1100cc car, but this retired because of a burnt-out starter motor.

The works Coopers beat the Elevens at Goodwood on Easter Monday and in the British Empire Trophy at Oulton Park, but thereafter the pendulum of success swung in favour of the Elevens. One of the finest successes of Team Lotus during the year was in the Coupe Delamare de Bouteville, a one-and-a-quarter hours race preceding the Rouen Sports Car Grand Prix. In the absence of serious opposition Chapman was the overall winner at 87.93 mph. Cliff Allison was second and won the 1100cc class and Harry Schell finished third with Sopwith's FWB-powered car. Team Lotus returned to Le Mans with a trio of entries. To comply with the new Le Mans regulations, chassis frames had been widened at the centre to allow the use of full-width open cockpits and the compulsory full-width screens were fitted. On the Elevens these fully enclosed the cockpits with the side portions attached to the drop-down doors. Despite heavy rain during the night hours, all three cars survived until the Sunday morning. The 1500 of Chapman/Fraser was eliminated by big-end failure, Allison/Hall retired after a collision with a large dog, but the second 1100 of Bicknell/Jopp finished seventh overall and first in the 1100cc class at an average speed of 89.97 mph.

Other highlights of the season were the fantastic duel at Goodwood on Whit Monday between Chapman with his Team Lotus car and

Mike Anthony's special Eleven-Bristol seen here at Goodwood in 1956 leading a Cooper-Climax and a Connaught A-series. (Geoffrey Goddard)

The three works Elevens at Le Mans in 1956. Amongst those present are Reg Bicknell (second from left), Peter Jopp (third from left), Cliff Allison (fourth from left), Graham Hill (extreme right) and Colin Chapman (second from right). Nos. 36 and 35 are the 1098cc cars (No. 36 driven by Jopp/Bicknell won the 1100cc class) and 32 was powered by a 1460cc Climax FWB engine. *(Geoffrey Goddard)*

Another view from Le Mans 1956 with the 1500cc car and one of the 1100s in front of the pits. *(Geoffrey Goddard)*

Hawthorn with the Ecurie Demi-Litre car, during which they spun in formation at Madgwick, collided and rejoined the race, with Chapman winning by a good margin after Hawthorn stopped at the pits for the car to be checked. In June Bicknell finished third in the City Cup race at Porto behind Salvadori (works Cooper) and Nogueira (Porsche). Ecurie Demi-Litre entered their Eleven in a couple of continental Endurance races, the Supercortemaggiore Grand Prix at Monza, where the car non-started because of gearbox trouble, and the Reims 12 Hours race, where Bueb/Mackay Fraser led until the loss of first and second gears. This Eleven was effectively destroyed at Oulton Park in August when, cornering too fast, Hawthorn lost control in the *Sporting Life* Trophy, hit the bank, the car flipped and disintegrated, with parts striking Salvadori's Cooper. The cars also ran in Formula 2 races during the year, with Chapman finishing second to Salvadori's new Cooper in the inaugural Formula 2 race at Silverstone on the day of the British Grand Prix, and Chapman and Flockhart (the latter entered by Coombs) taking third and fourth places in the Gold Cup race at Oulton Park.

Towards the end of the year Lotus went record-breaking at Monza with Fraser at the wheel of an 1100cc car and whole string of class records were taken, including the 100 miles at 137.5 mph.

In November *The Autocar* road-tested one of the Le Mans entries, the 1100 driven by Allison/Hall. The magazine achieved a mean maximum speed of 111.75 mph, acceleration from 0–60 mph in 10.9 sec, 0–100 mph in 38.9 sec and the standing quarter-mile in 17.9 sec. Overall fuel consumption was a remarkable 47.8 mph. *The Autocar* commented: 'There is no reason why the car should not on occasions be used for local shopping or, in fine weather, for taking the younger member of the family to school – and no reason either to suppose that the Lotus would be harmed by such employment, for it has all the normal components and an engine which is far from being temperamental. On the other hand a milkman does not usually buy a racehorse to draw his float, nor does an esquimo choose a whippet.'

There were also a number of interesting variants on the Eleven theme. Alex McMillan raced an Eleven with a Fiat-based 1100cc Stanguellini engine, optimistically claimed to develop 95 bhp at 7300 rpm and with a Fiat gearbox. After he had found his Maserati 150S far too heavy for British short-circuit events, Brian Naylor transferred the engine to an Eleven. Mike Anthony, the Brighton furrier, who had raced earlier Lotus cars with success, had tried to persuade Chapman to build him a Bristol-engined Eleven. Chapman was far too busy to go along with this experiment, so Anthony built and developed a car himself with the Bristol engine laid on its side. This was transported on the back of a lengthened Standard Vanguard transporter which deliberately aped the high-speed transporter used by Mercedes-Benz in 1955. Despite its immaculate preparation and superb appearance, the special Anthony car achieved very little success.

## Series 2

Nineteen fifty-six had established Lotus very firmly on the international racing map and the company moved forward into 1957 both with a new single-seater for Formula 2 and an improved version of the Eleven. The new Series 2 featured double wishbone and coil spring front suspension, as on the Formula 2 cars, and there was a strengthened de Dion rear axle to cope with the much greater power of the newly available 1475cc twin-cam Coventry Climax FPF engine. Externally Series 1 and Series 2 cars are not readily distinguishable, but usually (but not necessarily) the fixed bottom panels below the door and running from front to rear wing sections were left unpainted on Series 2 cars.

Lotus now offered the choice of four models, the 'Le Mans 150' with the twin-cam FPF engine, the 'Le Mans 85' with stage 2 Climax 1100 engine, the 'Club 75' with Climax 1100 engine, drum brakes and live rear axle, and the 'Sports 45' with Ford 1172 engine, drum brakes and live rear axle.

In British sports car events, the 1100cc and 1500cc classes were almost totally dominated by Lotus entries. The year started well internationally with a class win at Sebring by a 1100cc car driven by Chapman/Sheppard/Dungan, which finished 11th overall.

At Le Mans were five Lotus entries and for this race a number of changes were made to the cars. Because of the regulations, which specified a full-width screen, two proper seats and a

The Series 2 Eleven first appeared in the UK in the 1957 British Empire Trophy at Oulton Park, held that year as three separate races. The 2000cc event was won by Ron Flockhart (Series 2 entered by John Coombs, FWB 1460cc engine, wire wheels) from Colin Chapman (Team Lotus Series 2, FWB 1460cc engine, 'wobbly-web' wheels). *(T. C. March)*

At Le Mans this Team Lotus car with 744cc Climax FWC engine and driven by Cliff Allison and Keith Hall (seen here at the wheel) won the 750cc class and the Index of Performance. That great character (and fine sports car driver) Duncan Hamilton laps the Lotus with his D-type Jaguar. Hamilton/Masten Gregory finished sixth with the Jaguar. *(LAT)*

flexible tonneau, Chapman devised a layout whereby the windscreen curved backwards at the top in a line with the rear bodywork, which was raised to the height of the rear wings; a flexible tonneau over the passenger seat linked the top of the screen to the top of the rear body. Of the entries the 1500cc to be driven by Mackay Fraser/Jay Chamberlain suffered a dropped valve in practice and non-started, so these drivers took over the 1100cc car to be driven by Ashdown/Stacey. They finished ninth overall, won the 1100cc class and were classified second in the Index of Performance. Other Elevens, the private entries of Dalton/Walshaw and Hechard/Masson, finished 13th and 16th overall, taking second and fourth places in the 1100cc class. The third Lotus entry was a car powered by the 744cc Coventry Climax FWC engine and driven by Cliff Allison/Keith Hall; this finished 14th overall, winning the 750cc class and the Index of Performance. It was one of the finest performances in Lotus racing history.

From Le Mans, Team Lotus travelled to Rouen to compete once again in the Coupe Delamare de Bouteville. The race was won by Ron Flockhart with John Coombs's 1500cc

The 1957 Autosport Series production Sports Car Championship was dominated by Ian Walker with this yellow Eleven, the specification of which was something of a hybrid and included a Ford 1172cc engine with a Willment overhead inlet valve head. Note the carburetor intakes poking through the bonnet. This Eleven had originally been one of 1956 Team Lotus cars and had won the 1100cc class at Le Mans. Although seen here at Oulton Park with open cockpit, etc., in Sports trim, at the final round of the Championship, the three-hour race at Snetterton, it ran with streamlined headrest, metal tonneau and wrap-round cockpit surround. *(T. C. March)*

Eleven, but Jay Chamberlain took second place with the Team Lotus entry and Chapman, with the car that had won the 1100cc class at Le Mans, finished second in this class at Rouen after a pit stop for water. In addition Allison drove the 750 to a class victory.

Team Lotus decided to run a stripped sports car in the Formula 2 race at Reims, arguing that the superior aerodynamics of the sports car would give it an advantage on this high-speed circuit. Sadly Mackay Fraser was killed at the wheel of this car when he lost control and crashed at the very fast Garenne Curve.

The Eleven Series 2 remained in production in 1958 and continued to dominate the 1100 class. With a single exception, the cars were no longer fielded by Team Lotus, which concentrated on the 15 sports-racing car and single-seater racing. The exception was Le Mans, where two 750cc cars were entered. Both were fitted with the new Coventry Climax FWMA 745cc engine, a live rear axle to reduce transmission power loss, drum rear brakes and magnesium-alloy wheels. During practice the FWMA engine broke on the works car of Stacey/Dickson and so the 1957 744cc engine

was substituted. The second car was a nominally private entry for Masson/Hechard. There were also two 1100 cars entered for Ireland/Taylor by Team Lotus and the private entry of Frost/Hicks. Only one of the four entries finished, the works 750 in 20th and last place.

Undoubtedly the Eleven was one of the most successful of all Chapman's designs.

**Specification (Series 1, 1956):**
ENGINE: Coventry Climax FWA 1098cc or FWB 1460cc.
GEARBOX: Lotus/A30 4-speed.
CHASSIS: multi-tubular space-frame.
FRONT SUSPENSION: swing axles and coil spring/damper units.
REAR SUSPENSION: de Dion axle and coil spring/damper units.
WHEELBASE: 7ft 1in.
FRONT TRACK: 3ft 10.5in.
REAR TRACK: 3ft 11in.
OVERALL LENGTH: 11ft 2in.
OVERALL WIDTH: 5ft 0in.
KERB WEIGHT: 9.1 cwt.

# 12

*Formula 2 and Formula 1, 1957–9*

Although Formula 2 did not officially start until the 1957 season, there were a number of Formula 2 races during 1956 which were dominated by the one serious single-seater contender, the Coventry Climax-powered Cooper. Lotus revealed their Formula 2 car at the 1956 London Motor Show and this was incomplete in that it had a mock-up of the new twin-cam Coventry Climax FPF 1475cc engine and Lotus trans-axle.

The basis of the car was a multi-tubular space-frame, incorporating Reynolds 531 tubing for the main longitudinal members, a very rigidly attached undertray which increased rigidity and with new front suspension of the double wishbone type, with a wide-based lower member and the upper member formed by a transverse tubular link. Initially, there was a de Dion rear axle at the rear, as used on the Eleven, located however by single radius rods and an A-bracket. When the first car was completed, it incorporated a BMC gearbox in unit with the engine. Girling disc brakes were fitted front and

rear, inboard at the rear. The car was also characterized by the new Lotus 'wobbly-web' cast magnesium-alloy disc wheels of considerable strength and low weight. These were of the bolt-on type as Chapman did not envisage wheel changes, even in long races, because of the low weight of the car.

Although a car with de Dion rear axle was raced by Mackay Fraser at Brands Hatch and the Crystal Palace over the 1957 Whitsun weekend, on the third car to be built (raced by Allison at Goodwood on Easter Monday), and subsequent cars, this was replaced by the Chapman strut layout whereby each of the rear hubs was located by three members, a coil spring/damper unit controlled vertically by the hub casting, a fabricated forward-facing radius arm which located the hub fore and aft and a fixed-length half-shaft which located the hub laterally.

After a number of experiments, a new gearbox was designed for the team by Richard Ansdale and this mated directly to a hypoid crown wheel and pinion and a ZF limited slip differential. The engine was inclined downwards towards the clutch to achieve a 5in drop in the transmission line. The new gearbox was all-indirect with the

Construction of 12 Formula 2 cars in the tiny Lotus works at Tottenham Lane, Hornsey. Colin Chapman can be seen in the background of this photograph studying (for the camera) the installation of the Climax FPF engine.

At the Easter Goodwood meeting in 1958 Jack Brabham (Works Cooper) leads Graham Hill (Lotus 12) and they finished this Formula 2 race in this order in first and second places. *(LAT)*

The 12's best performance was in the 1958 Belgian Grand Prix in which Cliff Allison finished fourth. The 12 enjoyed a trouble-free race apart from a loose exhaust pipe. As the first three cars all had mechanical problems and could not have completed another lap, it was almost a Lotus victory. *(LAT)*

gate arranged in a series of letter 'Zs' sequentially in motorcycle-style. This gearbox, which became known as the 'queerbox', was disliked by most drivers and gave endless problems. During 1957 Keith Duckworth, then a student helping out during his holidays, was set to work on the gearbox. He introduced a positive stop gear-change mechanism and sorted out the problems. After 1957 a spiral bevel final drive was substituted. The body was styled by Williams & Pritchard from a sketch by Chapman and its neatness and balance made it one of the very best-looking of all front-engined racing cars. In addition the 12 was exceptionally light, which led to many problems, including chassis breakages.

Team Lotus entered the 12s in a total of eight races during 1957, but they proved no real match for the rival Coopers. Herbert Mackay Fraser finished second at Brands Hatch on Whit Sunday, Allison and Hill took third and fifth places in the Woodcote Cup at Goodwood in September and the following month Allison took second place in the Gold Cup race at Oulton Park. Apart from the prototype, Team Lotus used four different 12s during 1957 and a further three cars were sold to private purchasers. A further four cars were completed in 1958.

It was not until 1958 that Lotus entered Formula 1, but very little success was gained during the year in that category. Allison was definitely the star driver of the team, considerably overshadowing Graham Hill, and he took sixth place in the Dutch Grand Prix at Zandvoort and fourth in the Belgian race at Spa-Francorchamps. At Spa the first three cars all had problems and could not have completed another lap, so it was very nearly a Lotus victory. Throughout the season the team used the 1.9-litre Climax engine, but subsequently took delivery of a 2207cc unit. This engine was used by Allison in both of his World Championship points-scoring races.

In Formula 2 Hill and Allison took second and third places in the Lavant Cup at Goodwood. Allison was fourth with a Formula 2 car in the Richmond Trophy at Goodwood, Hill was fourth in the Formula 2 class of the Aintree 200 race, Allison finished fifth on aggregate in the Kentish 100 race at Brands Hatch and Ivor Bueb with his private car took a number of places. Although private owners continued to race their 12s in 1959, Team Lotus entered a 12 in only one race, the Lavant Cup at Goodwood on Easter Monday, when Graham Hill took fourth place.

Colin Chapman's first single-seater was less than satisfactory or successful, but it was soon to be superseded by a new design for Formula 2 and Formula 1 that was to be beset by even greater problems.

**Specification:**
ENGINE: Coventry Climax FPF (various capacities).
GEARBOX: Lotus 5-speed.
CHASSIS: multi-tubular space-frame.
FRONT SUSPENSION: double wishbones with upper wishbone formed by transverse tubular link and coil spring/damper units.
REAR SUSPENSION: strut system, with coil spring/damper units, controlled vertically by hub castings, forward radius arms and fixed length half-shafts.
WHEELBASE: 7ft 4in.
FRONT AND REAR TRACK: 4ft 0in.
OVERALL LENGTH: 10ft 11in.
WEIGHT: approx 660 lb dry.

# 13

*Type number not allocated, but usually regarded as referring to the Eleven Series 2*

# 14 Elite

*Production GT Car, 1957–63*

The Elite represented the greatest achievement in Chapman's short career. It was by any standard an exceptionally fast and technically advanced design of superb appearance. With the Elite the Lotus company crossed the divide from being a specialist constructor of competition cars to becoming a serious production car manufacturer. It scored a string of successes in International racing, more than was achieved by any of the earlier sports-racing cars. For most drivers, however, it provided a nightmare of unreliability and problems, for it was, in the words of Colin Chapman, 'a racing car for the road', and, its unique monocoque apart, an evolution of the existing competition cars. And the financial problems that it caused Lotus almost resulted in the company's premature demise.

In its production form the Elite, a unique glass-fibre monocoque, incorporated only three major moulds – the body, including roof, wings and boot; the 'chassis' formed by the floor pan and wheel wells and incorporating the metal sub-frame that mounted the front suspension and the mounting for the final drive; and an elaborate moulding that comprised the engine bay, transmission tunnel, formed the boot and mounted the windscreen 'hoop' and jacking points. These three moulds were joined by epoxy resin. There were separate moulds for other components, including the doors, bonnet and boot lid.

The monocoque of the first prototype was much more complex for it incorporated nearly 60 different mouldings, but intensive work reduced these to the three mentioned above. The first prototypes also incorporated steel and aluminium bonded between layers of glass-fibre for strengthening, but testing proved that this was unnecessary. The coupé body, with aerodynamically efficient lines and delicate and attractive styling, was largely the work of Peter Kirwan-Taylor, with aerodynamic refinements by Frank Costin and translation from drawings to clay model by John Frayling; the car entered production without styling changes from the clay model.

To power the new car Chapman entered into an arrangement with Coventry Climax, who agreed to supply a new version of their familiar single-cam engines, the FWE with a capacity of 1216cc (76.2 x 66.6mm) and a power output of 75 bhp at 6100 rpm. Transmission was by a BMC B-series gearbox, essentially the MGA, but with an alloy casing incorporating the bell housing for the Climax engine. Suspension design followed that of the 12 Formula 2 car, with double wishbones and coil spring/damper units at the front and Chapman strut suspension at the rear. Girling 9.5in, disc brakes were fitted front and rear, inboard at the rear, and there were Dunlop 15in 48-spoke wire wheels with knock-off hubs front and rear.

The prototype Elite appeared at the Earls Court Show in 1957 (where it proved to be the sensation of the Show) and after display in the Lotus showroom at Hornsey for some months it was broken up. Two further prototypes were completed and loaned to Ian Walker and John Lawry, who raced them extensively as part of the Elite development programme, and other prototypes were extensively tested by the factory. The first production cars were not delivered until December 1958. These early cars were built in the small premises at Edmonton where the construction of the first prototype had taken place. The first cars were sold to well-known personalities, including band leader Chris Barber, Ian Scott-Watson of the Border Reivers team (for Jim Clark to drive), John Whitmore, Graham Warner (of The Chequered Flag sports car dealers) and Keith Hall. The new Cheshunt factory did not open until October 1959 and it was there that serious production was undertaken.

The production cars can be summarized as follows:

*Series I (designation adopted subsequently)*
Specification as described above and with body/chassis unit by boatbuilders Maximar. Choice of pale green, light blue, dark blue, red, grey and later white exterior colour finish. Production by Maximar continued to July 1960. Total production 280 units. Price in 1960, basic £1387 (£1966 with purchase tax). When road-tested by *The Motor* in 1960 a mean maximum speed of 111.8 mph was achieved, with 0–60

Jim Clark at the wheel of the Elite that he drove for The Border Reivers in the Production Sports Car race at the Gold Cup meeting at Oulton Park in 1959. This was one of the very early production cars that was supplied to Clark's close friend Ian Scott-Watson. *(T. C. March)*

The sales catalogue for the Series 1 Elite.

mph in 11.4 seconds, 0–100 mph in 41.1 seconds and the standing quarter-mile covered in 18.4 seconds. Overall fuel consumption was 34.1 mpg.

### Series II

From July 1960 to the cease of production, body/chassis units were supplied by Bristol Aeroplane Plastics and a total of 749 units were delivered, split between the various versions of the Series II, with 20 to 30 units unused when production ceased in the autumn of 1963. The Series II featured modified suspension, with longer, larger-diameter springs at the front, and at the rear a new strut arrangement incorporating a triangular wishbone in place of the original kinked radius arm. This resolved rear end steer, which had been found to develop on cars with a high racing mileage. There were also longer, larger-diameter springs. Many other minor changes were made then and progressively during production of the Series II, including throttle cables (instead of levers), twin SU carburettors (from late 1962), Royalite thermoplastic interior (from 1962, to replace the original vinyl), a smaller steering wheel and an umbrella-type handbrake (replacing the original and rather more effective fly-off handle on the transmission tunnel).

### Series II SE

Announced at the 1960 Earls Court Show, the SE was powered by a version of the FWE engine developing 85 bhp and fitted with the new ZF S4-12 gearbox with synchromesh on all four gears and a separate aluminium bell housing. There were other minor changes and, unless the customer specified otherwise, a silver roof. In 1962 the basic price was £1425, compared with £1299 for the standard model. Both prices are for the cars in kit form.

### Series II, Super, 95, 100 and 105

A very small number of cars were built from 1962 onwards as what amounted to 'factory-built competition cars'.

It appears that there are no records of precise numbers available. The Super 95 (with 95 bhp engine) first appeared in May 1962, and was superseded in the same year by the Super 100 and by the Super 105 in 1963.

Throughout the production life of the Elite, Lotus struggled to make the cars reliable and struggled to achieve reasonable sales levels, partly because of the high price compared with the Elite's mass-production rivals. In the United States there were special problems and the final

Graham Warner (with The Chequered Flag's LOV 1) and Tom Dickson battle for the lead in the *Autosport* Championship race at Mallory Park in May 1960. On this occasion Warner was narrowly beaten. *(T. C. March)*

collapse of Jay Chamberlain's import company (a collapse directly attributable to difficulties in selling the cars) nearly brought down Lotus with it. In an effort to keep sales moving, from October 1961 the cars were sold in kit form. This had the added advantage that no purchase tax was payable. In this way Lotus managed to keep sales moving until production finally stopped in September 1963. For some time afterwards 20 to 30 body/chassis units were littered round the Cheshunt works. One was built up by David Lazenby (General Manager of Lotus Components) with a Lotus twin-cam engine (as used in the Elan) and the remainder were it seems eventually sold and built up into cars. Because of the supply of replacement body/chassis units for cars that had been damaged, there is no accurate record of the number of cars completed.

Although Chapman estimated that Lotus lost £100 for every Elite sold, and it was certainly not a commercial success, its racing record makes it one of the most successful of all Lotus competition sports cars. The Elite's international racing career began at the Nürburgring in 1959 when Peter Lumsden (with Peter Riley as co-driver), won the 1300cc GT class of the 1000 Kilometres race. This same duo appeared shortly afterwards at Le Mans and in the 24 Hours race won the 1500cc class, finished eighth overall, took fifth place in the Index of Performance and second in the newly introduced Index of Thermal Efficiency.

The following year, 1960, the 1300cc GT class of the Nürburgring was won by the Elite of John Wagstaff/Alan Stacey with Peter Lumsden/Peter Sargent second. For Le Mans Lotus prepared a special Elite, powered by a 1960cc FPF Climax twin-cam engine, for Michael Taylor, who was to be partnered by Team Lotus Formula 1 driver Innes Ireland. Taylor was badly injured when his 18 Formula 1 car crashed badly in practice at Spa because of steering failure and so his place was taken by Jonathan Sieff. During practice at Le Mans, Sieff, feeling his way with a 1.2-litre Elite, crashed heavily and suffered severe injuries. In

## Join the Elite

The finest compact Grand Touring car on the roads today, the Lotus Elite, proven by success after success on the world's racing and rally circuits, gains unanimous praise for its advanced specification, superb styling and finish, low running costs combined with fantastic performance and perfect day-to-day utility.

120 m.p.h. and 34 m.p.g. are only two characteristics imparted by a specification which includes all-round independent suspension, 4-wheel disc brakes, OHC Coventry Climax engine, all-synchromesh gearbox and many other unique and advanced features.

Insurance, Finance and Part Exchange facilities can be arranged by the Factory Sales Department together with demonstrations at the factory or at your home. When purchased in component form the Lotus Elite can be built for £1,299 (*with six months' warranty*).

**The Factory Sales Department, Lotus Components Limited, Delamare Road, Cheshunt, Herts.**
**Waltham Cross 26181**

Advertisement for the Elite placed by Lotus Components Limited in *Autosport* in August 1962. This was the Series 2 car with Bristol body built from July 1960 onwards.

any event the 2-litre car had been handling badly and it was withdrawn. All was not lost, however, for the new 1300cc GT class was won by the Elite of Masson/Laurent with the similar car of Wagstaff/Marsh second in the class. The complicated formula of the Index of Thermal Efficiency was such that the winners were Wagstaff/Marsh with Masson/Laurent second.

Well to the fore in 1961 was Team Elite, formed specially to race Elites with works backing, and David Hobbs, whose red and blue car was fitted with Hobbs Mechamatic automatic transmission designed by his father. During practice at the Nürburgring Peter Arundell wrote off one of the Team Elite cars, but Hobbs/Pinckney won the 1600cc sports car class (they were forced to run in this class because the non-standard automatic transmission made the Hobbs Lotus ineligible for the 1300cc GT class), and the 1300cc GT class was won by the Elite of Lumsden/Riley.

At Le Mans the Team Elite-entered car of Bill Allen/Trevor Taylor won the 1300cc class, but more attention was focussed on the UDT-Laystall entry of Cliff Allison/Mike McKee. This car, running in the 850cc Sports class, was powered by the Climax FWMC 742cc twin-cam engine developing 81 bhp at 8000 rpm and the aim was to win the Index of Performance. It retired in the tenth hour because of overheating and a broken oil pump drive.

In 1962 the 1300cc GT class at the Nürburgring was won by an Alfa Romeo, but Wagstaff/Fergusson finished second in the class. At Le Mans Hobbs/Gardner won the 1300cc GT class and finished eighth overall. Although the Elite was now being overtaken by more recently developed rivals, in 1963 Wagstaff/Baird won the 1300cc GT class at the Nürburgring and Wagstaff, again partnered by Fergusson, won the 1300cc class at Le Mans. Nineteen sixty-four was the last year of Elite success in international events and at Le Mans the Elite of Hunt/Wagstaff finished 22nd overall and took the Elite's fifth and final class win at Le Mans.

Outside this brief account of the Elite's international racing successes, the cars were immensely successful in British (and American) National events. Apart from Team Elite, formed in 1960 and managed by David Buxton, and David Hobbs with his Mechamatic automatic transmission Elite, who regularly competed in international races, many of the more successful Elites were seen exclusively in British events. The most successful drivers were Graham Warner (LOV 1, black and white) and Les

This Team Elite entry at Le Mans in 1963 was driven by Wagstaff/Fergusson. It finished tenth overall, won the 1300cc GT class and finished third in the Index of Thermal Efficiency – despite an off-course excursion into the sand at Mulsanne corner on the first lap. Wagstaff again drove the class-winning Elite at Le Mans in 1964. *(Nigel Snowdon)*

Leston (pale green, DAD 10) and the successes – and their duels – were too numerous to relate here. Leston's car was one of a small number fitted with the very clean, aerodynamic front end developed by Frank Costin and first fitted to the private Elite of Malle/Carnegie that was entered – and retired – at Le Mans in 1961. In all about five cars featured this nose, which was said to improve aerodynamics to the extent that it was worth 15–20 bhp more than a standard car. Despite the shortcomings of the Elite as a production car, these were more than compensated for by its track performances.

**Specification (1960):**

ENGINE: Coventry Climax FWE 1216cc (76.2 x 66.6mm).
GEARBOX: BMC B-series with alloy casing.
CHASSIS: glass-fibre monocoque.
FRONT SUSPENSION: double wishbones and coil spring/damper units.
REAR SUSPENSION: strut system with coil spring/damper units, controlled vertically by hub castings, trailing radius arms and fixed-length drive-shafts.
WHEELBASE: 7ft 4.25in.
FRONT TRACK: 3ft 11in.
REAR TRACK: 4ft 0.25in.
OVERALL LENGTH: 12ft 4in.
OVERALL WIDTH: 4ft 11.25in.
OVERALL HEIGHT: 3ft 10.5in.
KERB WEIGHT: 13.25 cwt.

# 15

## Sports-Racing Car, 1958–60

The 15 represented a refined and improved version of the Eleven, intended to take larger-capacity engines, with many of the technical features of the 12 single-seater. As usual the chassis was a multi-tubular space-frame, constructed from 1 in and ¾in round and square tubes with the prop-shaft tunnel and the floor forming stressed integral parts of the frame. At the front there was double wishbone and coil spring suspension, as seen both on the team's Formula 2 cars and the Eleven Series 2, while at the rear there was the strut suspension based on three members, the drive-shaft which located the wheels laterally, a forward-facing radius arm and the strut member formed by the coil spring/damper unit, converging into an aluminium casing behind the wheel. As offered to private customers, the 1.5-litre Climax FPF engine was installed, but the works cars initially used 2-litre engines and later the full 2.5-litre Climax FPF. Transmission was by the Lotus-designed gearbox and combined ZF final drive used in the Formula 2 cars, with positive stop gear-change and all five forward gears in line. Reverse was selected by a separate linkage with the knob behind the passenger seat to prevent accidental engagement.

Because the Climax engine was canted to the right at 60 degrees from the vertical, it was possible to ensure a very low bonnet line, although the engine layout necessitated the use of special manifolding for the twin Weber carburettors. Again, although credited often to Frank Costin, the body was the work of Williams & Pritchard. It was exceptionally smooth, a vast improvement on the style of the Eleven, but retaining the same basic lines, with an exceptionally aerodynamic windscreen blending smoothly into the cockpit and with a streamlined headrest. Three tanks for oil and fuel, together with the battery and the spare wheel were mounted in the tail, and the spare wheel was fitted under the headrest. The works cars used Lotus 'wobbly-web' magnesium-alloy wheels and these could be supplied on customer cars, but centre-lock wire wheels were the standard fitting. Girling disc brakes were fitted front and rear, inboard at the rear.

For much of the 15's first season, 1958, the cars were plagued by mechanical problems. Graham Hill drove the 15 on its début in the Unlimited Sports Car race at Goodwood on Easter Monday, but retired because of gearbox trouble, and in the next outing in the British Empire Trophy at

The 15 made its début at Oulton Park in the British Empire Trophy race in 1958. Here Cliff Allison is at the wheel. In their original, advanced form the cars were plagued by unreliability. The body, although Costin-inspired, was the work of Chapman and bodybuilders Williams & Pritchard. *(T. C. March)*

Graham Hill (Team Lotus-entered 15 with 2.5-litre Climax engine) and Jack Brabham (Coombs-entered Cooper Monaco 2-litre Climax) battle for the lead in the Sports Car race at the British Grand Prix meeting at Aintree in 1959. Hill won from team-mate Stacey with Brabham third. *(T. C. March)*

Oulton Park, Hill failed to qualify for the final because of a pit stop caused by a loose plug and Allison retired in the final because of loss of oil pressure. More problems followed at Aintree, but Hill won the 1500cc Sports car race at the May Silverstone meeting. In the Unlimited race Allison retired with a 2-litre car.

Two 15s were entered at Le Mans by Team Lotus and by this race the layout had been much revised. The engines were now canted a mere 17 degrees to the left from the vertical and this resulted in a substantial body bulge that disrupted the smooth airflow of the body design. In this race the cars were also fitted with higher tails, said to be more aerodynamic, and inflatable tonneau covers running from the top of the windscreen to the tail. The 2-litre car driven by Allison and Graham Hill was very fast

in practice, but retired after three laps because of gasket failure. The second 15 with 1.5-litre engine driven by Chamberlain/Lovely was slowed by a persistent engine misfire and retired after Chamberlain had spun into the bank near the Dunlop bridge and was rammed by a Ferrari.

One of the more successful cars was John Coombs's private 2-litre 15, which Salvadori drove into second place at the Sports Car race at the British Grand Prix meeting at Silverstone; Allison was third with a works car, winning the 1500cc class. Another victory for Salvadori with the Coombs car followed in the Gold Cup sports car race at Oulton Park. Coombs's car was superbly prepared and very well developed, whilst it was only too obvious that Team Lotus was simply trying to do too much, competing in both Formula 2 and Sports car racing, and there was simply no time nor sufficient resources for adequate development and preparation.

A Series 2 15 was announced in August 1958, said primarily to be intended for export. The Series 2 featured the 1.5-litre Climax engine mounted 17 degrees to the left of the vertical as on the Le Mans cars, together with a BMC B-series 4-speed gearbox mounted in unit with the engine and the normal H-pattern gear-change; a final drive with BMC gears was used in a Lotus chassis-mounted casing.

For the 1959 season Lotus produced a Series Three version of the 15, which was again intended as a customer car (originally Team Lotus was not going to run in sports car events) and was offered with the 1.5-litre and 2-litre Climax FPF engines angled 17 degrees to the left as on the Series 2 cars and with the BMC-based 4-speed gearbox. The principal changes were stiffening of the chassis frame, and suspension modifications, whereby the upper front wishbones had been reversed so that they now passed behind the wheel centres, making space for a larger radiator and oil cooler. The front track was one inch narrower.

Team Lotus relented on the decision not to run a works car and Graham Hill regularly drove a 15 in British events, but without a great deal of success. He finished third at Oulton Park behind two Cooper Monacos, the real force in this class of racing at the time, second at Aintree to Salvadori's Cooper and retired at Silverstone in May with transmission failure while leading the race. Team Lotus fielded a 2.5-litre 15 for Graham Hill/Derek Jolly at Le Mans and although it was in seventh place at the end of the second hour, it started to jump out of fourth gear and as a result Jolly over-revved the engine. A 2-litre 15 was driven by Ireland/ Stacey, but after being delayed by a broken

wishbone it retired with engine failure. Both of the Le Mans 15s featured the Lotus 5-speed gearbox which was available as an extra on customer cars.

After scoring a victory with a 2.5-litre car in a minor event at Mallory Park, Hill won the Sports Car race at the British Grand Prix at Aintree, but admittedly Salvadori did not run in this event. Further successes for Hill followed at Brands Hatch on August Bank Holiday Monday and at the International Brands Hatch meeting at the end of August. In the United States Jay Chamberlain, the Lotus distributor, raced a 2-litre 15 with considerable success.

Lotus continued to offer the 15 in 1960, but it was now only raced by private owners and was not really competitive. Amongst those to race the 15s that year were Tommy Dickson, David Piper and Michael Taylor. The days of the 15 were really over by 1961, but in 1962 test pilot 'Dizzy' Addicot raced with considerable success a 15 powered by a Buick 3.5-litre engine and this was the forerunner of the 'big-banger' Group 7 cars of the mid-1960s.

**Specification (Series 1, 1958):**
ENGINE: Coventry Climax FPF 1475 or 1960cc.
GEARBOX: Lotus 5-speed.
CHASSIS: multi-tubular space-frame.
FRONT SUSPENSION: double wishbones and coil spring/damper units.
REAR SUSPENSION: strut system, with coil spring/damper units, controlled vertically by hub castings, forward radius arms and fixed length half-shafts.
WHEELBASE: 7ft 4in.
FRONT TRACK: 3ft 11in.
REAR TRACK: 4ft 0in.
OVERALL LENGTH: 11ft 5in.
OVERALL WIDTH: 5ft 0in.
WEIGHT: approx. 980 lb dry.

# 16

*Formula 1 and Formula 2, 1958–9*

Based on the experience gained with the 12, Chapman put in hand a much more advanced Formula 1 car at the beginning of the 1958 season. This was the most advanced and sophisticated of all front-engined 2.5-litre Grand Prix cars raced during the years 1954–60, but it was to prove an almost total failure, firstly because of its unreliability and secondly because the day of the front-engined car was over. Jack Brabham with the rear-engined Cooper was to win the 1959 World Championship and from that point onwards the traditional front-engined racing car was finished.

The 16 featured a multi-tubular space-frame, wider and stiffer than that of the type 12, again with Reynolds round-edge tubing for the lower longitudinal members and constructed mainly from 20-gauge tubing but with 18-gauge tubing used in the more highly stressed areas of the chassis. Later the chassis was modified by the addition of detachable tubes to support the fuel tank and gearbox (replacing the original sling arrangement) and there was a detachable tube mounted diagonally across the engine bay. The suspension was broadly similar to that of the 12, but the rear strut system incorporated longer radius rods. Girling disc brakes were mounted outboard at the front and inboard at the rear.

Although originally credited to Frank Costin, the bodywork again was sketched out by Colin Chapman and built by Williams & Pritchard. What Chapman had penned was the smoothest and most striking front-engined single-seater, with the very light bodywork constructed in 22-

Innes Ireland with the 16 in 1.5-litre Formula 2 form leads Ivor Bueb's British Racing Partnership Cooper-Borgward in the 1959 International Trophy at Silverstone. Ireland finished fourth in the Formula 2 class. *(T. C. March)*

In the 1959 British Grand Prix at Aintree Alan Stacey (Lotus 16) leads Harry Schell (BRM). Stacey finished eighth.
(T. C. March)

gauge aluminium sheet and closely wrapped round the chassis tubing. The bodywork was so light that it constantly cracked and split, distorted out of shape and was very easily damaged. The body featured a very small nose inlet, with a duct on the right-hand side enclosing the exhaust pipe and another on the left-hand side in which the alloy oil pipes forming the main cooler were enclosed. Because the body, which closely aped Costin's design for the Vanwall, although it was even smoother and more shapely, lacked proper ducting, not only were the drivers cooked in the cockpit but the cars constantly overheated.

In an effort to minimize the height and frontal area of the car, the Climax FPF engine was initially canted at 62 degrees to the right, and offset 5½ degrees from the chassis centre-line. The 'queerbox' was used in its latest form, with a lateral offset between the gearbox input and output shafts.

By the time the 16 was first raced at Reims, Climax had made it only too clear that they were unhappy with the engine arrangement and so hastily Lotus redesigned one of the cars so that a Formula 2 engine was mounted 17 degrees to the left and angled across the frame centre-line at 6½ degrees right front to left rear. Graham Hill drove a 2-litre 16 with the laid-down engine in the Formula 1 Grand Prix, but retired with a holed radiator, whilst the modified Formula 2 car was involved in a minor accident at the start of the race which dented the nose, closing off the air intake and holing the oil tank. Over-heating eliminated both 1.9-litre 16s entered in the British Grand Prix, Allison finished tenth in the

German race and in Portugal Allison non-started with his 16 after a practice crash; Hill was also eliminated in the Portugese race by an accident. Following the damage to Allison's car at Oporto, there was only the one 16 available for the last two races of the season, Monza and Ain Diab, and whilst Hill was still running at the finish of both races, he was too far behind to be classified.

The 16 appeared only twice in Formula 2 races in 1958, in the Formula 2 category at the German Grand Prix in which Hill retired and in the Kentish '100' race at Brands Hatch in August, in which Hill again retired.

For 1959 Chapman settled on an arrangement with the engine canted 17 degrees and offset 10½ degrees. In addition to the two cars raced in 1958 (one of which had been written off) six cars were built for 1959. John Fisher bought the car displayed at Earls Court in 1958 for Bruce Halford to drive in Formula 2 races. The car that had first appeared at the French Grand Prix in 1958 was sold to David Piper and Bob Bodle. The third private car was Anthony Brooke's and this was built up by him on what probably was the chassis of the car crashed by Allison in Portugal. There were five new cars raced by Team Lotus in 1959.

Lotus had been joined by Len Terry as designer/draughtsman and he introduced a number of changes to the 1959 cars, including an angled fire wall/bulkhead at the front of the cockpit, which helped the drivers to keep a little cooler and stiffened the chassis cockpit area. In addition the top-left chassis rail was kinked so as to clear the carburettors when the engine was removed. Subsequently the chassis was further stiffened by a fabricated and perforated sheet hoop around the dash panel. All the 1959 cars (other than that supplied to Fisher) had a revised front suspension of the so-called 'reverse type' with the anti-roll bar to the rear and kinked to clear the engine. At the rear there was now a new wider wishbone which replaced the original fixed-length shaft radius rod. During the year the bodywork was modified and outside exhaust systems were adopted.

Initially the Formula 1 team consisted of Graham Hill and Pete Lovely, but the latter drove only in one race, the International Trophy at Silverstone, and failed to qualify at Monaco before returning to the United States. His place was taken in the team by Innes Ireland. Both Innes Ireland and Alan Stacey had come to an arrangement with Lotus whereby each of them had a Formula 2 16 which they built up themselves from parts provided at cost, on the basis that a percentage of their income from racing the car was paid to Team Lotus. Retirement followed retirement throughout the year, but there were some highlights. In the Dutch Grand Prix at Zandvoort, Ireland and Hill took fourth and seventh places, and Ireland was sixth in the United States Grand Prix at Sebring. In Formula 2 the picture was a little better, with a second place by David Piper in the Preis von Zeltweg race in Austria, and a second place on aggregate by Hill in the Kentish '100' race at Brands Hatch.

By the end of 1959 Chapman had decided to abandon the front-engined layout for Formula 1, but 16s appeared in three races under the banner of Team Lotus in 1960. A pair of 16s were entered in both the Argentine Grand Prix and in the Buenos Aires City Grand Prix, whilst a Formula 2 car was driven by Stacey at Siracusa.

## Specification:

ENGINE: Coventry Climax FPF (various capacities).
GEARBOX: Lotus 5-speed.
CHASSIS: multi-tubular space-frame.
FRONT SUSPENSION: double wishbones with upper wishbone formed by transverse tubular link and coil spring/damper units.
REAR SUSPENSION: strut system, with coil spring/damper units, controlled vertically by hub castings, forward radius arms and fixed length half-shafts.
WHEELBASE: 7ft 4in.
FRONT AND REAR TRACK: 3ft 11in.
OVERALL LENGTH: 11ft 8in.
WEIGHT: approx. 1080 lb dry.

# 17

*Sports-Racing Car, 1959*

Lotus introduced a new contender in the 1100cc class of Sports Car racing in 1959 – the 17, a replacement for the now outdated Eleven, which was smaller, lighter, lower and more aerodynamic than its predecessor. Len Terry, who had joined Lotus was primarily responsible for the design, which featured a Lotus-style space-frame constructed from ⅝in and ¾in square and round 20-gauge tubing, with, as on the 15, the floor and the prop-shaft tunnel acting as stressed members. On the 17 for the first time Lotus adapted strut-type front suspension, with lower wishbones and almost vertical coil spring/ damper units. The rear suspension was again of the strut-type as used on the 15. Terry was also responsible for the design of the bodywork and this was constructed of aluminium and glass-fibre. The power unit was the Coventry Climax FWA 1098cc (stage 3) or the FWM 747cc engine, angled 10 degrees to the left. The gearbox again was the BMC B-series in a special Lotus casing in unit with the engine. A ZF limited slip differential was available as an extra. A single light alloy 8-gal fuel tank and SU fuel pump were mounted in the rear, together with the battery. Magnesium-alloy wheels were fitted front and rear, together with Girling disc brakes, mounted inboard at the rear.

Although the 17 undoubtedly proved unreliable and development was slow, its real prospects of a success in its class were thoroughly scotched by the new Lola that proved all-conquering in 1959. The 17 first appeared at Aintree in April, when it was driven by Alan Stacey, who came through from the back of the grid to take the lead, but retired because of gearbox trouble. This was a portent of Team Lotus fortunes with the 17 throughout the year. Two cars were entered at Le Mans, privately owned but entered in the name of Team Lotus and powered by the 745cc engines. Driven by Alan Stacey/ Keith Greene and Michael Taylor/Jonathan Sieff, both were eliminated by overheating problems. That Lotus struggled all year to make the cars a success was undoubted, but at the end of 1959 the company gave up and left the 1100cc class to Lola.

**Specification:**
ENGINE: Coventry Climax FWA 1098cc or FWM 745cc.
GEARBOX: 4-speed, BMC casing with Lotus gears, in unit with the engine.
CHASSIS: multi-tubular space-frame.
FRONT SUSPENSION: strut-type with coil spring/ damper units, wishbones and radius arms.
REAR SUSPENSION: strut-type with coil spring/ damper units, radius arms and fixed length drive-shafts.
WHEELBASE: 6ft 10in.
FRONT TRACK: 3ft 6in.
REAR TRACK: 3ft 9in.
OVERALL LENGTH: 10ft 11in.
OVERALL WIDTH: 4ft 7.5in.
WEIGHT approx. 750 lb. dry.

Alan Stacey with his Team Lotus 17 in the 1100cc Sports Car race at the International Trophy meeting at Silverstone in May 1959. He retired because of brake problems. The 17s were plagued by indifferent handling and were no match for the rival Lolas. *(T. C. March)*

# 18

*Formula 1, 2 and Junior, 1960*

During 1959 Chapman realized that his front-engined cars, for all their sophistication, were never likely to prove competitive in Formula 1 and that the way to go was to produce a rear-engined car, following the example of Cooper, whose design had been created through practical experience rather than any clear sense of direction. Not only was the 18 what might be described as the 'thinking man's Cooper' but it proved to be a successful all-round design equally suitable for Formula 1, Formula 2 and Formula Junior. The chassis was a properly triangulated space-frame using mainly very strong 18-gauge tubing, with some 16-gauge mild steel round tube. There was a fully triangulated front suspension bay (carrying a light forward sub-frame mounting the radiator, oil tank and body mounts), a cockpit area with strengthened side-bays and braced engine bulkhead, and with two straight tubes at the rear converging to meet the rear suspension pick-ups and with a detachable Y-frame that could be unbolted for engine and gearbox removal.

At the front suspension was by unequal-length wishbones and coil spring/damper units, whilst at the rear there were non-splined half-shafts, reversed lower wishbones, twin radius rods and coil spring/damper units, with anti-roll bars front and rear. The fuel was carried in a 22-gal aluminium tank above the driver's legs and there was a secondary 9½-gal tank behind and to the right of the driver's seat. Disc brakes were fitted front and rear, 10½in. at the front and 9½in, at the rear, the latter mounted inboard. The engine was the Coventry Climax FPF 2495cc and transmission was by the 'queerbox' in its latest form. The body was built in glass-fibre by Williams & Pritchard from an aluminium prototype shell, and it hugged the frame closely, giving the 18 a very square, squat appearance.

The 18 first made its appearance at the Boxing Day meeting at Brands Hatch in 1959 in Formula Junior form. The car was driven by Alan Stacey, but in practice the Cosworth engine blew and the engine from Graham Warner's Gemini was hastily substituted. In the race Stacey spun off, but recovered to come through to finish third. It was not a promising début, but 1960 was to prove that the new 18 was a truly outstanding car in every category in which it competed.

The first appearance of the 18 in Formula 1 form was in the Argentine Grand Prix and in this race Innes Ireland was second fastest in practice and led the race until he ran into mechanical problems; he finished sixth with one brake not working and deranged steering. At Goodwood on Easter Monday the 18 appeared in all three of its forms. The works Formula Junior car won its race in the hands of Jim Clark, and

At the May Silverstone meeting in 1960 Innes Ireland scored his second win with the Formula 1 18 in the International Trophy race. *(T. C. March)*

in fact the works team consisting of Clark, Trevor Taylor and Peter Arundell won most of the year's races.

Innes Ireland won the Formula 1 race at Goodwood, the Richmond Trophy, from Moss's Cooper and also won the Formula 2 Lavant Cup from Moss's Porsche. Ireland followed this up with another win in the International Trophy at Silverstone and by the Monaco Grand Prix Rob Walker had taken delivery of an 18 for Stirling Moss to drive. In practice Moss took pole position and he won the race from McLaren's Cooper, despite having to stop at the pits for a plug lead to be replaced and despite the fact that the engine mountings had broken, with the result that the front of the engine was being held on only by the water hose. This was a first World Championship victory for Lotus, but it had been achieved by a private entrant, the same private entrant who had scored Cooper's first World Championship victory in the Argentine in 1958. In the Dutch race Moss was forced to stop to change a wheel after it had been shattered by a lump of concrete kerbing thrown up by Brabham's Cooper; he lost two laps, and rejoined the race to finish fourth. Brabham won, with Ireland in second place.

Next came the Belgian Grand Prix, which was to prove a complete disaster for Lotus. Practice was marred by two terrible crashes; on Moss's car a rear stub axle failed, the 18 shed a wheel and Moss suffered severe injuries, which meant that he missed several races during the season. The Argentine 18, now driven by Mike Taylor as a

Trevor Taylor with his Team Lotus Formula Junior 18 at the International Trophy meeting at Silverstone in May 1960. Although he led the race, he finished second behind team-mate Jim Clark. *(T. C. March)*

private entrant, crashed badly when a faulty weld on the steering column broke, and he suffered broken ribs, clavicle and neck. In the race not only did Chris Bristow crash fatally at the wheel of his Cooper, but Lotus works driver Alan Stacey, apparently struck in the face by a bird, crashed with fatal results. Ireland retired his 18 and new to the team Jim Clark finished fifth.

Mainly because of the slow, straight-line speed of the 18, the works cars were out of the picture in the French Grand Prix and Clark, Flockhart (brought into the team for this one race) and Ireland finished fifth, sixth and seventh. At this race the works 18s were fitted with a tapered nose-section and enclosed carburettors, which was achieved by canting the engine to the right, and both alterations were intended to improve aerodynamics. Next came the British Grand Prix, where the works 18s driven by Surtees and Ireland finished second and third. All three works cars retired in the non-Championship Silver City Trophy at Brands Hatch on 1 August.

In 1960 the German Grand Prix was held as a Formula 2 race and so the next round in the Championship was the Portuguese Grand Prix, where Moss was back at the wheel of a car built up by the Walker mechanics around a new

chassis frame. Walker's car was also now fitted with a Colotti gearbox, which necessitated moving the rear brakes to an outboard position. In practice for the race Clark crashed badly, but the team managed to patch up his car and he drove fairly easy race to finish third behind the works Coopers of Brabham and McLaren. Ireland finished sixth whilst Surtees, who had taken pole position, spun out of the race because his foot slipped off the brake pedal as a result of a fuel leak. In Portugal Moss was very much off-form and he spun off when a brake grabbed. He tried to re-start his car by going downhill on the pavement against the direction of the race, and as a result was disqualified.

The British Formula 1 teams boycotted the Italian Grand Prix because it was run on the full Monza circuit with bankings and in their absence Ferrari enjoyed a walk-over. In minor events, however, Ireland won the Lombank Trophy at Snetterton (with Clark second) and Moss won the Gold Cup race at Oulton Park. Two further successes were to come for Moss in 1960, in the Watkins Glen Formule Libre race in October and in the United States Grand Prix at Riverside Raceway, where he won from Innes Ireland.

During 1960 18s with the 1.5-litre Climax FPF engine won Formula 2 races at Oulton Park

In 1961 Stirling Moss scored two brilliant victories, amongst the finest in his career, with Rob Walker's outdated Lotus 18 in the face of overwhelmingly strong Ferrari opposition. Here he is seen at Monaco where he scored his second successive win. In 1960 he ran as number 28; in 1961 he was number 20. *(David Phipps)*

in April (Ireland), the Crystal Palace in June (Trevor Taylor) and the 'Kentish 100' at Brands Hatch in August (Clark).

In Formula Junior the 18s almost completely dominated the year's racing. Team Lotus entered cars for Jim Clark, Trevor Taylor and, later in the year, Peter Arundell. Clark and Taylor were joint first in the British National Championship organized by *Motor Racing* magazine, Taylor and Clark took first and second places in the BARC Championship and Clark won the John Davy Championship.

Although there was a new 21 model for Formula 1 in 1961, in the early part of the season the works team continued to rely on the 18s. Not much in the way of success was gained, although Clark did win the Pau Grand Prix in April. Team Lotus also continued to race 18s in InterContinental events with 2.5-litre Climax engines and in a couple of Formula 1 races later in the year when the team was short of 21s because of accident damage. Stirling Moss continued to drive the Rob Walker 18 and in a year dominated by the immensely powerful V6 Ferraris, he succeeded in winning the Monaco Grand Prix (in addition to taking pole position and setting fastest lap), taking fourth place in the Dutch Grand Prix, winning the Silver City Trophy at Brands Hatch and scoring another remarkable World Championship victory in the German Grand Prix at the Nürburgring, by when his car had been fitted with new, rather more stylish bodywork and some 21 features. More minor successes for Moss followed in the Kanonloppet in Sweden, the Danish Grand Prix at Roskilde and the Modena Grand Prix. Moss also took second places behind Clark in the Rand Grand Prix at Kyalami, the Natal Grand Prix and the South African Grand Prix at East London.

Many private owners continued to race 18s well through 1963 and Moss was still at the wheel of an 18, albeit much modified, in the early part of 1962, and it was with this car fitted with a Coventry Climax V8 engine that he suffered the near-fatal accident in the Richmond Trophy at Goodwood in April that brought his long racing career to an end.

**Specification (Formula 1):**
ENGINE: Coventry Climax FPF 2495cc.
GEARBOX: Lotus 5-speed.
CHASSIS: multi-tubular space-frame.
FRONT SUSPENSION : unequal-length double wishbones and coil spring/damper units.
REAR SUSPENSION: non-splined half-shafts, reversed lower wishbones, twin radius rods and coil spring/damper units.
WHEELBASE: 7ft 6in.
FRONT TRACK: 4ft 4in.
REAR TRACK: 4ft 5.25in.
OVERALL LENGTH: 11ft 3in.
OVERALL WIDTH: 4ft 8.5in.
WEIGHT: approx. 980 lb dry.

# 19

*Sports-Racing Car, 1960–2*

Directly developed from the 18 rear-engined Formula 1 car raced by Lotus in 1960, the 19 appeared in August of that year. The chassis was very similar to that of the 18, a multi-tubular space-frame constructed from 1in and ¾in 18- and 16-gauge tubing and built up in three sections, the same way as the single-seater: a forward section that carried the mounting for the front suspension, with ahead of it a lighter frame carrying the water and oil radiators and the oil tanks; behind this was a sheet and tubular scaffold frame which was linked to the rear section by the centre cockpit area; to the rear of the cockpit the third section consisted of the engine bulkhead and the tubular rear engine bay. Front suspension was by double wishbones and coil spring/damper units and at the rear there were lower wishbones, with the unsplined drive-shafts providing a transverse location, parallel radius arms and coil spring/damper units. The body was constructed in aluminium and glass-fibre with quickly detachable nose-section and a one-piece engine cover. Originally the engine was the 2.5-litre Coventry Climax FPF used with the latest form of the Lotus 5-speed gearbox.

Stirling Moss tested the first car and then drove it to victory in a 56-mile race at Karlskoga in Sweden. Only 12 of these cars were built, partly because of the relative scarcity of the 2.5-litre engines. Nine cars, including the prototype, were sold in the United States and three were sold to the UDT-Laystall team to be raced in British events. The production cars were not delivered until the 1961 season. They scored many successes in both Britain and the United States over a period of years and certain of the cars sold in the United States were re-engined with American power units.

The 19B was a one-off sports-racing car built for Dan Gurney, with strengthened and modified suspension and powered by the Ford V8 engine. He raced it during 1962–3 and in the 1962 Daytona Continental Three Hours Road Race scored a win after the engine broke its crankshaft just before the start of the last lap and he crossed the line on the starter motor.

**Specification:**
ENGINE: Coventry Climax FPF 2495cc 4-cylinder.
GEARBOX: Lotus 5-speed.
CHASSIS: multi-tubular space-frame.
FRONT SUSPENSION: double wishbones and coil spring/damper unit.
REAR SUSPENSION: reversed lower wishbones, unsplined drive-shafts providing transverse location, parallel radius arms and coil spring/damper units.
WHEELBASE: 7ft 6in.
FRONT AND REAR TRACK: 4ft 1in.
LENGTH: 11ft 9in.
WEIGHT: 10 cwt.

Although the 19s won many races, they were mainly minor events. Innes Ireland won the 50-mile Sports Car race at the Gold Cup meeting at Oulton Park in 1962 with this 19 entered by the UDT-Laystall team. *(T. C. March)*

# 20

## *Formula Junior, 1961*

At the Racing Car Show held in London in January 1961 Lotus Components revealed their new Formula Junior car for the second full season of this class of racing to be held in Great Britain. Although the design closely followed that of the successful 18, there was a stark contrast in external appearance. Both chassis and suspension followed that of the 18, but changes included the top right and lower left main longitudinal members serving as water pipes between engine and radiator, there were now fabricated side tanks to carry the fuel in place of the scuttle tank of the 18 and the engine bay was stiffened by a detachable Y-shaped member. The body was a sleek aerodynamic design, contrasting strongly with the box-shape of the 18, and was built by Williams & Pritchard in three glass-fibre moulds. At the beginning of the year the power unit was the Cosworth-developed Ford 105E, developing around 85 bhp, but later in the year the team produced a 1100cc engine based on a linered-down version of the 1340cc Ford Classic 109E engine and developing 100 bhp. This was first seen in Trevor Taylor's car at Reims, and became more widely used as the season progressed. The gearbox was now a Renault 4-speed, replacing the 3-speed gearbox modified to take four gears that had been used in the 1960 Formula Junior version of the 18. Drum brakes were fitted to front and rear and there were Lotus cast magnesium 'wobbly-web' wheels, 13in at the front and 15in at the rear.

A version of this design with 1498cc Ford engine and disc brakes for Formule Libre and USA Formula B racing was known as the 20B. Total production of the 20, including 20B cars, amounted to 118 and the price quoted for the ordinary 20 in component form was £1450.

Team Lotus drivers Trevor Taylor and Peter Arundell enjoyed a great deal of success with the cars during 1961. Taylor won more races, eight, including victories at Goodwood, Reims and

The battle for the lead in the Formula Junior race at Silverstone in May 1961 between Peter Arundell (the most successful driver that year) and Jim Russell. Arundell stopped at the pits and Russell won the race.
*(T. C. March)*

Solitude, whilst Arundell won seven races, including the probably most prestigious Junior race of the year, the Prix Monaco Junior. In addition Jo Siffert, with his private 20, also won seven races during the year.

**Specification:**
ENGINE: Cosworth-modified Ford 105E 997cc developing 85 bhp.
GEARBOX: Renault 4-speed.
CHASSIS: multi-tubular space-frame.
FRONT SUSPENSION: double wishbones and coil spring/damper units.
REAR SUSPENSION: reversed lower wishbones, unsplined drive-shafts providing transverse location, parallel radius arms and coil spring/damper units.
WHEELBASE: 7ft 6in.
FRONT TRACK: 4ft 1in.
REAR TRACK: 4ft 0in.
LENGTH: 11ft 7in.
WEIGHT: 7.19 cwt.

# 21

*Formula 1, 1961*

From the very successful 18, Lotus developed the 20 Formula Junior car, which was exhibited at the Racing Car Show in January 1961, and this was the link between the 18 and the 21. Originally the 21 had been designed to take the new Coventry Climax V8 engine complying with the new 1500cc Grand Prix formula that came into force that year. It soon became apparent, however, that British constructors' opposition to the new Formula had resulted in substantial delay in starting work and development on both the Coventry Climax and the BRM V8 engines. Accordingly Lotus were forced to redesign the car to take an improved version of the 4-cylinder 1497cc FPF engine, the Mark II which was used with a ZF gearbox that had been intended for the V8-powered car. The chassis followed the design principles of the 18, including the incorporation of perforated stress-panels at the dashboard and at the rear end and with a Y-frame bolted across the top of the engine bay. To comply with the new Formula 1 minimum weight requirement of 450kg, the 21 was heavier.

At the front the suspension incorporated fabricated top rocking arms actuating inboard-mounted coil spring/damper units and at the rear there was also a new layout, with a top link which produced the necessary roll-centre height. The rear suspension also incorporated the new Metalstik rubber couplings. The FPF engine, which now incorporated the strong bottom end of the 2.5-litre version, was canted 18 degrees to the right in the frame to provide a lower engine cover. Partly because there were now 30-gal fuel tanks in aluminium cells which were attached to the chassis frame by bungees, Chapman had drawn smoother, more curvaceous lines than those of the 18. Other changes were that both front and rear brakes were now mounted outboard, the frame tubes were used to carry oil and water because of the limited cockpit space and the driver sat in a much more inclined position, so that his head was lowered by two inches or thereabouts. Another change was the adoption of 15in wobbly-web wheels, instead of the 13in wheels used on the 18.

The problem faced by Team Lotus throughout 1961 was the sheer power of the Ferrari Tipo 156s that dominated the year's racing, apart from the two wins scored by Moss with Rob Walker's 18 at Monaco and the Nürburgring (by when the Walker car incorporated certain 21 features). From the first appearance of the 21 at Monaco, the season for both Jim Clark and Innes Ireland proved disappointing. Ireland failed to start at Monaco because of a bad

Although an interim car to take the 4-cylinder Climax FPF Mk II engine for the 1961 season, design features of the 21, especially the suspension, were to persist on Lotus competition cars for many years. Here Jim Clark is seen in the 1961 Gold Cup race at Oulton Park in which he retired because of suspension problems. *(T. C. March)*

practice crash, the result of him becoming confused over the new arrangement of the gearchange whilst Clark finished a poor tenth. The best performances during the year were third place by Clark in the Dutch Grand Prix at Zandvoort, second by Clark (behind Moss) in the Silver City Trophy at Brands Hatch in June, third and fourth places by Clark and Ireland in the French Grand Prix at Reims, a win by Ireland in the non-Championship Solitude Grand Prix, and fourth place by Clark in the German Grand Prix; later in the year Ireland won the Flugplatz Rennen race at Zeltweg, and Ireland scored the team's first victory in a Championship race at the United States Grand Prix at Watkins Glen in October – but Ferrari did not enter this race. Clark won the non-Championship races at Kyalami, Westmead and East London in South Africa in December. Trevor Taylor also won the Cape Grand Prix at Killarney with Clark second on 2 January, 1962.

Private owners, including Jack Brabham and Jo Siffert (entered by Scuderia Filipinetti), continued to race these cars with limited success in 1962.

The problem with the 21 was not any deficiency in design or development, but simply that the cars were underpowered compared with their Ferrari rivals.

**Specification:**
ENGINE: Coventry Climax FPF Mk II.
TRANSMISSION: ZF 5-speed gearbox and combined final drive.
CHASSIS: multi-tubular space-frame.
FRONT SUSPENSION: upper fabricated cantilever rocking arms, lower wishbones and outboard coil spring/damper units.
REAR SUSPENSION: upper links, twin radius rods, reversed lower wishbones and outboard coil spring/damper units.
WHEELBASE: 7ft 6in.
MAXIMUM TRACK: 4ft 5.25in.
OVERALL LENGTH: 11ft 9in.
WEIGHT: 8.91 cwt.

# 22

## Formula Junior, 1962

The 1962 Formula Junior Lotus, the 22, was a modified version of the 20, but the standard engine, the 1098cc Cosworth-Ford, was inclined 30 degrees to the right in the frame so as to achieve a significant reduction in the height of the rear bodywork and at the same time provide a better induction tract. There was the choice of a 4-speed Renault or VW gearbox, Girling disc brakes were fitted front and rear, the oil system was also now taken through the chassis tubes, and there was now a ½in rear anti-roll bar. Power output of the Cosworth-Ford engine was guaranteed to be 100 bhp at 7500 rpm. Disc brakes had been adopted because these had now been homologated on the production Triumph Herald car and were fitted outboard at the rear because of lack of space for inboard rear calipers. The track was slightly wider and the price was £100 more than the 20, £1550, to cover the extra cost of the disc brakes and the 1100cc Cosworth engine.

The Team Lotus works entries were driven by Peter Arundell, Alan Rees and Bob Anderson. Arundell had a magnificent season, winning a total of 18 races out of the 25 in which he was entered and in addition taking three second places. Neither Rees nor Anderson achieved much in the way of success. In addition, Ian Walker Racing ran private 22 cars for Mike Spence and Peter Ryan. Ryan, a Canadian, was sadly killed in a collision with the Gemini of Bill Moss at Reims. Lotus totally dominated the season, despite a strong challenge from the works Brabhams and the Coopers entered by Ken Tyrrell, but such was the success of Lotus that the magazine *Das Auto Motor und Sport*, through an article written by its Editor, Richard von Frankenberg, alleged that Lotus were using 1450cc engines. The origins of the story lay in an interview with Alan Rees, injured in a crash at the Nürburgring, who when questioned under sedation refused to sell the engine from his crashed car on the grounds that it belonged to the works. Understandably Chapman and Team Lotus took the accusations very seriously and accepted a challenge thrown down by von Frankenberg to take a 22 to any circuit which he chose, to repeat their race-winning speeds and to allow the size of the engine to be checked. There

The 22, the 1962 Formula Junior car, was just as successful as its predecessors. Peter Arundell is seen on his way to a win with the 22 in the Formula Junior race at the Gold Cup meeting at Oulton Park. Following is Tony Maggs (Cooper-Austin).

was to be a wager that would cover all expenses and if Team Lotus won, von Frankenberg would withdraw his allegations.

The circuit chosen by von Frankenberg was Monza and Arundell had to match the speeds that he had achieved in the Monza Lottery Grand Prix, an average of 113.47 mph over 30 laps and his fastest lap 1 min 50.8 sec (115.99 mph). Arundell averaged 115.16 mph for the 30 laps on a circuit that was less than perfect, for the day was very cold and there were patches of ice under the trees on the circuit, and his fastest lap was 1 min 50.4 sec. Afterwards Arundell completed three extra laps, recording a best time of 1 min 40.8 sec (117.14 mph). When the engine was dismantled by the scrutineers, it was found that it had a capacity of 1092.348cc (85 x 48.15mm), it was 3kg over the minimum weight limit (of 400kg) and von Frankenberg was forced to retract his allegations and to pay to Lotus the sum of £1000.

**Specification:**
ENGINE: Cosworth-modified Ford 105E 1097cc developing 100 bhp.
GEARBOX: Renault 4-speed.
CHASSIS: multi-tubular space-frame.
FRONT SUSPENSION: double wishbones and coil spring/damper units.
REAR SUSPENSION: reversed lower wishbones, unsplined drive-shafts providing transverse location, parallel radius arms and coil spring/damper units.
WHEELBASE: 7ft 6in.
FRONT TRACK: 4ft 3.5in.
REAR TRACK: 4ft 2in.
LENGTH: 11ft 7in.
WEIGHT: 7.88 cwt.

# 23

## *Sports-Racing, 1962–4*

Based on the 22 Formula Junior car, Lotus produced in 1962 the 23 sports-racing car with the same 1097cc Cosworth-Ford modified engine claimed to develop 103 bhp (although cars were also built with 997 and 1599cc engines), Renault or VW-based 4-speed gearbox and final drive unit, the multi-tubular space frame widened to form a two-seater and with similar suspension. The glass-fibre bodywork complied with the then current Appendix J, Group 4 sports car regulations and, in addition to the standard 9-gal fuel tank, extra fuel tanks could be accommodated for use in long-distance races. The car was also very inexpensive, £1650, in component form.

The 23 first made its mark in the Nürburgring 1000 Km race, where a car was entered in the name of the Essex Racing team, under the supervision of Mike Costin. This 23 was fitted with a 1498cc twin overhead camshaft engine, based on the Ford 116E block soon to be used in the Ford Classic, developing around 140 bhp and to become the standard production

Lotus engine. The drivers at the Nürburgring were Formula 1 team members Jim Clark and Trevor Taylor.

At the start of the race in damp and very slippery conditions Clark led away from the Le Mans start, he was still leading at the end of lap 1 from strong Ferrari and Porsche opposition and by the end of lap 8 had a lead of over two minutes. The field closed up as the track dried out and on lap 12, suffering from fumes from a leaking exhaust, Clark failed to correct a slide at Kesselchen and the Lotus finished its race in the ditch. It was quite a remarkable performance for such a small capacity car to lead the field in a major international race.

There were two 23s entered at Le Mans, a works car with 997cc twin-cam Lotus engine and from UDT-Laystall an entry with 745cc Climax engine. At scrutineering the cars were rejected on the grounds that the front wheels had four-stud fixing and the rear wheels six-stud, so that the spare could be used on only one axle. Chapman modified the cars to to take the four-stud wheels at the rear, but when they were presented again for scrutineering, the scrutineers refused to look at them and claimed that the rear wheels had been designed for six-stud fitting and

Jim Clark at the wheel of Ian Walker Racing's 1.5-litre Lotus 23 at Oulton Park in September 1962. After a delayed start he fought his way through the field, headlamps ablaze, to finish second to Innes Ireland's Lotus 19. *(T. C. March)*

The 23 and 23B enjoyed long careers in British racing. One of the most successful drivers in later years was Tommy Weber, whose 23B was powered by a BRM Formula 2 engine. Here Weber (No. 118) is being lapped by Sadler (Lotus 30) in the 1966 Tourist Trophy at Oulton Park. *(T. C. March)*

so with four studs they must be dangerous. The RAC intervened on behalf of Lotus, but the cars were excluded from the race. It was only too clear that the exclusion had been a deliberate move to protect the interests of the French teams that normally contested the Index of Performance. Chapman made a vow that he would never again race at Le Mans and he never did so.

Later in 1962 there appeared the 23B version with strengthened chassis and this was usually fitted with the Lotus-Ford 1594cc twin-cam engine. In all 131 of these cars were manufactured.

Probably the most successful 23 was that of Mike Beckwith entered by Normand Racing, and the Ian Walker Racing Team also enjoyed successes with their 23s. The Le Mans UDT car, powered by a 997cc Lotus twin cam engine and driven by Rosinski/Consten won its class in the Montlhèry 1000 Km in 1962. In 1963 Normand ran a team of three cars for Mike Beckwith, Tony Hegbourn and Jim Clark and Clark's successes included wins at Snetterton, Oulton Park and the Crystal Palace.

**Specification (1962):**
ENGINE: Cosworth-modified Ford 1097cc (85 x 48.4mm) developing 100 bhp at 7500 rpm.
GEARBOX: Renault or VW 4-speed.
CHASSIS: multi-tubular space-frame.
FRONT SUSPENSION: double wishbones and coil spring/damper units.
REAR SUSPENSION: reversed lower wishbones, unsplined drive-shafts providing transverse location, parallel radius arms and coil spring/damper units.
WHEELBASE: 7ft 6in.
FRONT TRACK: 4ft 3.5in.
REAR TRACK: 4ft 2in.
OVERALL LENGTH: 11ft 7in.
OVERALL WIDTH: 4ft 9in.
OVERALL HEIGHT: 2ft 8in.
WEIGHT: 7.9 cwt.

# 24

## Formula 1, 1962

This was the first Lotus Formula 1 car to appear in 1962, but it was soon to be superseded by the monocoque 25. The 24 was broadly similar to the 21, but it was designed to take the new Coventry Climax FWMV V8 twin overhead camshaft engine. The space-frame was now built by Arch Motors (who had replaced Progress Chassis as Lotus chassis builders, who built only one 24), there were new cast front suspension uprights (replacing the Triumph components used previously) and new rack and pinion steering whereby the track-rod was level with the top rocker arm and improved air flow through the front suspension. Other changes were a scuttle fuel tank mounted above the driver's legs because of the higher fuel consumption of the FWMV and there were rubber doughnut couplings on the inboard end of the drive-shafts.

Team Lotus used the 24 at the beginning of the season and Jim Clark scored a number of successes, including a win in the Lombank Trophy at Snetterton in April, a win in the Aintree 200 race the same month and second place in the International Trophy at Silverstone, where he was beaten by a narrow margin by Graham Hill (BRM), whilst his team-mate Trevor Taylor took second place in the Dutch Grand Prix at Zandvoort. By this stage Clark was at the wheel of the first of the new 25s, but Taylor continued to race the works 24 for much of the season. He was one of the unluckiest of number two drivers in Team Lotus, crashing badly at Spa and achieving nothing much during the remainder of the year.

In all about 15 24s were built by Lotus, and it was to be the mainstay of private teams, some who were very disappointed when Lotus so swiftly afterwards produced the monocoque 25. Amongst purchasers were Jack Brabham, the UDT-Laystall team, whose cars were usually powered by BRM engines, and Jo Siffert, who raced a car for Scuderia Filipinetti. Innes Ireland, dropped by the Lotus team, achieved a measure of success with his UDT-Laystall car

Jim Clark at the wheel of his Team Lotus space-frame 24 in the International Trophy at Silverstone in May 1962. Right on the finishing line he was pushed back into second place by Graham Hill (BRM) in one of the closest finishes ever seen at Silverstone. *(T. C. March)*

Original colour of the 12 and 16 when raced by Team Lotus is unavailable. This photograph was taken in 1968. Dave Boorer is seen with his ex-Stacey car, 366, at the VSCC Silverstone meeting in April. *(Guy Griffiths)*

Stirling Moss at the wheel of Rob Walker's 18 in the 1960 Gold Cup race at Oulton Park which he won.
*(T. C. March)*

Another view of an 18 in the 1960 Gold Cup. This is Innes Ireland with a works car which he retired because of brake failure. *(T. C. March)*

Masten Gregory leads Mike Hailwood in the 1963 British Grand Prix at Silverstone. Both were at the wheel of 24s entered by Reg Parnell (Racing), but Gregory's car was BRM-powered and Hailwood used a Climax V8 engine. Hailwood finished eighth and Gregory 11th. Gregory's car appears to have an ex-UDT-Laystall nose-cone, characterized by the shield-shaped intakes. *(Guy Griffiths)*

The 1963 British race was won by Jim Clark with his works 25. He also won the World Championship for the first time that year. *(Guy Griffiths)*

Mike Spence at the wheel of his Team Lotus 33 before the start of the 1965 British Grand Prix at Silverstone. He finished fourth. *(Guy Griffiths)*

Jim Clark in pole position on the starting grid for the 1965 British Grand Prix. Alongside him are Hill (BRM), Ginther (Honda) and Stewart (BRM). Clark won the race for the fourth year in succession. *(Guy Griffiths)*

The original 49 of 1967 was sleek and purposeful and the lack of rear engine cover was distinctive. Jim Clark is seen at the 1967 British Grand Prix. *(Chris Willows)*

An atmospheric shot of Graham Hill with the 49 taken in the paddock at the 1967 British Grand Prix. *(Chris Willows)*

Graham Hill with the 49 in the 1968 Race of Champions at Brands Hatch. This was the sole Gold Leaf Team Lotus entry, but Hill retired. *(Nigel Snowdon)*

At Monaco in 1968 Graham Hill with the longer wheelbase, Hewland-gearbox 49B (49B/5) scored a fourth victory in the race. *(Nigel Snowdon)*

Jo Siffert with Rob Walker's 49B on his way to a win in the 1968 British Grand Prix at Brands Hatch – the last win by a private owner in a World Championship race. Following is Chris Amon with his Ferrari V12. *(Nigel Snowdon)*

Jack Oliver on his way to third place with the 49B in the Gold Cup race at Oulton Park in August 1968. This photograph shows clearly the high rear aerofoils adopted by all the teams that year. *(Nigel Snowdon)*

Graham Hill in practice for the 1969 Monaco Grand Prix. Before the race, won by Hill for the fifth time, high-mounted rear aerofoils were banned. *(Nigel Snowdon)*

In the 1971 Race of Champions at Brands Hatch the gas-turbine 56B was driven by Emerson Fittipaldi. He retired after the car had bottomed badly and damaged the right rear suspension. *(Nigel Snowdon)*

The unsuccessful four-wheel-drive 63, seen here driven in the 1969 British Grand Prix by John Miles. Miles finished ninth, with the gearbox jammed in third for the last 30 laps. *(Guy Griffiths)*

In the 1962 British Grand Prix Jack Brabham (about to launch his own Formula 1 car) with 24/947 leads Innes Ireland (24/943) entered by the UDT-Laystall team. Brabham finished fifth, but Ireland was 16th and last. *(T. C. March)*

and his successes include a win in the rather parochial race at the Crystal Palace in June, third place in the Reims Grand Prix at the beginning of July, third place in the Danish Grand Prix at the Roskildering in August, and third place in the Mexican Grand Prix in November. Private owners continued to race 24s throughout the years of the 1500cc Grand Prix formula.

**Specification:**
ENGINE: Coventry Climax FWMV V8.
TRANSMISSION: ZF 5-speed gearbox and combined final drive.
CHASSIS: multi-tubular spaceframe.
FRONT SUSPENSION: upper fabricated cantilever rocking arms, lower wishbones and inboard coil spring/damper units.
REAR SUSPENSION: upper links, twin radius rods, reversed lower wishbones and outboard coil spring/damper units.
WHEELBASE: 7ft 6in.
MAXIMUM TRACK 4ft 5.25in.
OVERALL LENGTH: 11ft 10in.
DRY WEIGHT: 8.92 cwt.

# 25

## *Formula 1, 1962–5*

Revolutionary by Formula 1 standards, the 25 was, with its immediate successor the 33, and together with BRM's V8, the most successful car of the 1500cc Grand Prix Formula 1961–5. Having introduced the 24 for 1962, Chapman almost immediately superseded it by this new monocoque car, with two stressed pontoons joined by the undertray, front and rear bulkheads, a stressed panel carrying the instruments and with additional tubular cross-bracing at the front. The monocoque extended the full length of the car and the engine was enclosed in it as a semi-stressed member. The concept of a monocoque for racing was by no means original and indeed the Jaguar D-type of 1954 featured a monocoque centre-section. Because of the use of rubber fuel bags inside the two pontoons, there was a substantial saving in weight.

The suspension was as on the 24, but a minor change was that the rear coil spring/damper units were now mounted ahead of the drive-shafts instead of behind them. The power unit was the Coventry-Climax FWMV V8 twin-cam 1497cc engine and transmission was by twin-plate Borg & Beck clutch and a ZF 5-speed combined gearbox and final drive unit, with synchromesh on second to fifth gears. Chapman again adopted Metalastik bonded-rubber couplings so as to avoid the use of sliding-spline drive-shafts. One of the biggest problems with the 25 was the fact that the cockpit was so cramped, necessitating the use of pendant pedals and extra cockpit space was provided by the use of a 12in-diameter steering wheel. That the 25s were retained solely for the works team during the years 1962–3 heightened the irritation and frustration of the private teams, who had already bought the 24.

From 1962 Jim Clark was joined at Team Lotus by Trevor Taylor, but whilst Clark enjoyed an extremely successful season, taking second place to Hill in the World Championship, Taylor's year was dogged by misfortune. Clark first appeared with the 25 in the Dutch Grand Prix, where he finished a poor ninth, and he retired at Monaco, but subsequently he won the Belgian race at Spa-Francorchamps, retired at Reims (a non-Championship race), retired in the Championship French Grand Prix at Rouen,

won the British race at Aintree, was fourth in the German Grand Prix at the Nürburgring and also won the United States Grand Prix. He scored minor successes with the 25 in the Gold Cup race at Oulton Park, which he won, and he also won the Mexican Grand Prix after taking over Trevor Taylor's car; in this race Clark was disqualified for receiving a push-start. His final win in 1962 came in the Rand Grand Prix. Taylor achieved nothing during the year with the 25, other than a third place in the Solitude Grand Prix, a second place in the Rand Grand Prix and a victory over Clark in the Natal Grand Prix, all non-Championship races.

Only detail changes were made to the 25s for 1963. The original carburettor Climax V8 engine had been replaced by an improved fuel-injected version, the later monocoques were in lighter-gauge sheeting than the prototype car, and 1963 cars featured side ducts on the glass-fibre nose-cones. The main result of these changes was a reduction in weight and great efforts had been made to improve the reliability of the 25. Early in the year Clark scored a number of successes, including second place to Hill in the Lombank Trophy at Snetterton, wins at Pau and Imola, a third place at Aintree where he took over Taylor's car, and a win in the International Trophy at Silverstone. Clark retired in the first round of the World Championship at Monaco, but won at Spa, Zandvoort, Reims and Silverstone. In three of these races Clark took pole position and in three he set fastest lap of the race.

After third-string team-member Arundell had finished third at Solitude, Clark finished second to Surtees (Ferrari) in the German Grand Prix. Another minor win for Clark followed at Karlskoga, and Arundell finished second in the Mediterranean Grand Prix at Enna in Sicily. At another non-Championship race, the Austrian Grand Prix at Zeltweg, a new 25, chassis R6, appeared in much modified form, with the latest flat-crank Climax V8 engine featuring a low-level exhaust system a Hewland 5-speed VW-derived gearbox, together with modified suspension. The use of the Hewland gearbox was not continued. Clark retired at Zeltweg, but he subsequently won the Italian Grand Prix (setting fastest lap), the non-Championship Gold Cup race at Oulton Park (where he took pole position and set fastest lap), finished third in the United States Grand Prix at Watkins Glen (and set fastest lap). He rounded off the

In 1962 Jim Clark with the monocoque Climax V8-powered Lotus 25 scored the first of four successive wins in the British Grand Prix which was held that year at Aintree. *(T. C. March)*

season with a win in the Mexican Grand Prix (at which he also took pole position and set fastest lap) and in South Africa (where he again won and took pole position). Clark won the Drivers' World Championship with 54 points (the maximum) to the 29 of Graham Hill (BRM), and Lotus dominated the Constructors' Cup with 54 points (the maximum) to the 36 of BRM.

For 1964, with design control in the hands of Len Terry, who had rejoined Lotus, work was continuing on the 33, an improved version of the 25, but parallel with work on this car, developments of the 25 appeared. At Snetterton in March 1964 Team Lotus entered the first of the 25B cars, which featured revised suspension incorporating lower rear radius rods, lower rear links, 13in cast magnesium spoked wheels with smaller brake discs and new suspension uprights. The ZF gearbox/final drive unit was retained, but there was an improved gear linkage. Although the 33 first appeared at Aintree in April, for much of the year both Clark and his new team-mate Peter Arundell used the 25s. Clark's favourite mount was chassis R6, incorporating all the latest modifications, but also the top radius rod repositioned on the hub carrier at the same level as the lateral link. Unofficially this car was known as the 25D, whilst Arundell's usual chassis, R4, with the earlier suspension, but smaller wheels, the new suspension uprights and modified gearbox was usually referred to as the 25C. Later in the year Clark's 25D was fitted with modified Mercedes-Benz sliding-spline drive-shafts.

During 1964 Reg Parnell (Racing) became the first private team to run a 25, when R4 was lent to them for the Austrian Grand Prix, following Arundell's severe crash in the Formula 2 race at Reims. Later in the year they were sold two ex-works 25s, featuring the later modifications,

Mike Spence was number two at Team Lotus in 1964 and here he is seen with the modified 25B car that he drove into ninth place, three laps behind his winning team-mate in the British Grand Prix. *(Nigel Snowdon)*

and they were raced with BRM V8 engines and Hewland transmissions.

Clark's successes with the 25 during the year included a win in the *News of the World* Trophy at Goodwood at the end of March, together with wins in the Dutch, Belgian and British Grands Prix. In addition he won the non-Championship Solitude Grand Prix at Stuttgart and finished second in the non-Championship Mediterranean Grand Prix at Enna. Arundell showed promise prior to his bad crash, taking several third places, including the Monaco Grand Prix, and later in the year Mike Spence, who replaced him in the team, finished sixth at Monza and fourth in the Mexican race. Of these successes the performances at Solitude and Monza were with 33s.

For the next two seasons plus Team Lotus was to rely on the 33, but private owners continued to race the modified 25s with limited success.

**Specification (1963):**
ENGINE: Coventry Climax FWMV V8.
TRANSMISSION: ZF 5-speed gearbox and combined final drive.
CHASSIS: 'bath-tub'-type monocoque.
FRONT SUSPENSION: upper fabricated cantilever rocking arms, lower wishbones and inboard coil spring/damper units.
REAR SUSPENSION: upper links, twin radius rods, reversed lower wishbones and outboard coil spring/damper units.
WHEELBASE: 7ft 6in.
MAXIMUM TRACK: 4ft 5.25in.
OVERALL LENGTH: 11ft 10in.
WEIGHT: 8.88 cwt (dry).

# 26 Elan (also 26R, 36 and 45)

*Production sports car, 1962–71*

Once it had become obvious that the Elite was not proving the commercial success that Chapman had hoped, he turned his mind to a successor that would be economic to build, would combine reliability and performance and hopefully would have a long production life. Above all Chapman wanted the new car to have a twin overhead camshaft engine and after lengthy discussions, Harry Mundy, then Technical Editor of *The Autocar*, but previously with BRM and Coventry Climax and who had designed the Facellia twin-cam engine, agreed to design a light alloy twin-cam head to mate with the Ford 1500cc block. Preliminary development work was carried out with the Ford 109E 1340cc engine, but the production versions were based on the five-bearing 116E unit. The first 22 Elans were fitted with 1498cc (81.5 x 72.75mm) engines, but from May 1963 onwards all cars had larger 1558cc (82.55 x 72.55mm) engines and the engines in the first cars were replaced. The overhead camshafts were driven by a single roller chain, with the existing side-mounted camshaft driving the distributor and oil pump. Carburation was by two twin-choke Weber or Dell'Orto carburettors or, for overseas markets, two constant-vacuum Zenith-Strombergs. The Zenith-Strombergs were however fitted to cars sold on the British market from November 1968 to August 1969. The power output of the original engine was 100 bhp, but the 1558cc unit developed 105 bhp at 5500 rpm in standard tune, 115 bhp at 6000 rpm in Special Equipment form and 126 bhp at 6500 rpm in later Sprint form. The light alloy cylinder heads were originally produced for Lotus by J.A. Prestwich (manufacturers of JAP engines), but after this company had been taken over by Villiers, the jigs and tools were passed to Lotus so that they could manufacture themselves at Hethel.

For the Elan Chapman conceived a very simple, very rigid backbone form of construction, with a relatively narrow, but deep central section (acting as the propeller-shaft tunnel), a deep 'two-prong' section at the front and with a box-section cross-member and integral suspension uprights. To the rear there was a much shorter 'two-prong' section, linked by a cross-member and with integral suspension uprights. The front

Sir John Whitmore with this Elan entered by Ian Walker finished sixth overall and second in the 2000cc class behind another Elan driven by Peter Procter in the Ilford Films Trophy for GT cars at the 1964 British Grand Prix meeting at Brands Hatch. *(T. C. March)*

At the International Trophy at Silverstone in May 1964 Graham Warner at the wheel of The Chequered Flag's competition Elan shed a wheel in the race for Grand Touring cars. Although it is not to be seen in this photograph, Warner's Elan carried the same registration number as his famous Elite, LOV 1. Following the Elan is Graham Hill, race winner with the Ferrari 250 GT0/64 entered by Maranello Concessionaires. *(T. C. March)*

fork mounted the engine and Ford 4-speed all-synchromesh gearbox. At the front there were pressed steel unequal-length double wishbones and coil spring/damper units, whilst at the rear there was strut-type independent suspension, incorporating wide-based triangulated tubular lower wishbones and built-in coil spring/damper units. Rack-and-pinion steering was fitted. There was a chassis-mounted hypoid bevel final drive, Girling disc brakes (at the rear mounted inboard of the damper units close to the Rotoflex rubber doughnut-type universal joints) and bolt-on steel wheels.

The body, built in glass-fibre, was constructed in two sections, the upper main body and the floor pan and wheel arches. These two parts were laminated into a one-piece moulding during construction and the then one-piece body, forming a saddle over the backbone chassis, was bolted at 16 points and provided some extra stiffening for the structure. The Elan was announced at the 1962 Earls Court Show at a price, including purchase tax, of £1495 or, maintaining the tradition started with the Elite, at £1095 in kit form. From May 1963, when the larger engine was adopted, a hardtop was available as an optional extra.

From its announcement the Elan was recognized as an enthusiast's sports car, very compact, with quick high-geared steering (2½ turns lock-to-lock), superlative, beautifully balanced handling, 0–60 mph acceleration of around 8.7 sec and a top speed of about 115 mph (without rev limiter, about 7 mph less with rev limiter). It was not, however, a car with a high standard of finish (vinyl or similar plastic trim only was available) and it was rather crude and noisy compared with some of the then available opposition.

Throughout its production life the Elan was progressively modified and the developments can be summarized as follows:

**Series 2:** Introduced November 1964. The principal changes were larger front brake callipers, full-width wood veneer facia with lockable glove box and quick-release filler cap. Centre-lock wheels were an optional extra. The price was £1435 including purchase tax and £1179 in component form.

**Series 3:** In September 1965 the 36 fixed head coupé was introduced, with detail changes including the boot lid extended to the lip above

An interesting variant of the Elan was a competition fixed head coupé developed by Ian Walker Racing. This car, painted red, was driven by hill climb exponent David Good. He is seen at The Three Clubs meeting at Wiscombe Park in June 1965 on his way to winning the class for Grand Touring cars up to 1600cc. *(The Author)*

the rear vertical panel, the battery mounted in the boot and later in the model's production life, extractor grilles in the sides of the coupé roof behind the trailing edges of the doors. A close-ratio gearbox became optional on both open and closed models in November 1965 (many would have said that a 5-speed gearbox was needed), and in January 1966 both became available in SE (Special Equipment) form with 115 bhp engine, the close-ratio gearbox, servo-assisted brakes, centre-lock wheels and repeater flashers (on the front wheel arches) as standard. It was not until June 1966 that the 45 Series 3 convertible was introduced, featuring framed windows and the other features of the fixed head coupé. The price of the fhc when introduced was £1613 including purchase tax.

**Series 4:** Introduced in March 1968, the Series 4, available in both fhc and convertible forms, incorporated flared wheel arches (to accommodate low profile tyres), rocker facia switches and a bulge in the bonnet (as on the Plus 2).

**Elan S4 Sprint:** Fitted with the 'Big Valve' engine developing 126 bhp, designed by Tony Rudd, this model was introduced in 1971 at

£1663 (fhc) and £1686 (convertible) in component form. Other features included strengthened drive-shaft couplings, drive-shafts and differential and there was a two-colour paint scheme.

The last six Elans were fitted with 5-speed gearboxes.

Production of the Elan ceased in August 1973. For much of the information in this section the author was heavily dependent on *The Lotus Elan and Europa* by John Bolster (Motor Racing Publications Ltd., reprinted 1985).

There is much confusion about production figures for the Elan, but the figures have been carefully analysed by Paul Robinshaw and Christopher Ross (*The Original 1962–1973 Lotus Elan*, Motor Racing Publications Ltd., 1989) as follows:

Series 1: 900 (including 52 26R competition cars)
Series 2: 1250 (including 45 26R competition cars)
Series 3: 2650
Series 4: Between 2976 and 3000
Sprint: Between 900 and 1353

Sales catalogue for the Lotus Elan Series 4.

## 26R

This was the competition version of the Elan and much of the development work was carried out by Graham Warner's The Chequered Flag and the team's car, carrying the same registration as the team's Elite, LOV 1, was driven by Warner, Mike Spence and Jackie Stewart. Differences between the 26R and production cars included lighter bodies with much thinner glass-fibre panels, a power output of around 140 bhp, and modified steering and suspension.

The cars were raced by a large number of teams, including SMART (Stirling Moss Automobile Racing Team), Ian Walker Racing, the Willment team (John Miles with the team's car powered by the 158 bhp BRM Phase 2 version of the Lotus engine won the 1966 *Autosport* Championship) and very many private owners, but in the main successes were limited to Club events. As mentioned above, there was a total of 97 26R cars.

**Specification (1963 Series 1):**
ENGINE: Lotus-Ford 1558cc twin overhead camshaft.
GEARBOX: Ford 4-speed.
CHASSIS: central steel box-section backbone with front and rear fork extensions, each linked by boxed cross-member.
FRONT SUSPENSION: pressed steel, unequal-length double wishbones and coil spring/damper units.
REAR SUSPENSION: strut-type, with tubular lower wishbones and coil spring/damper units.
WHEELBASE: 7ft 0in.
FRONT TRACK: 3ft 11.1in.
REAR TRACK: 4ft 0.44in.
OVERALL LENGTH: 12ft 1.25in.
WIDTH: 4ft 8in.
WEIGHT: 14 cwt.

# 27

## *Formula Junior, 1963*

For the last year of Formula Junior, Lotus developed a new and very advanced car that it was hoped would also serve as the production car for the new Formula 2 to be introduced for the 1964 season. The new 27 was a development of the 25 Formula 1 car, but differed in many respects, mainly in the interests of production economy.

The monocoque was built up of 18-gauge aluminium sheet flat interior panels, to which glass-fibre outer panels were pop-riveted, a steel fabricated front bulkhead enveloping the inboard front suspension, an aluminium sheet centre bulkhead (forming the seat back) and a second steel fabricated bulkhead with a tubular tie-bar at the rear. Front suspension was by fabricated upper rocking arms, wide-based lower wishbones, modified Triumph Herald uprights and inboard coil spring/damper units. At the rear there were the familiar reversed lower wishbones, single top links, twin radius rods, magnesium uprights and inclined coil spring/damper units.

The Cosworth engine featured a fully counterbalanced forged steel crankshaft. As

*Autosport* commented in its description of the car by John Bolster, 'These are expensive to buy but much cheaper than the repairs after a loud bang and a pool of oil.' The VW-based Hewland Mk 4 gearbox was fitted. Girling disc brakes were mounted outboard front and rear and there were 13in cast magnesium 'wobbly-web' wheels front and rear. The 27 was much more compact than its immediate predecessor, the 22, and the most sophisticated of all Formula Junior cars. Bolster finished his description of the car with these words, 'A price of £1890 is quoted for the new Lotus in Formula Junior form. That is a far cry from the original ideas of the founders of this racing category, but for what is virtually a slightly reduced Grand Prix car, it is by no means expensive. If ever a car looked a winner, this is it.'

Sadly, this proved not to be the case immediately. In 1963 the works Junior team was run by Ron Harris and entered in the name of Ron Harris-Team Lotus with Peter Arundell, Mike Spence and John Fenning as drivers. Arundell won the first race of the year at Oulton Park, but it was soon revealed that the car handled badly because the monocoque was insufficiently rigid. It was decided to replace the outer glass-fibre skins of the monocoques with rolled aluminium panelling and as the season progressed the 27s

Mike Spence at the wheel of his Ron Harris-Team Lotus Formula Junior 27 at Silverstone in May 1963. Alongside him is Bill Bradley (Lola). Spence's 27 was an early all glass-fibre car lacking structural rigidity and he failed to feature in the results. *(T. C. March)*

became more and more of a match for the very successful Brabhams. Arundell won the race at the British Grand Prix meeting and then five races in succession to snatch the British Formula Junior Championship by one point from Denis Hulme (Brabham).

Delivery of production cars was delayed while the works cars were sorted. Private owners scored limited success during the year, and it is not clear just how many of these cars were made.

**Specification:**
ENGINE: Cosworth-Ford 1097cc.
GEARBOX: Hewland Mk 4 VW-based 5-speed.
CHASSIS: monocoque constructed from 18-gauge aluminium inner panels, with fabricated steel front and rear bulkheads, aluminium-sheet centre bulkhead and rolled aluminium outer panels.
FRONT SUSPENSION: upper rocking arms, lower wishbones and inboard coil spring/damper units.
REAR SUSPENSION: reversed lower wishbones, single top links, twin radius rods and outboard coil spring/damper units.
WHEELBASE: 7ft 6in.
MAXIMUM TRACK 4ft 3.5in.
OVERALL LENGTH: 11ft 7in.
WEIGHT: 7.87 cwt.

# 28

## *Lotus-Cortina*

The origins of the Lotus-Cortina Mk I lie in the design by Harry Mundy, then Technical Editor of *The Autocar*, of a twin overhead camshaft cylinder head for the Ford 'Kent' engine. The first prototype engine, based on the 1340cc three-bearing Ford engine, developed 97 bhp at 5500 rpm. When it became known that Ford would have available from the autumn of 1962 the 116E engine of 1499cc and with five-bearing crank, all Lotus efforts were concentrated on that unit. The first public appearance of the engine was in the Lotus 23 entered in the 1962 Nürburgring 1000 Km race in the name of the Essex Racing Team and with which Clark led the field until he slid off the road, mainly as the result of exhaust gasses entering the cockpit from a fractured exhaust.

Mundy's design retained, in accordance with his instructions, the complete bottom end of the Ford engine, and the twin overhead camshafts were driven by chain from the nose of the crankshaft, whilst the original Ford camshaft, mounted in the side of the cylinder block, was retained to drive the oil pump and distributor

through skew gears. Two horizontal twin-choke Weber Tipo 40 DCOE curburettors were fitted. In this form power output was 100 bhp at 5700 rpm. At an early date Chapman decided that capacity should be increased and so the standard size became 1558cc (82.55 x 72.8mm) and power output in this form was 105 bhp at 5500 rpm.

Chapman was approached by Walter Hayes of Ford, whom he knew well, from the days when Hayes had been Editor of the *Sunday Dispatch*, to see whether Lotus would assemble 1000 Cortina GT cars at Cheshunt with the twin-cam engine so that the model could be homologated in the then Group 2. Caught between the dying Elite and the yet to be borne Elan, Chapman responded enthusiastically.

The new car, always known as the Lotus-Cortina, except to Ford, who gave it the official title of Cortina-Lotus, first became available in 1963. Apart from the installation of the 1558cc engine and the close-ratio Ford 4-speed all-synchromesh gearbox fitted to the Elan, at the front there were new spring and damper rates which reduced ride height, whilst at the rear there were more fundamental changes, including location of the axle by twin tracking arms and an A-bracket and springing by vertical coil spring/damper units. Other changes made by

The production Lotus-Cortina photographed at Brands Hatch in 1963. Passing is a Lotus Elite.

Chapman included light alloy skin panels for the two doors, the bonnet and boot lid and light alloy castings for the clutch housing, remote control extensions and the differential housing. All Lotus-Cortinas were painted white with a green stripe on the sides and the tail panel. Lotus badges were displayed on the rear wings and on the right side of the radiator air intake and there were quarter-bumpers. There were also interior changes, including a central console over the new remote control gear-change, bucket seats, pistol-grip handbrake and wood-rimmed, alloy-spoked steering wheel. The basic price was £910. There is no clear record of the date that production started or the rate of production (although at one stage it was rather improbably claimed that Lotus were turning the cars out of Cheshnut at the rate of five a day).

There were a number of problems with the early cars, including loosening of the differential housing (so that it lost all its oil and wrecked the final drive) and oil leaks affected the rubber bushes in the mountings of the A-bracket and could cause the rear suspension to collapse.

During production a number of changes were made to solve problems and accord with Cortina production changes. In July 1964 Lotus substituted a two-piece prop-shaft for the original one-piece, the light alloy transmission castings were replaced by standard Ford cast iron components

The Lotus-Cortina had been homologated as a touring car by the Gold Cup meeting at Oulton Park in September 1963. Jack Sears and Trevor Taylor took third and fourth places (first and second in their class) behind the Ford Galaxies of Dan Gurney and Graham Hill. (T. C. March)

Sir John Whitmore with his Team Lotus Lotus-Cortina in the Saloon Car race at the Grand Prix meeting at Brands Hatch in July 1966. He finished fourth behind a trio of much larger-capacity American Fords. *(Guy Griffiths)*

and the Cortina GT gearbox with uprated second gear cluster was adopted in place of the Elan gearbox.

In October 1964 the Lotus-Cortina adopted the Aeroflow ventilation system used on current production Ford bodyshells. The 1965 Ford-Cortina GT rear suspension by semi-elliptic leaf springs and twin radius arms replaced the coil spring rear suspension in June 1965. The final changes came in October 1965 when self-adjusting rear brakes and Corsair 2000E gear ratios were fitted. A special equipment engine developing 109 bhp was also offered.

Total production (as stated by Graham Robson, *The Sporting Fords, Vol 1*, Motor Racing Publications Ltd., Second Edition, 1989) was as follows, apart from a very small number of pre-production prototypes:

| | |
|---|---|
| 1963: | 228 |
| 1964: | 563 |
| 1965: | 112 |
| 1966: | 991 |

These figures include 97 racing Lotus-Cortinas completed by Lotus Components Limited.

The maximum speed of the Mark 1 was approximately 106 mph, with 0–60 mph acceleration in 9.9 sec, the standing quarter-mile in 17.4 sec and an overall fuel consumption of around 21 mpg.

Although less than the necessary number of cars had been built, the Lotus-Cortina was homologated in Group 2 in September 1963. The cars were first raced that year and there was a serious campaign in 1964, by Team Lotus in the UK and by Alan Mann Racing in Europe on behalf of Ford and in the United States Ford also raced the cars. In Group 2 competition from power output was 145/150 bhp. Very many successes were achieved, including a win by Jim Clark in the British Saloon Car Championship, a win by Stewart/Beckwith in the Marlboro 12 Hours race in the United States, first and second places by the Alan Mann cars of Sir John Whitmore/Peter Procter and Henry Taylor/Peter Harper in the Brands Hatch Six Hours race (as well as a string of successes on the Continent). The cars also won International races in Australia, New Zealand and South Africa. In the Tour de France a Lotus-Cortina built up by Ford's Competition department at Boreham and driven by Vic Elford/David Seigle-Morris finished fourth and won its class.

In 1965 the Lotus-Cortinas were homologated in Group 2 with leaf spring rear suspension and the engines were tuned by BRM. The Team Lotus cars were driven by Jim Clark and Jack Sears; the latter finished fourth overall in the Championship and won his class. Sir John Whitmore, driving Alan Mann cars, won the European Touring Car Challenge, with victories

The Lotus-Cortina Mark 2 of 1967 onwards, which was built in its entirety by Ford.

shared with Sears in the Nürburgring Six Hours race and solo victories in the Mont Ventoux hill climb and at Zolder and Snetterton. Throughout the year the recently homologated Alfa Romeo GTAs presented an ever-stronger threat.

Team Lotus raced the cars in 1966 in Group 5 form. These cars had engines modified by BRM and the specification included dry sump lubrication and Lucas fuel injection; power output was 180 bhp at 7750 rpm. Other changes included modified suspension geometry and coil spring/damper units replaced the standard MacPherson struts. Team Lotus won the Entrant's award in the British Saloon Car Championship and although Whitmore for the Alan Mann team won races at Aspern and Zolder and the hill climbs at Mont Ventoux and Eigenthal, Alfa Romeo won the European

Touring Challenge. Rally successes in 1966 included wins by Soderstrom/Palm in the Acropolis and RAC British rallies with a car entered by Ford.

In 1967 the Mark 2 Lotus-Cortina was announced. This was not allocated a Lotus Type number, because all production was undertaken at Dagenham. It was not a car in which Lotus themselves took much interest, apart from racing. Production continued until 1970 and a total of 4032 cars was built.

Team Lotus raced cars with Cosworth FVA Formula 2 engines and during 1967 they were driven by Graham Hill, John Miles and Jacky Ickx, who battled all year with Vic Elford (Porsche 911), but before the end of the year the team had sold the cars to Brian Robinson.

# 29

## *Indianapolis, 1963*

It was with American driver Dan Gurney's encouragement and support that Chapman concluded a deal with Ford to run a pair of cars at Indianapolis in 1963. Detail design of the 29 was the work of Len Terry and in most respects the car was a strengthened and enlarged version of the 25. The monocoque was based on that of the 25 (but with lengthened wheelbase to comply with the USAC minimum of 8ft 0in) with similar but strengthened suspension (and with pick-up points that permitted an asymmetrical suspension offset to the left by 2.875in. to suit the left-hand banked corners of the Indianapolis circuit). The Ford V8 engine was based on the push-rod 4260cc production Fairlane unit, but with alloy crankcase, cylinder block and heads, slightly reduced bore and mechanically operated

valves and a power output of about 370 bhp. Transmission by a Colotti Tipo 37 combined 4-speed gearbox and final drive.

After the prototype had been tested at Snetterton with stack exhausts and symmetrical suspension, further testing was carried out at Ford's test track at Kingman in Arizona. During qualifying at Indianapolis Gurney crashed heavily and was forced to drive the prototype in the race. The race was won by Parnelli Jones (Watson-Offenhauser Willard Battery Special), but Clark led briefly during refuelling stops, Jones should possibly have been disqualified for dropping oil (the debate remains unresolved) and after Clark had been badly delayed while the yellow flag was out, he finished second, 19 seconds in arrears. Gurney took seventh place, delayed by an unscheduled pit stop to tighten the rear wheels.

Subsequently the cars ran at Milwaukee, where Clark took pole position and led

The first of the Lotus Indianapolis contenders, the 29 raced at the Speedway in 1963. Dan Gurney, seen here with his crew, finished seventh, whilst Jim Clark took second place.

throughout and Gurney finished third. In the Trenton '200' both cars retired after dominating the race. The car that had been crashed in qualifying at Indianapolis by Gurney was sold to Lindsey Hopkins and with this 29 fitted with a Ford four-cam engine Bobby Marshman led the field in the 1964 500 race until eliminated by a transmission oil leak. In the 1965 race Al Miller finished fourth at Indianapolis with this car and he was eliminated with it in the multiple crash at the start of the 1966 race.

**Specification:**

ENGINE Ford V8 4200cc.

TRANSMISSION: Colotti Tipo 37 combined 4-speed gearbox and final drive.

CHASSIS: monocoque based on two side pontoons constructed from 16-gauge aluminium-alloy sheet with welded steel cross-member fabrications front and rear.

FRONT SUSPENSION: upper rocking arms, lower wishbones and inboard coil spring/damper units.

REAR SUSPENSION: reversed lower wishbones, top links, twin radius rods and coil spring/damper units.

WHEELBASE: 8ft 0in.

MAXIMUM TRACK: 4ft 5.25in.

OVERALL LENGTH: 13ft 0in.

WEIGHT: 11.16 cwt approx.

# 30

*Group 7 Sports, 1964–65*

For 1964 Lotus developed a Group 7 sports car, that is for the group of 'big banger sports cars' which enjoyed a run of popularity in the mid-1960s. Chapman based his design on a backbone-type chassis, broadly similar in shape to that used for the Lotus Elan and inspired by its design. At the front a transverse box-section carried the suspension and at the rear there were two diverging arms to form a Y-shape and mount the Ford engine. The deep box-section girder panelled in 20-gauge steel sheet formed the main centre backbone member and this housed a 30-gallon rubber fuel tank, but additional 9-gallon tanks could be installed in the sills of the one-piece glass-fibre body. The front suspension was by unequal-length double wishbones and combined coil spring/damper units. For the rear Lotus switched to a system of upper wishbones,

reversed lower wishbones, lower radius rods which passed through slots in the arms of the backbone and coil spring/damper units.

Lotus had entered into an arrangement to buy the V8 engines from Ford in the 271 bhp Hi-Performance form and modified them with a specification that included four Weber carburettors and with a resultant power output of approximately 350 bhp. Transmission was by a ZF combined 5-speed all-synchromesh gearbox and final drive unit and the gearbox and rear suspension were supported by a box structure linked to the engine bay. If the gearbox ratios had to be changed, it was necessary first of all to dismantle the rear suspension. There were twin radiators behind low-set intakes in the nose. The wheels were 13-in four-spoke, evolved from the wheels used at Indianapolis and Girling 11in. disc brakes were fitted.

The first car was run by Ian Walker Racing on a semi-works basis, and driven into second place at Aintree on its début by Jim Clark. Clark also

Jack Sears at the wheel of the works 30 in the Group 7 Sports Car race at Silverstone in May 1965. This was one of the least successful of all Lotus models. *(T. C. March)*

The 30 driven by Jim Clark in the Tourist Trophy at Oulton Park in 1965. It blew its 5.3-litre engine in practice and ran in the race with a 4.7-litre unit installed. *(T. C. March)*

drove a 30 in North America, finishing third at Riverside Raceway, and he also led in the Tourist Trophy at Goodwood until forced to retire by brake and suspension problems. After the first three cars had been completed all later versions had a more rigid chassis with 18-gauge panelling. Overall very little success was gained during the year, but nevertheless a total of 21 of these cars were sold at the low price of £3495 in component form.

The 1965 version was the Series 2, which incorporated a number of modifications to the chassis, including a detachable centre-section to the bridge carrying the rear suspension. Twelve of these cars were built in 1965.

Clark scored wins with the 30 early in the 1965 season in the Senior Service '200' road race at Silverstone in March (stopped short of the scheduled distance because of torrential rain) and he also won at Goodwood on Easter Monday. Private cars were run by the JCB team and by Willment; little success was gained. The cars

were no real opposition for the rival McLaren-Oldsmobile or the Lola-Chevrolet.

**Specification:**
ENGINE: Ford V8 4727cc push-rod ohv developing approximately 350 bhp at 5750 rpm.
GEARBOX: ZF combined 5-speed all-synchromesh gearbox and final drive.
CHASSIS: girder box-section centre backbone with rear transverse box-section.
FRONT SUSPENSION: unequal-length double wishbones and coil spring/damper units.
REAR SUSPENSION: upper wishbones, lower reversed wishbones, lower radius rods and coil spring/damper units.
WHEELBASE: 7ft 10.5in.
FRONT AND REAR TRACK: 4ft 5in.
OVERALL LENGTH: 13ft 9in.
OVERALL WIDTH: 5ft 8in.
HEIGHT (to top of screen): 2ft 2.5in.
WEIGHT: 13.66 cwt.

# 31

## *Formula 3, 1964*

Because of the company's preoccupation with Formula 2, the new Formula 3 received little attention from Lotus. Lotus Components offered the 31, a slightly improved version of the 1962 Formula Junior car. Engines were to customer's choice. The Formula prescribed production-based 4-cylinder engines up to a maximum of 1000cc and only one carburettor, so most drivers used the previous year's Formula Junior engines sleeved down to 1000cc. Only 12 of the 31s were built. A number of minor successes were gained by 22s and 31s, but the year's racing was dominated by the Cooper-BMCs of the Tyrrell Racing Organisation and usually with Jackie Stewart at the wheel.

The 31 represented a rather half-hearted attempt to build a Formula 3 car in 1964 and the model achieved little success. Here Banting spins his 31 at Lodge Corner, Oulton Park, in September 1964. *(T. C. March)*

# 32 and 32B

## *Formula 2 and Tasman, 1964*

For 1964 there was a new Formula 2 for single-seater cars with a maximum engine capacity of 1-litre, unsupercharged and restricted to 4-cylinder engines running on commercial fuel. Unlike the new Formula 3, Lotus took the new category very seriously and developed the 32. As had been originally intended, it was based on the Lotus 27, using a similar version of the all-aluminium monocoque developed during 1963 for that car. However the monocoque incorporated 16-gauge steel sheet panelling and there were two 9-gallon rubber bag fuel tanks within the sides of the monocoque. The front suspension was directly adopted from the 24 and 25 Formula 1 cars, and there were changes to the rear suspension that included top radius arms mounted on tall uprights and fully adjustable suspension. The power unit was the Cosworth-designed SCA 4-cylinder 998cc engine (based on the Ford Anglia unit) with valve actuation by a single gear-driven overhead camshaft. Two Weber 40DCM2 dowdraught carburettors were fitted

and a power output of 115 was developed. This engine was canted at 25 degrees in the chassis.

During 1964 the cars were managed by Ron Harris and entered by Ron Harris-Team Lotus. The drivers included Jim Clark, but also Peter Arundell, Mike Spence and Peter Proctor, whilst Jackie Stewart, John Fenning and Brian Hart also drove for the team during the year.

Despite his Formula 1 commitments, Clark won at Pau, the Eifelrennen at the Nürburgring, Mallory Park and Brands Hatch, whilst Mike Spence won the Formula 2 class of the Aintree '200', Brian Hart won the Enna race in Sicily and Jackie Stewart won a race at Snetterton. The tragedy of the season was Peter Arundell's bad crash at Reims, where he suffered very serious injuries which in effect brought his racing career to an end, although after his apparent recovery from the accident, he appeared in Formula 1 without much success. Despite opposition from Brabham, Lola, Cooper and Alpine, Lotus won seven of the year's 18 main races, but the French Formula 2 Championship went to Jack Brabham (with one of his own cars). The main weakness of the Lotus effort, balanced on the one hand by the

The 1964 Formula 2 car was the 32 and the works team was run by Ron Harris, fielding up to four cars as the season progressed. Jackie Stewart, who had been driving Coopers for Ken Tyrrell in Formula 3, joined the team in mid-season and won the Vanwall Trophy at Snetterton. *(Michael Cooper)*

skill and ability of Clark, was the fact that Ron Harris was forced to split the team when dates clashed and he was plagued all season by transportation and organizational problems. This resulted in insufficient time for testing and developing the cars. In all during the year 12 32s were built.

The 32B was a one-off version of the 32 built for the Tasman Formula (the series of races held in New Zealand and Australia during their summer) with a 2495cc Coventry Climax FPF 4-cylinder engine built for Jim Clark to race in 1965, for Lotus had returned to the series after a three-year interval. There was a total of eight races in the Series and of these Clark won five; he was eliminated from the New Zealand Grand Prix when he was rammed by Bruce McLaren's Cooper, finished second at Sandown Park, Melbourne and finished fifth at Longford in Tasmania. By any standards it was an exceptional performance by a single driver/car entry.

**Specification:**
ENGINE: Cosworth SCA 998cc developing approximately 115 bhp.
GEARBOX: Hewland Mk 4 5-speed.
CHASSIS: monocoque constructed from 18-gauge aluminium inner panels with fabricated steel front and rear bulkheads, aluminium sheet centre bulkhead and rolled aluminium outer panels.
FRONT SUSPENSION: upper rocking arms, lower wishbones, and inboard coil spring/damper units.
REAR SUSPENSION: reversed lower wishbones, single top links, twin radius rods and outboard coil spring/damper units.
WHEELBASE: 7ft 6in.
MAXIMUM TRACK: 4ft 3.5in.
OVERALL LENGTH: 11ft 7in.
WEIGHT: 8.88 cwt.

# 33

*Formula 1, 1964–65*

As the 25 was developed, so the input from that development went into the evolution of the 33, its immediate successor. The changes included a monocoque that featured a stiffer unit, running straight, rather than kinking inwards towards the pedal box as on the 25. The various suspension modifications and changes incorporated in the 25B appeared on the 33. The wheelbase was lengthened by .75in, so as to make room for the latest flat-crank Climax V8 engine and the chassis numbers followed on in series from the 25s.

The first 33, chassis R8, was driven by Clark in the 1964 Aintree '200' race, but whilst Clark was battling for the lead, a back-marker pulled across his line and Clark was forced to take to the grass, badly damaging the car against the bank. The 33 was not raced again until the non-Championship Solitude Grand Prix in July, where Clark took pole position in practice, set fastest lap and easily won the race. Both Clark and Spence had 33s in the German Grand Prix at the Nürburgring, but no success was gained during the remainder of the year.

The year 1965 was to prove one of almost complete Clark domination and he started the season by winning the South African Grand Prix, his heat in the Race of Champions, the Syracuse Grand Prix and the *Sunday Mirror* Trophy at Goodwood. In all these races except the

Jim Clark and Team Lotus dominated the 1965 season. Clark won six Championship races and the Championship. Here he is seen in the British race at Silverstone, which he won for the fourth successive time. *(T. C. March)*

Lotus continued to race the 33 in 1966 and Clark drove a car with enlarged 2-litre Climax V8 engine. Here at Monaco he rose to second place before retiring because of failure of a rear suspension upright. *(Nigel Snowdon)*

Goodwood race, he set fastest lap and took pole position, but at Goodwood he had to be satisfied with fastest lap only. Clark missed the Monaco Grand Prix because of his Indianapolis commitments, but thereafter he won the Belgian Grand Prix (setting fastest lap), the French Grand Prix (pole position and fastest lap), the British Grand Prix (pole position), the Dutch Grand Prix (fastest lap), the German Grand Prix (pole position and fastest lap), and took second place in the Mediterranean Grand Prix at Enna in Sicily (fastest lap and pole position). During the remainder of the season Clark was out of luck, but he had clearly dominated that year's World Championship. In both the *Sunday Mirror* Trophy at Goodwood and the French Grand Prix Clark had been at the wheel of a 25.

Lotus continued to race the 33 during the first season or so of the new 3000cc Grand Prix

Formula. Clark was usually seen at the wheel of R14, the most developed of all the 33s, which was powered by a special 2-litre V8 engine built up for Lotus by Coventry Climax. During that year the 33s were outclassed by the Brabhams and Ferraris, but Clark finished fourth in the British Grand Prix, took third place in the Dutch Grand Prix and finished third in the Gold Cup at Oulton Park. In addition Mike Spence and Peter Arundell took first and third places in the South African Grand Prix (which in 1966 was a non-Championship race) and Spence finished fifth in the Italian Grand Prix.

Jim Clark drove R14 in the Tasman races in New Zealand and Australia in January and February 1967, scoring a total of five wins and three second places, and taking an easy win in the Tasman Championship. For 1967 Clark was joined in the Team Lotus Formula 1 team by

Jim Clark at the wheel of the 33-Climax 2-litre at Warwick Farm in 1967. Clark won that year's Tasman Championship.
*(Nigel Snowdon)*

Graham Hill and whilst Clark continued to race the 33 with the special 2-litre Climax engine, Hill drove a car with a 2.1-litre BRM V8 engine. Hill finished fourth in the International Trophy at Silverstone and second at Monaco, but at the next race in which the works team competed, the Dutch Grand Prix at Zandvoort, the new Ford-powered 49s made their race début.

Team Lotus was still using the 33 in the early part of 1967. The team had been joined by Graham Hill, who drove this 2-litre BRM-powered car into second place at Monaco.
*(Nigel Snowdon)*

### Specification (1965):
ENGINE: Coventry Climax FWMV 32-valve.
GEARBOX: ZF 5DS10 combined 5-speed gearbox and final drive.
CHASSIS: monocoque based on two side pontoons constructed from 16-gauge aluminium-alloy sheet with welded steel cross-member fabrications front and rear.
FRONT SUSPENSION: upper rocking arms, lower wishbones and inboard coil spring/damper units.
REAR SUSPENSION: reversed lower wishbones, top links, twin radius rods and coil spring/damper units.
WHEELBASE: 7ft 8in.
FRONT TRACK: 4ft 7in.
REAR TRACK: 4ft 8in.
OVERALL LENGTH: 11ft 10in.
WEIGHT: 8.8 cwt.

# 34

## Indianapolis, 1964

Ford – and Lotus – returned to Indianapolis in 1964 with the 34 cars, very slightly modified versions of the 1963 29s, but with four overhead camshaft Ford V8 engines, fitted with Hilborn-based fuel injection and a power output of around 410 bhp. There were now ZF 2-speed transmissions in place of the previous Colotti. The cars were fitted with new wheel castings and new Dunlop tyres. Lotus was under pressure to use new Firestone tyres, partly because of the speed of Marshman in qualifying with the 1963 29 running on Firestones. Clark

qualified for pole position, with Marshman second and Gurney on the second row.

After only one lap the 500 Miles race was red flagged after a serious accident involving seven cars and costing the lives of two drivers. When the race was restarted Clark led initially, was passed by Marshman, and then took the lead again. The Dunlop tyres shed sections of tread, a serious vibration developed and the left rear suspension of Clark's car collapsed. Gurney's car was withdrawn as a safety precaution.

Although Ford was at the time very disenchanted with the Lotus performance, they agreed that the cars should be raced in a number of USAC races during the remainder of the year. Parnelli Jones won with the 34 at

Jim Clark at the wheel of the 1964 Indianapolis contender, the 34. The car was very similar to the previous year's 29, apart from centre-exhaust, Ford V8 engine, new Lotus four-spoke cast alloy wheels, special Dunlop tyres and modified pressure refuelling nozzle in the left side below the cockpit. Gurney's car was withdrawn following suspension failure on Clark's car.

Milwaukee whilst A. J. Foyt with the second car retired with gear-change failure. Subsequently Parnelli Jones won at Trenton, where Clark retired because of engine problems. The car that Jones had driven at Trenton was acquired by Lindsey Hopkins for Bobby Marshman to drive, but Marshman crashed during practice at Phoenix and died from his burns. In 1965 A. J. Foyt drove one of the 34s into second place at Indianapolis.

**Specification:**
ENGINE: Ford V8 four overhead camshaft 4200cc developing 410 bhp.
GEARBOX: ZF combined 2-speed gearbox and final drive.
CHASSIS: monocoque based on two side pontoons constructed from 16-gauge aluminium-alloy sheet with welded steel cross-member fabrications front and rear.
FRONT SUSPENSION: upper rocking arms, lower wishbones and inboard coil spring/damper units.
REAR SUSPENSION: reversed lower wishbones, top links, twin radius rods and coil spring/damper units.
WHEELBASE: 8ft 0in.
FRONT AND REAR TRACK: 4ft 5.5in.
OVERALL LENGTH: 13ft 0in.
WEIGHT: 11.16 cwt approx.

# 35

*Formula 2, Formula 3 and Formula B, 1965*

For 1965 Lotus developed the 35, evolved from the 27 and 32 monocoques, and intended for Formula 2, Formula 3, American Formula B racing and, if required, the car could be fitted with a Coventry Climax 2.5-litre FPF engine for Tasman racing. Transmission was by a Hewland combined gearbox and final drive unit with four, five or six gears.

Once again in 1965 the Formula 2 cars were entered by Ron Harris-Team Lotus, who started the season using both 35s and 32s, but soon concentrated on the newer model. The Team Lotus drivers during the year included Jim Clark, Brian Hart, Peter Revson and Mike Spence. The 35 powered by the Cosworth SCA engine developing about 125 bhp was barely a match for the new BRM Formula 2 engine developing 127 bhp and certainly no match for the Honda unit that powered the works Brabhams. Only Clark was able to enjoy real success, scoring a total of five wins (at Pau, the Crystal Palace, Rouen, Brands Hatch and Albi), matching the score of the rival Brabhams and winning both *The Autocar* Championship and the Grands Prix de France Championship. Tim Parnell entered a 35 powered by the BRM Formula 2 engine and this was driven by David Hobbs. It proved unsuccessful and was later sold to John Coombs for Graham Hill to race.

The Willment and Ron Harris teams also entered 35s in Formula 3. The category was dominated by the Brabhams, but Revson succeeded in winning the Formula 3 race at Monaco. In all its various forms total production of the 35 amounted to 22 cars.

In 1965 the Lotus Formula 2 cars were again run by Ron Harris-Team Lotus, but the year was largely dominated by Brabham. Here Jim Clark is on his way to a mediocre sixth place at Oulton Park.

## Specification (Formula 2):

ENGINE: Cosworth SCA 997cc.
GEARBOX: Hewland combined 5/6-speed gearbox and final drive.
CHASSIS: monocoque based on the 27 and 32 series.
FRONT SUSPENSION: upper rocking arms, lower wishbones and inboard coil spring/damper units.
REAR SUSPENSION: reversed lower wishbones, top links, twin radius rods and coil spring/damper units.
WHEELBASE: 7ft 9.5in.
MAXIMUM TRACK: 4ft 4in.
OVERALL LENGTH: 12ft 3in.
WEIGHT: 8.27 cwt.

## 36

*Elan Fixed head coupé. See 26*

# 37 'Three-Seven'

*Clubman's Formula Sports Car, 1965*

Exhibited at the 1965 Racing Car Show, this was a much-modified Series 2 Seven with independent rear suspension, Elite differential, inboard Girling disc brakes at the rear, 13in magnesium-alloy 'wobbly-web' wheels and a Cosworth-modified Ford 116E 1499cc engine said to develop 125 bhp. Only the one example was built and it was raced with success in Clubman's events by John Berry.

## 38

*Indianapolis, 1965*

Ford backed Lotus for a third successive year in 1965 and Len Terry designed a new model to comply with the latest USAC regulations, which had been introduced following the serious accident at Indianapolis in 1964. The main change was a re-designed monocoque which formed a stressed-skin structure, thereby replacing the 'bath tub' monocoque pioneered with the 25 and its derivatives. The regulations also made two pit stops compulsory at Indianapolis and there was to be a refuelling system using gravity towers. Accordingly Terry adopted a three-cell fuel system, with two large tanks on either side and the third tank behind

Jim Clark at the wheel of the 38 with four-cam Ford engine with which he won at Indianapolis in 1965.

the driver's seat. The new 38 was powered by Ford's four-cam V8 engine, now producing 500 bhp, and transmission was still by the ZF 2-speed combined gearbox and final drive unit. Other features of the car were a lengthened, more penetrating nose-section, induction ram-pods, central exhaust system and a suspension offset 3in to the left. Weight was much the same as for the previous 34 car, 1250 lb, right on the weight limit.

During testing at Trenton, Roger McCluskey crashed with one of the cars when the throttles jammed open, but there has been some argument as to whether this could be attributed to Lotus or was the fault of Ford's engine assembly. At Indianapolis the two Team Lotus cars were driven by Jim Clark and Bobby Johns, whilst Dan Gurney had taken delivery of a 38, entered by his All-American Racers team. During qualifying Clark set a new record of 160.729 mph, but this was subsequently bettered by A. J. Foyt with his 34, who lapped in 161.233 mph. After two brilliantly organized pit stops, Clark won the race at 149.334 mph, with Parnelli Jones (updated 34) second and Miller (29) fourth. Gurney retired his 38 with engine failure and Johns finished seventh. The 38 made one European competition outing, when Clark drove a car fitted with a ZF 5-speed gearbox in the Ste. Ursanne–Les Rangiers hill climb.

Because the new 42 was not ready, Lotus entered the 38s at Indianapolis again in 1966. In addition two 38s were sold to American entrants, and these cars differed in that they had monocoques built by Abbey Panels of Coventry which lacked the rigidity of the works cars, although Lotus made great efforts to stiffen them and rework them before delivery to their new owners. Andretti decided not to run his new 38, but A. J. Foyt drove the other private owner car only to be eliminated in the start-line crash that spoilt that year's race. Clark spun twice with the 38 during the race, and eventually finished second to Graham Hill (Lola). Andretti retired with engine failure and Clark's team-mate Al Unser crashed.

In October Unser finished second in a USAC race at Mount Fuji in Japan to Stewart's Lola, but Clark did not start the race because of engine failure in practice. The 38s had led to the development of several imitative cars, but Lotus themselves still relied on the 38 in 1967, because the planned BRM engines of the 42 cars were not raceworthy. Clark was running in 18th place when the race was stopped because of rain. The race was restarted the following day. Clark retired because of engine problems. In all five 38s were built.

**Specification:**

ENGINE: Ford four-cam V8 4200cc developing 500 bhp.
GEARBOX: ZF combined 2-speed gearbox and final drive.
CHASSIS: full stressed-skin monocoque.
FRONT SUSPENSION: upper rocking arms, lower wishbones and inboard coil spring/damper units.
REAR SUSPENSION: reversed lower wishbones, upper links, twin radius rods and outboard coil spring/damper units.
WHEELBASE: 8ft. 0in.
MAXIMUM TRACK: 5ft. 0in.
OVERALL LENGTH: 13ft. 0in.
WEIGHT: 11.16 cwt.

# 39

*Tasman Formula, 1966*

In 1965, Lotus had built the 39 as a Formula 1 car to take the flat-16 Coventry Climax engine, but this engine was not developed to a race-worthy standard, primarily because the V8 Climax engine in 16-valve form was dominating the season's racing and in any event the 1500cc Grand Prix Formula ended that year. Lotus adapted the 39 for Tasman racing with a tubular frame at the rear to take the 4-cylinder 2.5-litre Climax FPF engine. Jim Clark drove the car in the 1966 Tasman series, winning at Warwick Farm, finishing second in the races at Levin and Sandown Park (Melbourne) and third in the Lady Wigram Trophy at Christchurch and the Australian Grand Prix at the Lakeside circuit at Brisbane. The series that year was dominated by the 2-litre V8 BRM of Jackie Stewart, for which the 39 was no real match. For 1967 the 39 was sold to Leo Geoghegan, who ran the car in the Tasman Championship through to 1970. For the 1968 season onwards he raced the car fitted with a Repco V8 2.5-litre engine. Only the one 39 was built.

**Specification:**
ENGINE: Coventry Climax 4-cylinder 2495cc FPF.
GEARBOX: Hewland combined 5-speed gearbox and final drive.
CHASSIS: monocoque based on two side pontoons.
FRONT SUSPENSION: upper rocking arms, lower wishbones and inboard coil spring/damper units.
REAR SUSPENSION: reversed lower wishbones, top links, twin radius rods and coil spring/damper units.
WHEELBASE: 7ft 7.5in.
MAXIMUM TRACK: 4ft 8.25in.
OVERALL LENGTH: 11ft 8in.
WEIGHT: 8.88 cwt approx.

The 39 was the 1966 Tasman car and it was subsequently sold to Leo Geoghegan. By 1969 Geoghegan had fitted a Repco V8 engine and tall rear wing. He is seen in the very wet Warwick Farm race in 1969 in which he finished fifth. *(Nigel Snowdon)*

# 40

## *Sports-racing, 1965*

As a result of the failure of the 30, Chapman and Lotus development engineer John Joyce evolved what was hoped to be the improved 40, with strengthened chassis and suspension, 5.3-litre Ford V8 engine and Hewland LG500 combined gearbox and final drive. The bodywork was modified and the 40 could be distinguished by two angled stack exhausts emerging from the decking of the engine cover.

The first car appeared in the Austrian Grand Prix at Zeltweg, where it was driven by Mike Spence, but retired, and it was also driven in the Guards Trophy at Brands Hatch by Jim Clark, who spun twice before retiring in the first heat and crashing in the second heat. Two works cars were sent to the United States for Clark and Richie Ginther and a new car was supplied to Holman & Moody to be driven by A. J. Foyt. Apart from a second place by Clark

at Riverside Raceway no success was gained. This was the last sports-racing Lotus, no match for the rival McLarens and Lolas and lacking development input because Lotus resources were too thinly spread.

**Specification:**
ENGINE: Ford V8 5.3-litre developing approx 410 bhp.
GEARBOX: Hewland LG500 combined 5-speed gearbox and final drive unit.
CHASSIS: girder box-section centre backbone with rear transverse box-section.
FRONT SUSPENSION: unequal-length double wishbones and coil spring/damper units.
REAR SUSPENSION: upper wishbones, lower reversed wishbones, lower radius rods and coil spring/damper units.
WHEELBASE: 7ft 10.5in.
FRONT AND REAR TRACK: 4ft 5in.
OVERALL LENGTH: 13ft 9in.
WEIGHT: not available.

Jim Clark at the wheel of the 40 in the Guards Trophy at Brands Hatch on August Bank Holiday Monday. He spun twice in the first heat before retiring with gear-linkage problems. In the second heat he hit the bank at Clearways as a result of brake trouble. *(LAT)*

# 41, 41B, 41C and 41X

*Formula 2, 3 and B, 1966–8*

In late 1965 Lotus Components introduced the 41 for Formula 3. It had been decided to abandon the monocoque design for cars in this class and there was a new space-frame chassis, derived from the design of the 22 and 31, with extra rigidity provided by sheet steel panelling around the pedal box and for the undertray. The cockpit was reinforced by front and rear stressed steel bulkheads. At the front there were conventional double wishbones with outboard coil spring/damper units and at the rear reversed lower wishbones, single top links, radius rods each side and outboard coil spring/damper units. The engine was the Cosworth MAE66 developing 100 bhp at 9500 rpm and with a Hewland Mk 4 4-speed combined gearbox and final drive. In accordance with past Lotus practice, the tubes of the space-frame carried oil and water between the engine and radiators. The wheels were six-spoke cast magnesium 13in and Girling 10.5in disc brakes were mounted outboard front and rear.

Chapman arranged for the works cars to be run by Charles Lucas, who had fielded a Brabham team in 1965, and they were entered as 'Charles Lucas–Team Lotus' with Piers Courage and American Roy Pike as drivers. Courage scored five important wins and Pike won two races. In addition Lotus Components ran a 41 in Formula 3 for Jack Oliver, who scored many wins in minor events. Other cars were entered by Ron Harris for Peter Revson, John Cardwell and Rob Slotmeker. Overall, however, the 41 was less successful than the rival Brabham.

**Specification, 1966:**
ENGINE: Cosworth MAE developing 100 bhp at 9500 rpm.
GEARBOX: Hewland Mark 4 combined 4-speed gearbox and final drive.
CHASSIS: multi-tubular space-frame with sheet steel stiffening.
FRONT SUSPENSION: double wishbones and coil spring/damper units.
REAR SUSPENSION: reversed lower wishbones, single upper links and coil spring/damper units.
WHEELBASE: 7ft 6in.
FRONT TRACK: 4ft 8.5in.
REAR TRACK: 4ft 8in.
OVERALL LENGTH: 12ft. 0in.
WEIGHT: 8.27 cwt.

Mo Nunn with his Lewis-Nunn Racing-entered 41 in the Formula 3 race at the International Trophy meeting at Silverstone in May 1966. He finished seventh after dropping back on the last lap. He is seen leading Viscount Fielding and Peter Gethin, both at the wheel of Brabhams. *(Nigel Snowdon)*

John Miles with the new 72 in the 1970 Belgian Grand Prix. He retired because of fuel-feed problems. The race was won by Pedro Rodriguez (BRM). *(Nigel Snowdon)*

In the 1970 German Grand Prix the winner, Jochen Rindt (Lotus 72), leads second-place man Ickx (Ferrari 312B). *(Nigel Snowdon)*

Emerson Fittipaldi with the 72 in the 1971 German Grand Prix. In this race he retired because of loss of oil pressure. *(Nigel Snowdon)*

Number two in the Lotus Team, now in John Player Special colours, in 1972 was Dave Walker, seen here with his 72D, in the French Grand Prix at Clermont-Ferrand. Walker finished, but was unclassified. *(Nigel Snowdon)*

In the 1972 Monaco Grand Prix Emerson Fittipaldi (72D) leads Hulme (McLaren M19A). Fittipaldi finished third. *(Nigel Snowdon)*

Emerson Fittipaldi with the 72D in the 1973 Brazilian Grand Prix. He won the race and set fastest lap. *(Nigel Snowdon)*

In the 1973 Monaco Grand Prix Fittipaldi with the 72E took second place and set fastest lap. *(Diana Burnett)*

Ronnie Peterson with the 72E in the 1974 Monaco Grand Prix. He scored a fine victory, his first of three that year. *(Nigel Snowdon)*

Jacky Ickx, who had a thoroughly miserable two seasons with John Player Team Lotus, seen at the wheel of his 72E in the pits at the 1974 British Grand Prix at Brands Hatch. This was one of his better races and he took third place.
(Diana Burnett)

In 1975 John Player Team Lotus was still struggling on with the 72E, as a result of the failure of the 76. Here, on the team's last race with the car, Ronnie Peterson is seen in the United States Grand Prix in which he finished fifth.
(Nigel Snowdon)

Tim Schenken was brought into the team to drive the 76 at the 1974 United States Grand Prix, but started after the grid had departed and was disqualified. *(Nigel Snowdon)*

In the 1976 Japanese Grand Prix Mario Andretti scored the only Lotus Formula 1 win of the year with the 77. This photograph was taken in practice. The race was wet. *(Nigel Snowdon)*

Mario Andretti in practice for the 1977 Spanish Grand Prix which he won with the 78 – it was another wet race. Andretti finished third in that year's World Championship. *(Nigel Snowdon)*

In 1978 Mario Andretti won the World Championship with the Lotus 79. Here he is seen early in the season in the United States Grand Prix (West) at Long Beach, where he finished second to Reutemann's Ferrari. *(Nigel Snowdon)*

Ronnie Peterson's last World Championship race victory was in the 1978 Austrian race, run initially in the rain, but the track dried out as the race progressed. The car was the Lotus 79. *(Nigel Snowdon)*

In 1979 Lotus relied on the existing 79 model for most of the year; the team now raced with Martini sponsorship and the cars were painted dark green. This is Carlos Reutemann in the Spanish Grand Prix in which he finished second ahead of team-mate Andretti. *(Nigel Snowdon)*

In 1967 Lotus Components ran a space-frame 41 Formula 2 car with Cosworth FVA engine for Jack Oliver. Here Oliver is seen in the BUA International Trophy at the Crystal Palace on Whit Monday. Oliver had differential problems and finished sixth. *(Nigel Snowdon)*

The 41X was a works development Formula 3 car with pronounced 'Indy'-style wedge-shaped body. On the car's début at the International Trophy meeting at Silverstone in May 1968 John Miles scored a convincing win from Roy Pike (Titan) seen closely following the Lotus. *(Nigel Snowdon)*

# 41B

*Formula 2 and Formula B, 1967*

This was the Lotus Components version of the 41 for American Formula B racing. In addition Lotus Components entered one of these cars in Formula 2 events for Jack Oliver.

# 41C

This was the 1967 version of the Formula 3 41. There were only minor changes and a total of 61 41s of all types were sold.

# 41X

*Formula 3, 1968*

In 1968 Lotus developed an improved version of the 41C incorporating Lotus 47 suspension uprights and wheels and glass-fibre body of distinct wedge-shape and clearly inspired by the 56 Indianapolis cars. The sole example built was entered for John Miles by Gold Leaf Team Lotus and during the year he scored wins at Silverstone, Brands Hatch, Croft and Zandvoort. Lotus had planned to put the 41X into production as the 55, but this did not proceed.

# 42F

## *Indianapolis, 1967*

For 1966 Maurice Phillippe, who had joined Lotus from de Havilland, designed under Chapman's supervision this Indianapolis car which was intended to take a BRM H16 4.2-litre engine under development by BRM for sale to customers. The monocoque was similar to that of the 38, but it terminated behind the cockpit with attachment points for the engine and gearbox assembly, which would also carry the rear suspension, with the engine crankcase taking rear suspension chassis loadings. The H16 engines were plagued with problems and never raced in 4.2-litre form. In the 1966 Indianapolis race Lotus used the 38s, and in 1967 it was decided to enter one 38 and one of the original 42 monocoques, modified to take the Ford V8 four-cam engine. A tubular space-frame engine bay was added to the monocoque to take the engine

and because the Ford was much longer than the H16, the car had a wheelbase of 8ft 10in.

In this form the car was known as the 42F and it was driven at Indianapolis by Graham Hill. Hill retired with piston failure, but was officially classified 32nd.

**Specification:**
ENGINE: V8 four-cam 4200cc.
GEARBOX: ZF combined 2-speed gearbox and final drive.
CHASSIS: stressed monocoque with tubular space-frame engine bay.
FRONT SUSPENSION: upper rocking arms, lower wishbones and inboard coil spring/damper units.
REAR SUSPENSION: reversed lower wishbones, upper links, twin radius rods and outboard coil spring/damper units.
WHEELBASE: 8ft 10in.
MAXIMUM TRACK: 4ft 8.5in.
OVERALL LENGTH: 13ft. 8in. approx.
WEIGHT: Not available.

Raced at Indianapolis in 1967, the 42F was something of a 'bodge-up' as it combined the chassis intended to take BRM's H16 engine with the four-cam Ford power unit.

# 43

## *Formula 1, 1966–67*

Although Lotus relied mainly on the 33 cars during 1966 and the early part of 1967 until the new Ford-powered 49 was ready, the team also built the 43 with stressed-section monocoque, front suspension similar to that of the 33 and rear suspension by reversed lower wishbones, lateral top links and coil spring/ damper units. The cars were built to take BRM's H16 highly complex engine, stressed to act as a chassis member and mounted on the rear bulkhead. Transmission was by a BRM 6-speed gearbox. Arundell drove the car in practice at the Belgian Grand Prix in 1966, but non-started after problems and retired with the car because of gear selector trouble in the French Grand Prix. With redesigned BRM transmission Clark drove the car in the Italian Grand Prix at Monza and rose to fifth place before retiring. At the United States Grand Prix at Watkins Glen Clark's engine broke in practice and he drove the BRM team spare to score the only Lotus World Championship victory of 1966 and the only World Championship victory scored by the H16

engine. The 43 again appeared in Mexico where Clark retired because of gear-change problems. The last appearance of the 43 as a works car was in the 1967 South African Grand Prix, where two were entered. Graham Hill retired after damaging the front suspension, which caused the car to bottom and wore a hole in an oil pipe, while Clark, delayed by overheating problems, retired with fuel metering trouble. The two cars were later sold to private owners and raced in Formula 5000 events.

**Specification:**
ENGINE: BRM H16 2996cc.
GEARBOX: BRM combined 6-speed gearbox and final drive.
CHASSIS: stressed monocoque.
FRONT SUSPENSION: upper rocking arms, lower wishbones and inboard coil spring/damper units.
REAR SUSPENSION: reversed lower wishbones, lateral upper links, twin radius rods and coil spring/damper units.
WHEELBASE: 8ft 0in.
MAXIMUM TRACK: 5ft 0in.
OVERALL LENGTH: 13ft 2in.
WEIGHT: 9.87 cwt approx.

The 43, purely an interim Formula 1 car, scored a remarkable and unexpected victory in the 1966 United States Grand Prix with Jim Clark at the wheel.

# 44

## Formula 2, 1966

For 1966 Lotus developed this monocoque Formula 2 car based on the 35, but with the wider track from the 41 Formula 3 car. Once again the cars were entered by Ron Harris-Team Lotus and the new car did not appear until the Barcelona race. The 44, powered by the Cosworth SCA engine developing 140 bhp, was no match for the Honda-powered Brabham. Once again the most successful Lotus driver in Formula 2 that year was Jim Clark, who retired with engine problems on the model's début at Barcelona but subsequently took a number of places during the season. A second 44 was driven by a total of eight different drivers, none of whom achieved much in the way of success. Only three of these cars were built.

## Specification:

ENGINE: Cosworth SCA 997cc developing 140 bhp.
GEARBOX: Hewland combined 5/6-speed gearbox and final drive.
CHASSIS: monocoque.
FRONT SUSPENSION: upper rocking arms, lower wishbones and inboard coil spring/damper units.
REAR SUSPENSION: reversed lower wishbones, top links, twin radius rods and coil spring/damper units.
WHEELBASE: 7ft 9.5in.
MAXIMUM TRACK: 4ft 6in.
OVERALL LENGTH: 12ft 3in.
WEIGHT: 8.27 cwt.

The Ron Harris-Team Lotus 44 of Peter Arundell at the Crystal Palace on Whit Monday, 1966. Arundell finished sixth in the first heat, but crashed in the second heat and the car was too badly damaged for him to start in the final.
(Nigel Snowdon)

# 45

*Elan Drophead Coupé, known as the Series 3 and replacing 26. See 26.*

# 46 Europa (also 54 and 65)

*Production sports cars, 1966–71*

The Renault-powered mid-engined Europa which entered production in 1966 fulfilled a number of Chapman's aims. It was an inexpensive car that successfully aped the layout of contemporary Formula 1 cars, it reduced Lotus dependence on Ford for the supply of engines (and gave Renault a sporting link in addition to Alpine) and there were plans that it should prove ultimately the successor to the Seven. Chapman's concept of the steel backbone chassis of the Elan was retained, but forked only at the rear to take the unit engine and gearbox, with a very substantial front cross-member and a light, separate cross-member at the rear which bridged the gearbox and provided the upper pivot points for the rear coil

spring/damper units. As a result of negotiations conducted by Chapman's close friend Gérard ('Jabby') Crombac, Renault agreed to make available supplies of their 1470cc (76 x 81mm) light alloy push-rod engine used to power the production 16. As used by Lotus, power output was 82 bhp at 6000 rpm (80 bhp in Federal emission form). This was installed at the rear with the unit Renault 4-speed gearbox. As, however, the 16 was a front-wheel drive car, the engine and gearbox units were delivered with transposed crown wheel and pinion and mounted in the car turned through 360 degrees so that the front of the engine with its ancillaries and belt drives faced to the rear; this made the Europa much easier to work on than many mid-engined cars.

At the front the suspension was similar to that of the Elan, but the lower wishbones were cranked instead of straight and the upper pivots of the coil spring/damper units shared the bolts that secured the inner ends of the upper wishbones. The rear suspension was completely different from that of the Elan; fixed length drive-shafts doubled as upper links, there were light lower tubular members, fore and aft

The Europa was the first mid-engined Lotus road car, built from 1966 onwards with Renault engine. Initially the cars were for export. This is a Series 2 car.

The Europa production line at Hethel. This photograph was taken in 1968. *(Nigel Snowdon)*

location by box-section radius arms and the usual coil spring/damper units.

On the first cars, later known as the Series 1, the body, which was moulded in glass-fibre in the same way as the Elan's body, was permanently bonded to the chassis to increase rigidity and this gave immense problems when accident damage was repaired. The low body featured one-piece curved, fixed door windows and high body sides (which had little aerodynamic effect and gave the Europa the appearance of a fast van). Other features were a single 7-gallon fuel tank in the left forward corner of the engine compartment, disc brakes at the front, drums at the rear and bolt-on steel wheels. These first cars were for export only. Performance encompassed a maximum speed of approximately 110 mph and 0–60 mph acceleration in about 10 seconds.

In 1967 Lotus introduced the much improved Series 2 Europa (known as the 54). The principal changes were a detachable chassis, divided door windows of which the main panels were operated electrically, adjustable 'Grand Prix'-type hammock seats, modified instrument panel with wood facing and fully trimmed doors. The Europa became available in the UK in July 1969 at £1667 in completed form including purchase tax (£1275 in kit form) and in 1970 Lotus started to export a Federal-bodied Europa

to the United States (this was known as the 65). In 1971 the Renault-powered Europa was replaced by the twin-cam car (the 74, *qv*). Total production of all versions of the Europa, Renault and twin-cam, amounted to 9230 cars. For more information about the Europa, the reader is referred to *The Lotus Elan and Europa* by John Bolster (Motor Racing Publications Ltd, reprinted 1985) from which much of the above information was derived.

**Specification:**
ENGINE: Renault 16 1470cc.
GEARBOX: Renault 4-speed.
CHASSIS: central steel box-section backbone with fork extensions at the rear, linked by light cross-member.
FRONT SUSPENSION: pressed steel wishbones (lower cranked) and coil spring/damper units.
REAR SUSPENSION: upper and lower links (upper formed by fixed-length drive-shafts), trailing radius arms and coil spring/damper units.
WHEELBASE: 7ft 8in.
FRONT TRACK: 4ft 5.5in.
REAR TRACK: 4ft 5in.
OVERALL LENGTH: 13ft 1.5in.
WIDTH: 5ft 4.5in.
WEIGHT: 13 cwt.

# 47

*Competition Sports car, 1966–68*

Directly developed from the 46 Europa production car, the 47 was a pure competition car built for homologation in Group 4 as a Competition Sports car. The chassis was similar to that of the Europa, but lighter, which led to flexing and cracking. The T-section forward cross-member was deeper than that of the Europa and at the rear the arms of the Y-section member were shorter and with a welded box-section cross-member. This arrangement permitted the installation of the dry sump Lotus-Cosworth 13C 1594cc (83.5 x 72.75mm) twin overhead camshaft engine developing 165 bhp at 7000 rpm. Tecalemit-Jackson fuel injection was featured on the works cars, but most private owners ran cars with two twin-choke Weber 45 DCOE carburettors. A Hewland FT 200 5-speed gearbox/final drive unit was fitted.

Although the suspension layout was basically similar to that of the Europa, there were many differences, especially at the rear, which incorporated 59 light alloy uprights, separate upper tubular links, lower reversed wishbones and longer tubular upper and lower trailing arms. Disc brakes were fitted front and rear, inside the suspension uprights at the rear, and there were centre-lock magnesium-alloy wheels. Fuel capacity was 20 gallons, in two light alloy tanks behind the bulkhead. The body was a lighter version of the Europa.

For homologation in Group 4, Lotus had to lay down the parts for 50 cars, and although no precise figures are available, it would seem that the actual number completed was around 30.

John Miles drove the 47 on its début at Brands Hatch on Boxing Day 1966 and with this car entered by Lotus Components he won the Special GT race. Miles won eight minor British races with the 47 in 1967 and with a much

In the 1967 BOAC 500 race at Brands Hatch the Lotus 47 of Miles/Oliver is lapped by the Drury/Holland Ford GT40. Miles/Oliver finished ninth overall and won the 2-litre Prototype class. Note the air intakes emerging from the engine cover. *(Nigel Snowdon)*

developed car Miles/Oliver finished ninth in that year's World Championship BOAC 500 Miles race and also won the 2-litre class.

The fragility of the 47 in longer events led to the development of the improved 47A with strengthened chassis, much improved brakes, a detachable body shell (as on the S2 Europa) and seats that were no longer fixed.

In 1968 John Player sponsored a team of 47s in Gold Team Lotus colours and a number of successes were gained during the year. Miles won the 2-litre class (sixth overall) in the John Player's Trophy at Silverstone, he finished second in the 2-litre class at the International Trophy meeting at Silverstone and took third place in a race in Portugal. Oliver finished sixth overall and won the 2-litre class in the Guards Trophy at Brands Hatch and also took a sixth place and a class win at Croft. Generally, however, neither Lotus nor John Player were happy with the cars and switched to the experimental 62s in 1969. In addition the 47s achieved a substantial number of successes in Club events.

## 47D

A special car built for GKN with the backbone of the chassis lengthened 3in., Rover 3.5-litre V8 engine and ZF combined 5-speed gearbox and final drive. As initially fitted, the engine was tuned to produce 185 bhp, but development work by GKN's Vandervell Products Ltd, including increasing the capacity to 4.4 litres, boosted this to 292 bhp at 7000 rpm. In this form the car had 0–100 mph acceleration in 11.1 sec and a maximum speed of close to 180 mph. The car was regarded primarily by GKN as a development project, but, apparently, was also used as a high speed executive transport.

**Specification:**
ENGINE: Lotus-Cosworth 13C 1594cc.
GEARBOX: Hewland FT200 combined 5-speed gearbox and final drive.
CHASSIS: central steel box-section backbone with T-section front cross-member and Y-section rear members linked by welded box-section cross-member.
FRONT SUSPENSION: double wishbones and coil spring/damper units.
REAR SUSPENSION: upper tubular links, reversed lower wishbones, tubular upper and lower trailing arms and coil spring/damper units.
WHEELBASE: 7ft 7in.
FRONT TRACK: 4ft 5in.
REAR TRACK: 4ft 10in.
LENGTH: 13ft 1.5in.
WIDTH: 5ft 4in.
HEIGHT: 3ft 4in.
WEIGHT: 10 cwt approx.

This remarkable car, the 47D, specially built for GKN, was powered by a Rover V8 engine bored and stroked to 4.4 litres, fitted with a ZF 5-speed trans-axle and said to have a maximum speed of close to 180 mph.

# 48

## *Formula 2, 1967*

For 1967 there was a new Formula 2 with a capacity limit of 1600cc, and for this Lotus developed the 48, which was raced by Team Lotus. This featured a monocoque front section, but with space-frame engine bay and suspension similar to that of the 1966 44. The engine was the Cosworth FVA 1599cc unit, which was used with the ZF 5DS12 combined gearbox and final drive unit.

The model made its début in Tasman racing and Graham Hill drove the prototype in the Australian Grand Prix at Warwick Farm in February, but retired with final drive failure, because this prototype was fitted with the insufficiently strong Hewland Mk 5 trans-axle.

During the year, Jim Clark won races at Barcelona, Jarama and Keimola, as well as finishing second at Zolder and third at Karlskoga, Hameelinna and Albi. With a 48 Jack Oliver won the Formula 2 class in the German Grand Prix and finished fifth overall. Hill was rather less fortunate, but took second places at Snetterton, Oulton Park, Reims and in the Gold Cup race at Oulton Park. In all only four of these cars were built.

Lotus continued to race these cars in 1968 and Jim Clark was killed at the wheel of a 48 at Hockenheim in April. Graham Hill drove a 48 in eight races that year with no success, whilst the prototype that had first appeared in Australia in early 1967 was raced by Jack Oliver with sponsorship from the Herts and Essex Aero Club. Oliver finished second at Hockenheim and took fifth place in the Championship for non-graded drivers.

Graham Hill turned in a remarkable performance with the new Formula 2 48 in the Formula 1 Spring Cup race at Oulton Park in April 1967. He rose to second place in the final behind Brabham (F1 Brabham), but was delayed by a fuel injection problem and eventually finished eighth. He drove the 48 with great enthusiasm during the year, but was usually out of luck. *(T. C. March)*

Following Jim Clark's tragic death at Hockenheim with a 48 in April 1968, Lotus efforts in Formula 2 were very muted. However, Jack Oliver drove a 48, a semi-works car sponsored by Herts & Essex Aero Club, with some success. He is seen at the Crystal Palace where he finished fourth on Whit Monday, Oliver's car retained the traditional Lotus green and yellow colours. *(Nigel Snowdon)*

## Specification:
ENGINE: Cosworth FVA 1599cc developing
220 bhp.
GEARBOX: ZF 5DS12 combined 5-speed gearbox
and final drive.
CHASSIS: monocoque with tubular space-frame
engine bay.
FRONT SUSPENSION: upper rocking arms, lower
wishbones and inboard coil spring/damper units.
REAR SUSPENSION: reversed lower wishbones,
top links, twin radius rods and coil spring/
damper units.
WHEELBASE: 7ft 7.75in.
MAXIMUM TRACK: 4ft 10in.
OVERALL LENGTH: 12ft 5.5in.
WEIGHT: 8.27 cwt.

# 49

*Formula 1 and Tasman, 1967–70*

The 49 was probably the outstanding car of the early years of the 3000cc Grand Prix Formula that came into force for the 1966 season. Its development was only possible because of the willingness of Ford to back Cosworth in the production of an engine for Formula 1 on what was a very modest budget of £100,000 and on the basis that, for the first season only, Team Lotus would have the exclusive use of these engines. The 90-degree V8 produced by Cosworth was developed from the 16-valve twin-cam 4-cylinder FVA engine which Cosworth had already produced for Formula 2 in 1600cc form. Of very compact dimensions, with the water and oil pumps, distributor and other ancillary components mounted low beside the crankcase,

the engine was developed in consultation with Chapman and Maurice Phillippe, and fitted in to the Lotus concept that the engine should form an integral stressed unit with the monocoque.

The monocoque of the 49 was formed in 18-gauge L72 Alclad aluminium-alloy sheeting with the engine mounted on the rear bulkhead. At the front there was a fabricated bulkhead and in front of this a sub-frame supporting the oil and water radiators. Front suspension was by upper rocking arms, inboard coil spring/damper units, with a fabricated lower link and radius rod on each side. At the rear there were tubular frames with pick-ups on the cylinder heads, and a cross-frame which mounted the ZF 5DS12 5-speed combined gearbox and final drive. The transmission incorporated sliding-spline joints within the output shafts. The rear suspension consisted of single top links, reversed lower wishbones, twin radius rods and inclined outboard coil spring/

Jim Clark at the wheel of his 49 on the model's debut in the 1967 Dutch Grand Prix. He scored a fine win from the Brabhams of Brabham and Hulme. *(Nigel Snowdon)*

Graham Hill on his way to a win in the 1968 Monaco Grand Prix with the new and improved 49B, sporting Gold Leaf colours. *(Nigel Snowdon)*

damper units. The fuel was carried in a 10-gallon tank mounted behind the seat-support plates and there were 15-gallon fuel bags inside boxes. At the front there was a detachable glass-fibre nose-cone and this in fact constituted the only bodywork on the car and the entire engine and transmission were exposed.

The 49 was essentially a very simple car, but one of immense potential, although a good part of the 1967 season was spent in resolving teething troubles, and that year's World Championship went to Jack Brabham with the comparatively simple single overhead cam Repco-powered car of his own manufacture. Originally it had been hoped that the 49 would be ready in time for the Monaco Grand Prix, but its début was at Zandvoort in June. Jim Clark not only won the race, but set fastest lap, whilst Graham Hill, who had rejoined Lotus for 1967, retired. Subsequently during that season Clark won the British race, he finished third at Monza, won the United States Grand Prix, where his car crossed the line with the right-hand rear wheel leaning inwards because the suspension top link had failed, he won the Mexican Grand Prix and also the non-Championship Madrid Grand Prix at Jarama in November. Although Hill frequently led races, he was generally less lucky than his team-mate, and, failing to win a single Grand Prix in 1967, his best performances were in the Canadian Grand Prix, in which he finished fourth, the United States race, in which

he took second place (and also took pole position in practice and set fastest lap in the race), and the Madrid Grand Prix, in which he took second place.

In 1968 Jim Clark scored his 25th World Championship Grand Prix win in the South African Grand Prix, but it was to be his last Formula 1 appearance because he was killed in a Formula 2 race at Hockenheim in April. It was also the last race in which Lotus competed in its traditional green and yellow colours, for the team had secured John Player sponsorship and the team ran as Gold Leaf Team Lotus with the cars finished in that brand's red, white and gold colours. Following Clark's tragic death, Jack Oliver was brought in to the Lotus team.

At the International Trophy at Silverstone at the end of April, Jo Siffert appeared with the new 49 supplied to Rob Walker and raced in his dark blue and white colours, but in many of the season's races Siffert was to retire, although there was to be one fine victory for the Walker camp that year. Hill won the second round of the World Championship, the Spanish Grand Prix at Jarama in May, and he won again at Monaco the following month with the improved 49B car. The 49B featured a slightly more wedge-shaped appearance with upswept engine cowl. There was a stronger sub-frame to support the rear suspension, the cylinder heads of the DFV engine no longer carried direct suspension loads, the new Hewland FG400 gearbox had been adopted and there were 12in wide front

and 15in wide rear wheels

Nothing much was achieved in the Belgian and Dutch races, and at the French Grand Prix the Team Lotus 49Bs appeared with tall strutted rear aerofoils acting directly upon the rear suspension uprights. In 1968 such rear aerofoils were becoming very much the fashion, but few teams fully understood their potential, their aerodynamics or their dangers. During practice their danger was only too well demonstrated when Oliver was caught in the slipstream of another car, he lost control and hit a brick gatepost at close to 140 mph. Oliver was badly shaken, but otherwise unhurt. At the British Grand Prix both works drivers retired and victory went to Siffert with the Rob Walker entry, the last occasion on which a private entry has won a World Championship race. Later in the year Hill finished second in the German Grand Prix, fourth in the Canadian Grand Prix, second in the United States Grand Prix and won the Mexican Grand Prix. He won the Drivers' World Championship for the second time in his career. At the Mexican race Hill's car had been fitted with a fourth pedal to the left of the clutch pedal which enabled the driver to feather the rear aerofoil on the straights.

For 1969 the team was joined by Jochen Rindt and at the first of the season's races, the South African Grand Prix, the cars were fitted with front and rear wings of equal height and mounted directly on to the wheel uprights. Cable operation was used to feather them along the straights. Hill finished second in South Africa and finished second (having taken pole position) in the Race of Champions, whilst Rindt finished second in the International Trophy at Silverstone. Disaster struck the team in the Spanish Grand Prix, where the 49Bs were fitted with very high strutted wings which failed and resulted in both Hill and Rindt crashing.

Because of injuries Rindt missed the Monaco Grand Prix, where Dickie Attwood was brought into the team. It was only after practice had started that the decision was made to ban wings and the 49Bs were hastily fitted with wedge-shaped gearbox covers. Hill won his fifth Monaco Grand Prix victory, Siffert was third with the Walker car and Attwood took fourth place.

Siffert took another fine second place in the Dutch Grand Prix, and at the French race the new 63 4-wheel-drive car appeared in the hands of John Miles. Chapman was determined that the drivers would handle the 63s in the British Grand Prix, but eventually he gave way and both Rindt and Hill as usual drove 49Bs. That Hill's ability was past its best began to show itself in his 1969 performances, for he had

Jochen Rindt with a 2.5-litre 49 at Warwick Farm in the 1969 Tasman series. This car was a 49B, rather than an earlier 49T. The 49s were no match for Chris Amon's Ferrari, but here Rindt scored a rare race win. *(Nigel Snowdon)*

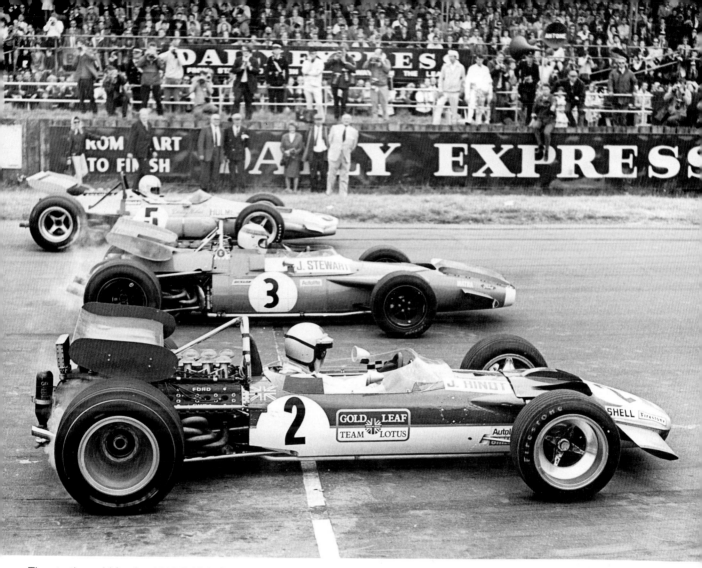

The starting grid for the 1969 British Grand Prix with Rindt (49B) in pole position, Stewart (Matra MS80) and Hulme (McLaren). Rindt finished fourth after a pit stop to have the left wing end-plate, which had been fouling the tyre, removed. *(Nigel Snowdon)*

finished a poor sixth in the French race, he was seventh at Silverstone and fourth at the Nürburgring. Rindt, hungry and excitable was trying too hard for a win, finishing fourth in the British race after a pit stop, and second in the Italian Grand Prix. In Canada Rindt finished third. Hill crashed badly at Watkins Glen after a tyre had punctured. He had spun on the previous lap, push-started the car and had been unable to re-fasten his seat belts. When he crashed, he was thrown out and suffered serious leg injuries. Jochen Rindt won the United States Grand Prix and Denis Jenkinson, the doyen of motor racing correspondents, who had bet that Rindt would never win a Grand Prix, and if he did he, Jenkinson, would shave off his famed beard, duly complied with his side of the bargain.

In the early part of 1970 Team Lotus raced the 49C cars, which featured 13in front wheels, new suspension uprights and revised steering geometry. Rindt and John Miles were the Team Lotus drivers, whilst Graham Hill was now handling Rob Walker's 49C. Apart from Jochen Rindt's brilliant victory in the Monaco Grand Prix, very little was gained by the 49Cs during 1970 and by the Dutch Grand Prix in June Team Lotus was entering the new 72s on a regular basis. Later in 1970 and in the early part of 1971, odd race appearances were made by Team Lotus with 49Cs and details are contained in the Appendix.

During the period 1966–69 Team Lotus regularly competed in the Tasman series of races held as international Formule Libre events in New Zealand and Australia. In 1968 and 1969 Team Lotus entered 49 cars powered by the 2.5-litre DFW version of the Cosworth Formula 1 engine and in this form they were known as the 49T. The 1968 Tasman series was won by Jim Clark, who scored a total of four race victories. In 1969 two 49Bs with 2.5-litre engines were

Graham Hill at the wheel of Rob Walker's Lotus 49C in the 1970 Dutch Grand Prix. The team enjoyed a thoroughly miserable season, for Hill was still recovering from his serious accident in the previous year's United States Grand Prix and the car was uncompetitive. *(Nigel Snowdon)*

entered for Jochen Rindt and Graham Hill. Rindt won the Lady Wigram Trophy at Christchurch and the Warwick Farm '100' at Sydney, and also finished second in the New Zealand Grand Prix and the Sandown Park race, whilst Hill was second at Christchurch and Teretonga. Overall, however, the cars proved no real match for the 2.4-litre Ferrari Dino of Chris Amon.

**Specification (1967):**
ENGINE: Cosworth-Ford DFV 90-degree V8.
GEARBOX: ZF 5DS12 combined 5-speed gearbox and final drive.
CHASSIS: monocoque constructed in 18-gauge aluminium-alloy sheet and with engine acting as integral stressed member.
FRONT SUSPENSION: upper rocking arms, fabricated lower links, radius rods and inboard coil spring/damper units.
REAR SUSPENSION: single upper links, reversed lower wishbones twin radius rods, inclined coil spring/damper units.
WHEELBASE: 7ft 11in.
FRONT AND REAR TRACK: 5ft 1in.
OVERALL LENGTH: 13ft 2in.
WEIGHT: 9.84 cwt.

# 50 Elan Plus 2

*Production Sports coupé, 1967–74*

Developed as a larger version of the Elan for the family man and with much more roomy interior and two small extra seats, the Plus 2 followed closely the specification of the Elan 2-seater. The chassis was of the same backbone construction, but larger, with the wheelbase increased by 12in, track by 7in, the length by 1ft 11in, and with an increase in weight of 3 cwt. The body was a very elegant fixed head coupé, retaining much of the style of the Elan fhc. As fitted to the Plus 2, the Lotus-Ford twin-cam engine, with two Weber 40 DCOE carburettors (Zenith-Strombergs were fitted only to cars with Federal emission equipment), developed 118 bhp at 6250 rpm. A brake servo was fitted as standard and there were centre-lock disc wheels. When announced the Plus 2 was priced by £1672 in component form and £1923 including purchase tax for the complete car. Maximum speed was a shade over 120 mph. 0–60 mph took about 8.2 sec, and fuel consumption averaged 25 to 28 mpg. Handling was exceptionally good, but the Plus 2 was rather susceptible to side winds. The original model remained in production until December 1969, but the first of a number of improved cars had already appeared.

**Plus 2S:** Apart from extra equipment and a higher standard of finish, there were few changes. The major difference, however, was that this was the first production Lotus to be sold only as a complete car. The Plus 2S was introduced in October 1968.

**Plus 2S 130:** Introduced in February 1971, this model was powered by the 'Big Valve' 126 bhp engine and distinguished by a self-coloured (as opposed to sprayed) silver roof. The price was £2626 including purchase tax.

**Plus 2S 130/5:** From October 1972 a 5-speed gearbox was optional, in which form the '/5' was added to the designation, and the new gearbox greatly improved high-speed cruising. In this form the price was £2826 including purchase tax.

Total Plus 2 production amounted to approximately 3300 cars.

The Plus 2 was the Elan for the family man (provided that the rear seat passengers were very short in the leg) and was in production between 1967 and 1974. This is a late Plus 2S 130.

Production of the Plus 2 at Hethel. This photograph was taken in 1968. *(Nigel Snowdon)*

**Specification (Plus 2S 130/5):**
ENGINE: Lotus-Ford twin overhead camshaft
developing 126 bhp at 6500 rpm.
GEARBOX: 5-speed with Austin Maxi gears in
Lotus casing.
CHASSIS: central steel box-section backbone
with front and rear fork extensions, each linked
by boxed cross-member.
FRONT SUSPENSION: pressed steel, unequal-
length double wishbones and coil spring/
damper units.
REAR SUSPENSION: strut-type, with tubular
lower wishbones and coil spring/damper units.
WHEELBASE: 8ft 0in.
FRONT TRACK: 4ft 6in.
REAR TRACK: 4ft 7in.
OVERALL LENGTH: 14ft 0in.
WIDTH: 5ft 3.5in.
WEIGHT: 17.5 cwt.

# 51 (also 51A and 51R)

*Formula Ford, 1967*

Formula Ford was introduced in 1967, a single-seater formula for cars powered by the Cortina GT push-rod engine, with narrow wheels and road tyres. Lotus produced the 51, based on the space-frame design of the 22 and 31, and this was marketed in conjunction with Motor Racing Stables at Brands Hatch. The price was £955. This beginners class of motor racing proved to be something of a rough and tumble and the fact that one of MRS drivers won five races means very little. What is more significant is that in 1967–68, despite very strong opposition from other manufacturers, a total of 218 Formula Ford cars was sold.

## Specification:

ENGINE: Ford Cortina GT.
GEARBOX: Ford 4-speed.
CHASSIS: multi-tubular space-frame.
FRONT SUSPENSION: double wishbones and coil spring/damper units.
REAR SUSPENSION: reversed lower wishbones, upper links, twin radius rods and coil spring/damper units.
WHEELBASE: 7ft 6in.
FRONT AND REAR TRACK: 4ft 1.5in.
OVERALL LENGTH: 11ft 8in.

## 51A

The 1968 Formula Ford car. The production total is included in the figure above.

## 51R

Version of the 51 with cycle wings, lighting and 'flower power' paint scheme exhibited at the 1968 Racing Car Show with a price tag of £1085. One of these cars was sold to an American customer.

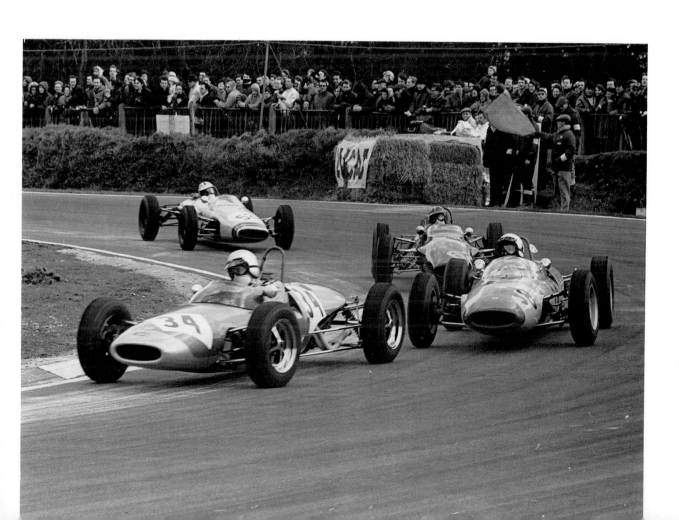

Two 51As, the 1968 Formula Ford car, seen at Brands Hatch in a supporting race to the Race of Champions in March 1968. *(Nigel Snowdon)*

# 52

## Proposed Production GT

A development of the Europa with Ford twin-cam engine in 1967 for sale in the UK, but not proceeded with. See 74 for the Europa TC announced in 1971.

# 53

## Sports-racing car, 1968.

Proposed car derived from the 23 and not proceeded with.

# 54

## Production GT, 1968.

The Series 2 Europa with detachable chassis and improved equipment and interior. See 46.

# 55

## Formula 3, 1968.

A one-off car for Gold Leaf Team Lotus. See 41X.

# 56

## Indianapolis, 1968

The gas turbine four-wheel-drive 56 was sponsored by Andy Granatelli through his STP company and was the result of a gradual build-up of enthusiasm for gas turbine cars and four-wheel drive. From 1964–67 the P104 Novi four-wheel-drive car built by Ferguson had run at Indianapolis without success, but with considerable promise, especially so far as lack of wheel spin was concerned, and in 1967 the Paxton Turbocar driven by Parnelli Jones had led at Indianapolis until eliminated by gearbox problems of a minor nature shortly before the finish.

Granatelli had a two-year exclusive agreement with United Aircraft of Canada for the use of their Pratt & Whitney industrial gas turbine engines. Because USAC had introduced a limit of 15.999 sq in inlet annulus area for Indianapolis cars, United Aircraft modified their engine by the removal of two of the three original axial compressor stages preceding the main centrifugal compressor. Although the cars would face stiff opposition from the many 2.8-litre turbocharged cars at Indianapolis, Chapman was convinced

Graham Hill at the wheel of the STP-sponsored 56 with Pratt & Whitney gas turbine engine and Ferguson four-wheel drive at Indianapolis in 1968. Three cars ran in the race, but none finished. Hill was eliminated because of suspension failure and was classified 19th.

that the 56, despite a power deficiency, would be a potential winner because of its speed through the corners.

The detail work on the car was the responsibility of Maurice Phillippe. The 56 featured a 'bath-tub' monocoque constructed in 16-gauge aluminium sheet with cross-bracing by a box structure at the front and a fabricated structure at the rear. Suspension front and rear was by double wishbones, top cantilever arms and inboard coil spring/damper units. The Ferguson four-wheel-drive transmission was used. Girling ventilated 10.25in disc brakes were fitted front and rear, driven by the half-shafts of the four-wheel-drive system.

Four of these cars were built, two to be entered as Team Lotus-STP entries and a third to be driven by an American driver for Granatelli's team. After the death of Jim Clark, and Jackie Stewart had injured his wrist in a Fomula 2 race, Mike Spence drove alongside Graham Hill, whilst the STP entry was driven by Greg Weld.

Sadly Mike Spence was killed during qualifying at the wheel of Greg Weld's car, when he went off-line, hit the wall broadside on, a front wheel was torn off and struck his head. Following the death of Jim Clark in April, the tragedy was almost too much for Lotus – and Chapman – to take. Weld withdrew from the race; Jo Leonard, Art Pollard and Graham Hill drove the cars in the race.

Leonard took pole position at 171.559 mph, whilst Hill was second fastest at 171.208 mph. At the start Leonard led briefly, but Hill was an early retirement when the front suspension failed and he hit the wall. After running second for much of the race, Leonard took the lead again, and was all set for victory with nine laps to run when the turbine died and the car coasted to a halt. Pollard's 56 also was eliminated by turbine failure. The cause in both cases was failure of the fuel pump drives; these incorporated phosphor bronze shafts which the manufacturers had insisted upon the cars being fitted with in place of the steel shafts which Lotus preferred. Hill's car had run, however, with a steel shaft in the fuel pump drive.

Granatelli ran the 56s in a number of other races during the 1968 season, but the future of turbine engines at Indianapolis was damned when USAC further limited turbines by the introduction of an inlet annulus area of 11.999 sq in for 1969. In addition it was also stated that from 1970 both four-wheel-drive and gas turbines would be illegal unless these items had been made solely for automobile use. One of the 56s reappeared at Indianapolis in 1968, with a turbocharged Offenhauser engine, but retired early in the race.

## Specification:

ENGINE: Pratt & Whitney gas turbine.
TRANSMISSION: Ferguson four-wheel-drive.
CHASSIS: 'bath-tub' monocoque constructed from 16-gauge aluminium sheet.
FRONT AND REAR SUSPENSION: double wishbones, upper cantilever arms and inboard coil spring/damper units.
WHEELBASE: 8 ft 6in.
FRONT AND REAR TRACK: 5ft 2.5in.
OVERALL LENGTH: 14ft 2in.
WEIGHT: 12.05 cwt.

# 56B

## Formula 1, 1968

Following the performance of the gas turbine cars at Indianapolis, Chapman discussed with United Aircraft the possibility of them developing an engine that would be equivalent to the 3-litre capacity limit of Formula 1. It was not until 1970 that this engine was ready, the spare type 56 Indianapolis monocoque was used and the car was not raced until 1971. Only very minor modifications were made to the car.

It was first driven by Emerson Fittipaldi in the 1971 Race of Champions, but on the bumpy Brands Hatch circuit it bottomed badly and was retired with damaged right rear suspension. It next appeared in the Rothmans Trophy at Oulton Park in the following month, April, driven by Reine Wisell, when smaller-diameter

tyres were fitted and there were minor suspension changes. Wisell rose to fifth place, but retired after a tyre failed and the suspension was again damaged. In the International Trophy race at Silverstone, Fittipaldi was back again at the wheel, but once more the car was eliminated by suspension problems in the first heat. In the second heat Fittipaldi finished third, and he was classified 13th on aggregate.

The car's next appearance was in the Jochen Rindt Gedachtnisrennen at Hockenheim in June, where Dave Walker was the driver. Because of engine failure during practice the car non-started. Walker then drove the 56B in the Dutch Grand Prix at Zandvoort, but slid off the road. Wisell was at the wheel at the British Grand Prix, but there the gas turbine lost power and the car was unclassified. Because of problems that still subsisted after Rindt's fatal crash at Monza in 1970, only a single Lotus, the

Emerson Fittipaldi with the Pratt & Whitney gas turbine-powered 56B Formula 1 car in the 1971 Race of Champions at Brands Hatch. He retired because of suspension failure. *(Nigel Snowdon)*

Stripped – the 56B in the paddock at Brands Hatch. *(Nigel Snowdon)*

Reine Wisell with the 56B in the Rothmans International Trophy race at Oulton Park in April 1971. Once again the car was eliminated by suspension failure. *(Nigel Snowdon)*

56B, entered in the name of World Wide Racing and painted black and gold, was fielded in the 1971 Italian Grand Prix for Fittipaldi. He finished eighth. The last appearance of the car was with Fittipaldi at the wheel in the Preis der Nationen Formula 5000 race at Hockenheim, in which he finished second and also set fastest lap.

The 56B had been purely experimental and it seemed that its goals were more than adequately fulfilled.

**Specification:**
As for 56, except Pratt & Whitney engine 'equivalent' to 3 litre Formula 1.

## 57

*Formula 1, 1968*

Proposed Formula 1 car with de Dion rear axle that did not proceed beyond the design stage.

## 58

*Formula 2, 1968*

This Formula 2 car with de Dion axle was completed and tested both with FVA 1600cc and, it is believed, with the Cosworth DFV 3-litre Formula 1 engine. The car was slow and the project was abandoned.

## 59 (also 59B and 59F)

*Formula 3, 1969*

Designed by Dave Baldwin, the 59 was intended for both Formula 2 and Formula 3. The basis of the design was a square-tube space-frame. At the front suspension was by double wishbones and outboard coil spring/damper units and at the rear there was the familiar Lotus layout of reversed lower wishbones, single top links and twin radius rods. Although Triumph Herald front suspension uprights were used, there were cast magnesium uprights at the rear. The Holbay Ford R68 engine was fitted and there was the usual Hewland gearbox and final drive unit. The bodywork was in glass-fibre and what distinguished the 59 was the unusual twin-nostril air intakes at the front.

Gold Leaf Team Lotus ran a pair of 59s with Holbay power for Roy Pike and Morris Nunn and a considerable number of these cars were entered with success by other teams. During the year Emerson Fittipaldi appeared at the wheel of a Formula 3 59 and soon found winning form.

**Specification:**
ENGINE: Holbay-Ford R68 997cc.
GEARBOX: Hewland combined 5-speed gearbox and final drive.
CHASSIS: multi-tubular space-frame constructed from square-section tubing.
FRONT SUSPENSION: double wishbones and coil spring/damper units.
REAR SUSPENSION: reversed lower wishbones, single upper links, twin radius rods and coil spring/damper units.
WHEELBASE: 7ft 8.75in.
MAXIMUM TRACK: 4ft 8in.
WEIGHT: 7.87 cwt.

Jochen Rindt with the Roy Winkelmann Racing Lotus 59B Formula 2 car has just passed Pescarolo (Matra MS7) in the Formula 2 race at Thruxton on Easter Monday 1969. He won the race, but Matras finished second, third and fourth. *(Nigel Snowdon)*

# 59B

*Formula 2, 1969*

This was the Formula 2 variant of the 59 with the Cosworth FVA engine, Hewland FT200 gearbox/final drive unit, larger fuel tanks, and, until the ban at the 1969 Monaco Grand Prix, a tall strutted aerofoil mounted on the rear suspension uprights. Lotus supplied these cars to Winkelmann Racing, and subject to Formula 1 commitments, they were usually driven by works Formula 1 drivers Jochen Rindt and Graham Hill. Despite a puncture in his heat, Rindt won the race at the Easter Thruxton meeting and followed this up with wins at Pau, Zolder and Langenlebarn. Hill won the Albi race. When the works drivers were not available Winkelmann entered other drivers, including John Miles, who was also a member of the Lotus Formula 1 team, Roy Pike and Alan Rollinson. Only one of these cars was sold to a private entrant. This was the car entered by Lotus dealer Len Street Engineering for Max Mosley, but it was written off in practice at the Eifelrennen.

**Specification:**
as for 59 except Cosworth FVA engine and Hewland FT200 combined gearbox and final drive.

Graham Hill drove a Winkelmann 59B in the 1969 Gold Cup race at Oulton Park, but retired because of a broken oil pressure gauge pipe. *(Nigel Snowdon)*

# 59F

*Formula Ford, 1970*

After one of these cars had been built up by Jim Russell's team, Lotus Components built a small number of 59-based Formula Ford cars with modified suspension and narrower wheels. The 59AF was the final version with wedge-shaped nose-cone.

One of the sensations of the 1969 season was Emerson Fittipaldi with his Formula 3 Lotus 59. He is seen at the Brands Hatch meeting on 1 September, 1969, leading Tim Schenken (Brabham). Fittipaldi finished third in this race behind Reine Wisell (Chevron) and Schenken. *(Nigel Snowdon)*

## 60

*The Seven Series 4. See 'Seven'.*

## 61 and 61M

*Formula Ford, 1969*

Although the 51 remained in production for some while in 1969, at the Racing Car Show Lotus Components exhibited the 61 with new multi-tubular space-frame strengthened by a stressed-steel undertray, typical Lotus suspension and a wedge-shaped body inspired by the Indianapolis cars. Lotus offered the Lotus-Holbay LH/105 engine guaranteed to develop 105 bhp, but the customer could fit any engine of his choice. The standard transmission was the Hewland Mk 6. These cars achieved a good measure of success, especially when entered by the Jim Russell Racing School Team (Dave Walker scored nine wins and gained the Les Leston Formula Ford Championship), but the most successful cars of the year were the Alexis and Merlyn. A substantial number of 61s were exported. Total production amounted to 248 cars.

### Specification:
ENGINE: Lotus-Holbay LH/105 Ford Cortina 1599cc developing 105 bhp.
GEARBOX: Hewland Mk6.
CHASSIS: multi-tubular space-frame.
FRONT SUSPENSION: double wishbones and coil spring/damper units.
REAR SUSPENSION: reversed lower wishbones, upper links, twin radius rods and coil spring/damper units.
WHEELBASE: 7ft 6in.
FRONT AND REAR TRACK: 4ft 3.5in.
OVERALL LENGTH: 12ft 6in.
WEIGHT: 7.32 cwt.

## 61M

*Formula Ford, 1970–71*

The production car for 1970–71, as for the 61 but with modified front to reduce frontal area.

The 1969 Lotus Formula Ford cars, the 61, seen here decked out in the colours of the Jim Russell Racing Drivers School.

# 62

*Prototype, 1969*

As part of the development programme for the new Lotus Type 907 engines destined to power the new Elite, two Group 6 Prototypes were designed by Martin Wade and raced by Gold Leaf Team Lotus in 1969. Although entered as Lotus Europas, the 47 version of which they superficially resembled (apart from much more bulbous rear bodywork and very flared wheel arches to accommodate wheels and tyres of Formula 1 size), they were very different under the skin.

In place of the backbone chassis of the 47 there was a multi-tubular space-frame with front suspension by double wishbones and coil spring/damper units and at the rear reversed lower wishbones, single upper links, twin radius rods and coil spring/damper units. Ventilated disc brakes of 12in diameter were mounted outboard front and rear and the wheel rims were 12in at the front and 15in at the rear.

The engine was based on the 4-cylinder Vauxhall Victor block, with a capacity of 1995cc, a twin overhead camshaft, 16-valve cylinder head, Tecalemit-Jackson fuel injection and a power output of 220 bhp at 8000 rpm. Transmission was by a ZF combined 5-speed gearbox and final drive. The glass-fibre body, with the complete front and rear body sections hinged to give access to the mechanics, featured a substantial spoiler on the tail and other spoilers on the nose.

In the Gold Leaf red, white and gold colours the 62s looked superb; they also sounded superb and went extremely well. The first car appeared in the 1969 BOAC race at Brands Hatch, and despite a host of teething problems, John Miles/Brian Muir drove it into 13th place and won the 2-litre Prototype class. Two cars appeared in many National and minor International races during the year and probably the best performances were a third place by Miles in the Tourist Trophy and a fourth place by the same driver in the Trophy of the Dunes at Zandvoort. The racing programme revealed weaknesses in

In the 1969 BOAC 500 race at Brands Hatch this new 62 was driven by John Miles/Brian Muir, but was delayed by a host of minor problems. Miles/Muir eventually finished 13th, but won the 2-litre Group 6 class. *(Nigel Snowdon)*

John Miles with his 62 on the starting grid for the Lombank Trophy race for Competition Sports Cars (Group 4) and Prototypes (Group 6) up to 2000cc at Brands Hatch on 1 September, 1969. Miles scored a convincing victory from Roger Nathan (Astra) and Roy Pike (with the second 62 alongside him on the grid). This photograph emphasizes the relationship to and the differences from the 47. *(Nigel Snowdon)*

the Victor block, which resulted in Lotus putting in hand design work on their own block, and with this function fulfilled the cars were not raced after 1969 by the works. One of the cars was however sold to jazz band leader Chris Barber and raced for him by Dave Brodie.

**Specification:**

ENGINE: Lotus-developed 1995cc twin overhead camshaft 4-cylinder developing 220 bhp.

GEARBOX: ZF 5DS2 combined 5-speed gearbox and final drive.

CHASSIS: multi-tubular space-frame.

FRONT SUSPENSION: double wishbones and coil spring/damper units.

REAR SUSPENSION: reversed lower wishbones, single upper links, twin radius rods and coil spring/damper units.

WHEELBASE: 7ft 7in.

FRONT AND REAR TRACK: 4ft 4in.

OVERALL LENGTH: 12ft 10in.

WEIGHT: 12.05 cwt.

# 63

## *Formula 1, 1969*

With the introduction of the 3000cc Grand Prix Formula in 1966, there was an awakening of interest by constructors in building a four-wheel-drive car, derived from the practical experience gained by Ferguson with their P99, which Moss had driven to a win in 1500cc form in the 1961 Gold Cup race at Oulton Park and by the use of the Ferguson transmission at Indianapolis. One of the problems faced by all Formula 1 constructors was getting the power of the 3-litre engines on to the road. As Chapman believed that the 49 had only a limited racing life, he implemented the 63 four-wheel-drive car which was produced by Maurice Phillippe and his staff for the 1969 season.

The design team produced a 'bath-tub' monocoque, with the driver positioned well to the front of the car, with the Cosworth DFV engine, reversed in the chassis, and with the clutch assembly behind the seat of the driver. The transmission was taken through a 5-speed Lotus-Hewland gearbox to a central torque-split unit on the left side of the car (in accordance with Indianapolis practice) and with propeller shafts driving off-set ZF final drives on front and rear axles. Because of the space occupied by the transmission, the fuel cells were within the pontoon side-boxes which extended along both sides of the engine.

Tubular sub-frames provided pick-up points for the front and rear suspension, which was by fabricated sheet wishbones and links, with inboard cranks operating coil spring/damper units. Although the 63 looked long and low, its wheelbase at 8ft 2in was only three inches longer than that of the 49. There were small 13in wheels front and rear and because of problems in achieving adequate steering lock, there was a double-crank swinging drag-link system incorporating conventional rack-and-

This view of the front end of the 63 shows clearly the drive arrangements, the drive-shaft mounted brakes – and the difficulty in reaching the pedals. *(Nigel Snowdon)*

John Miles in the pits at Silverstone for the 1969 British Grand Prix with the revolutionary, but hopelessly unsuccessful 63 four-wheel-drive Formula 1 car. *(Nigel Snowdon)*

pinion steering. One of the things that both Lotus Formula 1 drivers Hill and Rindt detested about the 63 was that to reach the pedals it was necessary for the driver to position his feet beneath the front axle tube.

Because of the reluctance of Hill and Rindt to drive the 63, Chapman brought John Miles into the team. He appeared with the 63 initially in the French Grand Prix at Clermont-Ferrand, but retired on lap 2; Chapman was determined that Rindt and Hill should drive 63s in the British Grand Prix at Silverstone; indeed so as to compel them so to do, he made arrangements for the sale of the team's 49s. However their resistance was so fierce that Chapman was forced to undo his deal and so the 63s were driven only by Miles and Bonnier (one of the would-be 49 purchasers). Miles finished tenth in the race, but Bonnier retired. At the German

Grand Prix Italo-American driver Mario Andretti drove a 63, and his enthusiasm for four-wheel-drive cars was well known. Unfortunately on the bumps and yumps of the Nürburgring the 63 was a considerable handful and on only the first lap the car grounded with full tanks and crashed.

Rindt had agreed to drive a 63 in the Gold Cup race at Oulton Park in August and he took second place behind Ickx (Brabham). Miles was back at the wheel in the Italian Grand Prix at Monza, but retired with engine problems. Although Rindt drove a 63 in practice for the Canadian Grand Prix, Miles alone drove one in the race and retired. Mario Andretti reappeared at the wheel of a 63 in the United States Grand Prix, but again retired. Miles also retired in the Mexican Grand Prix because of a misfiring engine.

By the end of the 1969 season Chapman had concluded that the combination of the heavy steering of the 63, the considerable weight penalty compared with the 49, power understeer and a general lack of feel, combined with the fact that the drivers preferred the torque-split set-up so that all the power went through the rear wheels (which was the equivalent of using the 63 as a rear-wheel-drive car only) made the venture pointless. Other constructors to build four-wheel-drive cars for 1969 were Matra (whose space-frame car appeared in a few races), McLaren (whose car ran only in the British race) and Cosworth, who did not race their car at all. Only two 63s were built and they were not raced after 1969.

**Specification:**
ENGINE: Cosworth DFV 2993cc.
TRANSMISSION: four-wheel-drive incorporating Lotus-Hewland 5-speed gearbox and ZF final drives front and rear.
CHASSIS: 'bath-tub' monocoque.
FRONT AND REAR SUSPENSION: fabricated sheet wishbones and links, vertical coil spring/damper units.
WHEELBASE: 8ft 2in.
FRONT AND REAR TRACK: 4ft 11in.
OVERALL LENGTH: 14ft 2in.
WEIGHT: 10.45 cwt.

# 64

## *Indianapolis, 1969*

Because of the limitations on turbines, STP and Lotus worked together on a new team of cars for the 1969 Indianapolis race, known as the 64. Initially USAC had banned four-wheel-drive cars, but relented to the extent that they permitted four-wheel-drive cars with wheel rims no wider than 10in. compared with the 14in of two-wheel drive. Lotus produced a monocoque, very similar to that of the 56, with similar suspension and with transmission closely related to that of the 63.

Lotus built four cars, three for the race and one as a spare. One was supplied to Mario Andretti, who after Firestone had an expenditure cut-back, agreed that his car should be taken over by Granatelli, but be prepared by his own team. The Team Lotus cars were to be driven by Graham Hill and Jochen Rindt. Although Andretti was very quick in qualifying, neither Hill nor Rindt could achieve good laps and Rindt spun off. In an effort to sort out the problems with the cars, large rear spoilers were fitted. Because of problems of overheating of the rear hubs, new finned hubs were made and fitted. Andretti crashed heavily when a right rear hub failed. It was revealed that the failure had been caused by inadequate heat treatment. Because there was insufficient time for new hubs to be made and tested, the cars were withdrawn from the race. Andretti qualified at the wheel of his Hawk-Ford and won. After the race there was a disagreement over the sale of the cars to Granatelli and they were eventually returned to Hethel.

The 2.6-litre turbocharged Ford-powered, four-wheel-drive 64 entered at Indianapolis in 1969, but withdrawn because of rear hub failure caused by poor heat treatment. It was the last appearance of Lotus at Indianapolis and a sad end to a long and distinguished career at the 'Hosier Bowl'. Mario Andretti is at the wheel.

## Specification:

ENGINE: Ford V8 2605cc four overhead camshaft turbocharged.
TRANSMISSION: four-wheel-drive incorporating Lotus-Hewland gearbox and ZF final drives.
CHASSIS: 'bath-tub' monocoque.
FRONT AND REAR SUSPENSION: fabricated wishbones, links, inboard coil spring/damper units.
WHEELBASE: 8ft 4in.
FRONT AND REAR TRACK: 4ft 2in.
OVERALL LENGTH: 13ft 4in.
WEIGHT: not available.

## 65

*Europa complying with Federal regulations for the Unites States market. See 46.*

## 66

*Not allocated.*

## 67

*Proposed car for the 1970 Tasman Championship that was not built.*

## 68

*Formula A, 1969*

Lotus thoroughly confused the issue by allocating the number 70 to the Formula A/Formula 5000 car (the new category for single-seaters powered by 'stock-block' engines of up to 5000cc) and then producing the first car in late 1969 as a Formula A car (the United States version of the Formula) under the designation 68.

The car was designed by Martin Wade and built by Lotus Components. It was based on a wedge-shaped monocoque with side-members in 16- and 18-gauge aluminium sheet, linked by an 18-gauge aluminium undertray, stiffened by folds in the inner skins of the side members, mild steel braces which also formed mounting points, a mild-steel box structure at the front and a sheet steel panel forming the back of the driver's seat. The power unit was the Shelby-developed Ford Boss V8 4945cc bolted to the monocoque and with tubular stay rods. The gearbox was the Hewland LG600. At the front, suspension was by substantial double wishbones (each formed by welded half-pressings), and outboard coil spring/damper units. For the rear suspension Lotus used single upper links, twin lower links, single radius rods each side and outboard coil spring/damper units. Lockheed 12in ventilated disc brakes were mounted outboard front and rear. By following the layout of the experimental 58, and mounting the radiator above the gearbox, it was hoped to create a near-perfect wedge shape. During testing it soon became apparent that this arrangement would result in overheating, so Lotus mounted a canted radiator in the nose with top ducting.

Koshland Competition took delivery of the first car and entered it for Mario Andretti in the Formula A race at Sebring in December. Andretti built up a substantial lead until the engine blew up. Andretti's plans to race the car in 1970 were thwarted by other commitments. The production car was, as mentioned, the 70 (*qv*).

Carlos Reutemann at the wheel of his 79 before the start of the wet United States Grand Prix at Watkins Glen in October 1979. He was eliminated by an accident. *(Nigel Snowdon)*

Lotus ran the very advanced 80 at only a few races in 1979 and its development problems were never resolved. Here is Andretti at Monaco, where he retired because of suspension failure. *(Nigel Snowdon)*

The Lotus 81 of Elio de Angelis in the 1980 Brazilian Grand Prix. He took a fine second place behind the Renault of Arnoux. *(Nigel Snowdon)*

Elio de Angelis with the Lotus 81 at the 1981 French Grand Prix at the Paul Ricard circuit. The Essex colours were particularly dazzling. *(Nigel Snowdon)*

Nigel Mansell with the 81 in the United States Grand Prix West in 1981. He raced this car after the twin-chassis 88 had been banned. He was eliminated by an accident. *(Nigel Snowdon)*

Elio de Angelis with the conventional 87 in the 1981 Monaco Grand Prix. He retired because of engine trouble. *(Nigel Snowdon)*

In the first of the 1982 races Team Lotus fielded the improved 87B. Elio de Angelis finished eighth in that year's South African Grand Prix. *(Nigel Snowdon)*

De Angelis's 88 at the 1981 United States Grand Prix West. The 88s were banned from the race. *(Nigel Snowdon)*

The Lotus 87 (nearest camera) and 88 at Silverstone during testing prior to the 1981 British Grand Prix. The cars are once again in John Player Special colours. *(Nigel Snowdon)*

Nigel Mansell with the 1982 91 in practice for the Canadian Grand Prix. He was eliminated on the second lap of the race by a collision with Giacomelli (Alfa Romeo). *(Nigel Snowdon)*

In the 1982 German Grand Prix Nigel Mansell finished ninth with the 91. *(Nigel Snowdon)*

At the start of the 1983 season Lotus still fielded a Cosworth-powered car, the 92, initially with computer-controlled 'Active' suspension, for Nigel Mansell. In the Brazilian Grand Prix Mansell finished a poor 12th. *(Nigel Snowdon)*

At Rio de Janeiro the team also entered the 93T with Renault turbocharged engine for Elio de Angelis. Here the car is seen in the team's garage. The Renault engine began to smoke badly on the warming-up lap and so de Angelis switched to his spare 92 and this resulted in his disqualification. *(Nigel Snowdon)*

Elio de Angelis in the 1983 Monaco Grand Prix with the turbocharged Renault-powered 93T. De Angelis was eliminated by drive-shaft failure. *(Nigel Snowdon)*

# 69 and 69F

*Formula 2, 3 and Ford, 1970–71*

For 1970 a change in the Formula 2 regulations made the use of bag-type fuel tanks compulsory. This meant that most cars required substantial modification, but Dave Baldwin re-designed the 59 so that a forward monocoque cell of quite bulbous proportions was mated to the space-frame engine bay. There were minor suspension modifications, a new wedge-nosed body and a low air intake for the radiator.

Following Roy Winkelmann's withdrawal from racing (the result of most of his staff joining the new March concern), Jochen Rindt formed his own team, Jochen Rindt Racing Limited, administered by Bernie Ecclestone to race the works 69s. Rindt won four races, at Thruxton, Pau, the Nürburgring and Zolder. Graham Hill, John Miles and other drivers also handled the Rindt cars during the year, but without achieving much. The other very successful Lotus driver was Emerson Fittipaldi, who ran for Jim Russell early in the season, but then switched to a car entered by Lotus Components and sponsored by Team Bardahl. He took a second place at Imola and a substantial number of third, fourth and fifth places, all of which were to lead to his place in the Gold Leaf Team Lotus Formula 1 team that year. Overall, however, the 69 was no match for the BMW, Brabham and Tecno opposition.

In 1971 the Formula 2 cars were to be run on behalf of the works by a new team, London International Racing Associates, run by journalists Justin Haler and Chris Witty, with Reine Wisell as driver. Wisell won at Pau, but this team soon found itself in financial difficulties and collapsed during the year. Another problem facing entrants of 69s was the fact that Lotus Racing was wound up early in the year following the resignation of its Managing Director, Mike Warner. Despite problems, including lack of spares, Emerson Fittipaldi with the Team Bardahl car scored wins at Madrid, the Crystal Palace and Albi and at the end of the year two races at Interlagos in Brazil.

In 1972 Emerson Fittipaldi continued to race the 69 as in 1971. The Formula had changed to a maximum capacity of 2000cc with a minimum sliding weight scale accordng to the number of cylinders. Fittipaldi's car (sponsored by Chapman's new toy, Moonraker Power Yachts) was powered by the very expensive and potent 1930cc Cosworth BDA, featured a full-width nose (as used by Fittipaldi in the 1971 Brazilian races) and was substantially modified as the season progressed. During the year Fittipaldi won races at Hockenheim, Rouen, the Österreichring and Interlagos.

The 69 was also built in space-frame form. In 1971 the Formula 3 regulations had changed and there was now a limit on capacity of 1600cc. As the regulations were drafted, the engines had

In 1970 Jochen Rindt Racing Limited, managed by Bernie Ecclestone, ran the new Formula 2 69s on behalf of the works and enjoyed a good measure of success. This is Rindt on his way to a win at Thruxton on Easter Monday. *(Nigel Snowdon)*

In 1971 a team of 69 Formula 2 cars was entered by Team Bardahl for Emerson and Wilson Fittipaldi (during the year the latter switched to a March). Here Emerson is seen at the Crystal Palace on 31 May, when he won the Formula 2 race. *(Nigel Snowdon)*

to breathe through a 20mm restrictor plate, which made the cars slow and boring, but this rule was changed in August and 21.5mm restrictors were then allowed. In Formula 3 form the 69 contained its fuel in rubber fuel bags within stressed alloy sheet side-boxes.

Gold Leaf Team Lotus ran a Formula 3 69 for Dave Walker and it featured a Novamotor-modified twin-cam Ford engine and inboard rear brakes. Walker started in 32 races and he won 25 of them. It had been the intention for Lotus Racing to sponsor an entry for Ian Ashley, but this did not proceed because of the closure of that side of the Lotus organization.

There was also a version of the 69, the 69F, for Formula Ford, and this featured narrower wheels and a chisel nose. Mo Harness, driving one of these cars for Jim Russell, won the 1971 Johnson Wax Euro-Trophy Championship.

Other versions of the 69 were available for American Formula B racing. A total of 57 cars of all types was built.

### Specification (Formula 2, 1970):
ENGINE: Cosworth FVA 1600cc.
GEARBOX: Hewland FT 200 combined gearbox and final drive.
CHASSIS: front monocoque and rear space-frame.
FRONT SUSPENSION: double wishbones and coil spring/damper units.
REAR SUSPENSION: reversed lower wishbones, single upper links, twin radius rods and coil spring/damper units.
WHEELBASE: 7ft 8.5in.
FRONT AND REAR TRACK: 4ft 8in.
WEIGHT: not available.

# 70

## *Formula 5000 and Formula A, 1970*

Although the prototype 68 had been fitted with a Ford engine, Lotus intended that the cars should also take the Chevrolet engine which had already proved immensely successful. Lotus Components entered a car in 1970 for Alan Rollinson and this was powered by a Vegantune-developed Chevrolet engine. Rollinson crashed heavily at Brands Hatch at Easter and the car broke in two. A second car was built up by Lotus Components with the Ford Boss engine, but driven by Dave Walker at Oulton Park towards the end of the season, it retired with clutch failure and at Brands Hatch, where it was to be driven by Rollinson, the rear suspension failed on the warming-up lap. Subsequently the car ran at Sebring and in the 1971 Tasman series. In the Tasman series the car finished fourth at Levin (David Oxton), second at Warwick Farm (Chris Amon) and fourth at Sandown Park (Chris Amon).

Only one 70 was entered privately in the UK, but driver Jock Russell soon found that it was no match for the rival Lolas, McLarens and Surtees. In the United States a few successes were gained and the most successful driver was George Follmer. With his Boss Mustang-powered car Follmer won at St Jovite and Mid-Ohio, finished second at Lime Rock and third at Elkhart Lake.

**Specification:**
ENGINE: Ford Boss Mustang V8 4945 cc developing approx 480 bhp.
GEARBOX: Hewland LG600 combined 5-speed gearbox and final drive.
CHASSIS: monocoque constructed from 18- and 16-gauge aluminium sheet.
FRONT SUSPENSION: double wishbones and coil spring/damper units.
REAR SUSPENSION: single upper links, twin lower links, single radius rods and combined coil spring/damper units.
WHEELBASE: 8ft 2in.
FRONT TRACK: 5ft 1in.
REAR TRACK: 4ft 10in.
OVERALL LENGTH: 12ft 8in.
WEIGHT: 11.6 cwt.

The new 70 with Vegantune Chevrolet engine made its début in the hands of Alan Rollinson in the first of the 1970 Formula 5000 races at the end of March. He was classified seventh on aggregate although he retired in the second heat. *(Nigel Snowdon)*

# 71

*Number not allocated.*

# 72

*Formula 1, 1970–75*

For the 1970 season Lotus developed the new 72, which, after disappointing early performances, proved to be perhaps the outstanding Formula 1 car of the 1970s. As usual Colin Chapman drew up the broad specification, while the design was by Maurice Phillippe. The 72 bristled with new features and with its 'shovel' nose and twin nose fins it was reminiscent of a hammerhead shark in outline, and the inboard front brakes, mid-mounted radiators and torsion bar suspension were all deviations from standard Formula 1 practice. In addition it was perhaps the lightest car (it was right on the minimum weight limit permitted) and the best handling, with a pitch-free ride and the ability to exploit the new softer, faster rubber compounds to the full.

The basis of the 72 was a light-alloy monocoque fabricated from 18swg magnesium alloy (used for the outer panels) and 20swg aluminium (the inner panels). A square-section tubular steel sub-frame reinforced the forward part of the monocoque and carried the suspension, whilst at the rear the Cosworth DFV engine was bolted to the monocoque rear panel. Suspension loads were fed through sandwich plates on the Hewland EG300 5-speed gearbox (but by Zandvoort in 1970 the lighter FG gearbox had been substituted).

Front and rear suspension was by compound torsion bars with the upper wishbones operating the linkages of the torsion bars. The front top and bottom wishbones were fabricated from welded nickel-chrome-molybdenum alloy sheet steel and there were Armstrong telescopic dampers. As originally built, there was pronounced 'anti-dive' and 'anti-squat' characteristics built into the design, but these features had been eliminated by the Belgian race. The solid brake discs were mounted inboard front and rear. The adoption of the side-mounted radiators was very much in accordance with the latest sports car practice and the aim was to achieve good air penetration by having as small a nose as possible. Another new feature of the 72 was the three-tier rear aerofoil.

In 1970 Jochen Rindt was joined in Gold Leaf Team Lotus by John Miles, whilst Graham Hill drove, initially, a 49C for Rob Walker, but this team had taken delivery of its own 72 by the Gold Cup race at Oulton Park in late August.

The new model made it début at the 1970 Spanish Grand Prix, but failed there and in the

The 72 Formula 1 car as shown to the press early in 1970. It was some while before the cars were properly sorted and could be regarded as race winners. *(Nigel Snowdon)*

It was not until the Dutch Grand Prix in 1970 that Rindt scored a win with the 72 leading across the line Stewart (March) and Ickx (Ferrari). *(Nigel Snowdon)*

International Trophy at Silverstone. The cars reappeared at the Belgian Grand Prix (although Rindt was still at the wheel of a 49C), and the 72 found its winning form at Zandvoort, where Rindt took pole position in practice and finished first in the race. He subsequently won the French, British and German Grands Prix. As the season progressed a number of modifications were made to the cars, including increased stiffening of the monocoque, repositioned rear dampers and, at Brands Hatch, an air collector box above the fuel injection system. These air-boxes were to become adopted by all the teams. Both cars retired in Austria, Rindt finished second in the Gold Cup at Oulton Park and then came the dreadful Italian Grand Prix. During practice Rindt ran his car without wings experimentally and in this form he crashed the car with fatal results. A prolonged Italian investigation finally decided that a front brake-shaft had failed, causing Rindt to lose control, but his fatal injuries were the result of badly installed safety barriers.

Lotus entries were scratched at Monza and Lotus withdrew from the Canadian Grand Prix. John Miles had now decided that he wished to discontinue his Formula 1 career and so Lotus

reappeared at the United States Grand Prix at Watkins Glen with the young team of Emerson Fittipaldi and Reine Wisell. Fittipaldi scored a remarkable victory after Pedro Rodriguez, leading the race with his BRM, made a late stop for fuel, and Wisell finished third. Rindt was the first, and hopefully the last, posthumous World Champion.

Fittipaldi and Wisell remained with the team in 1971. A number of minor changes were made to the cars. Steel suspension uprights replaced the original magnesium uprights, a new one-piece rear wing was adopted and at Monaco there appeared revised rear suspension to use the latest low-profile Firestone tyres. This arrangement incorporated twin radius rods, parallel lower links (in place of the original lower wishbones) and new upper links. In this form the car was known as the 72D. (The 72B was used to describe the 1970 car without anti-squat and the designation 72C was used for the 1970 car that lacked both anti-squat and anti-dive.)

The two youngsters in the Lotus Team simply were not up to scoring any wins in 1971, the first year since 1960 that Team Lotus had failed to win a Formula 1 race, but Fittipaldi finished second in the Austrian Grand Prix, third in the French and British races and fifth in the Monaco

Grand Prix. Wisell took fourth places in South Africa and Austria and finished fifth in Canada. In addition Fittipaldi took second place and set fastest lap in the Rothmans' Victory race at Brands Hatch, which was stopped short after Jo Siffert's fatal crash with his BRM.

For 1972 the 72Ds were painted in new black and gold colours and entered as 'John Player Specials'. Wisell was dropped from the team and he was replaced by Australian Dave Walker who had driven a Formula 3 car for Gold Leaf Team Lotus in 1971. Changes to the cars were few, but they now featured air-boxes of revised design, one-piece rear aerofoils of new design, revised oil tank design and suspension modifications. In addition the monocoques were re-skinned with 16-gauge sheet. The team also settled on 13in front and 15in rear wheels.

Although Walker's year with the team was one of dismal failure (his best performance during the year was fifth place in the non-Championship Brazilian Grand Prix), Fittipaldi enjoyed fine success and won that year's World Championship. After finishing second in the South African Grand Prix, winning the Race of Champions at Brands Hatch (as well as taking pole position and setting fastest lap), he won another non-Championship race, the International Trophy at Silverstone, where he also started from pole position. Thereafter his record consisted of a win in the Spanish Grand Prix, third at Monaco, a win (from pole position) in the Belgian Grand Prix at Nivelles, second place in the French race at Clermont-Ferrand, and wins in the British, Austrian and Italian races. In Italy only the one Lotus entry was made in the name of World Wide Racing. In addition Fittipaldi won the non-Championship Gran Premio Repubblica Italiano

Reine Wisell with his 72 in the 1971 Spanish Grand Prix on the Montjuich Park Circuit. He was delayed by gearbox trouble and finished 12th. Wisell was an immensely talented driver but always overshadowed by Fittipaldi and this seemed to prevent the full development of his career. *(Nigel Snowdon)*

In 1972 the French Grand Prix was held at the Clermont-Ferrand circuit and Emerson Fittipaldi with the modified 72D, now known as the John Player Special and painted black and gold, finished second and he won that year's World Championship. *(Nigel Snowdon)*

Another view of the 1972 72D, in this case the Rothmans 50,000 Formule Libre race at Brands Hatch, in which Fittipaldi took pole position on the grid and won. *(Nigel Snowdon)*

In the 1973 Spanish Grand Prix, Fittipaldi, despite a deflating left rear tyre, scored his eighth and Lotus's 50th Grand Prix victory. *(Nigel Snowdon)*

Despite the failure of the new 76 Ronnie Peterson scored three wins in 1974 with the obsolescent 72 at Monaco, Dijon and Monza. Here he is seen in the French race. *(Nigel Snowdon)*

at Vallelunga and the Rothmans 50,000 Formule Libre race at Brands Hatch.

For 1973 the cars were largely unchanged, but Walker was dropped from the team and Fittipaldi was joined by Ronnie Peterson. Another change was that Chapman had switched the team from Firestone to Goodyear tyres.

The team started the season in magnificent form with wins by Fittipaldi in both the Argentine and Brazil, together with a third place by Fittipaldi in South Africa. By the non-Championship Race of Champions at Brands Hatch the 72s had been rebuilt with double-skinned crash pads on either side, new undertrays and other changes necessary to comply with the new deformable-structure tank requirements. In this form the car was known as the 72E. Fittipaldi won the Spanish race, finished third in Belgium on the Zolder circuit and was second at Monaco, but his only other

successes during the year were second places in the Italian and Canadian races. Peterson soon found his form, taking third place at Monaco, second in the Swedish race and scoring a well-earned victory in the French Grand Prix at the Paul Ricard circuit. Thereafter he finished second in the British Grand Prix at Silverstone, won in Austria and Italy and rounded off the season with another win in the United States Grand Prix.

For 1974 Lotus developed the 76 which proved unsuccessful, so the team was forced to rely on the 72Es once more. Fittipaldi had left to drive for McLaren, but Peterson was joined in the team by Jacky Ickx. Bearing in mind just how old the design of the 72 was, the season's performances were remarkably good. Ickx finished third in Brazil and won the Race of Champions at Brands Hatch, a fine drive in pouring rain, whilst Peterson won at Monaco

Lotus still relied on the 72 in 1975, but failed to score a single win. Peterson is seen here on his way to a fourth place at Monaco. *(Nigel Snowdon)*

(and set fastest lap), the French Grand Prix, the Italian Grand Prix and finished third in Canada. During the remainder of the season the best that Ickx could manage was fifth place in France, third in the British Grand Prix and fifth in the German race. Only minor changes had been made to the cars during the year.

Because of the failure of the 76, the John Player Special team was forced to rely on the 72E again in 1975 and they retained the same drivers. In the Race of Champions Peterson was at the wheel of a new lightweight 72E, 72/9, and in this race he and Ickx finished third and fourth. Ickx took second place in the Spanish Grand Prix, stopped short after Stommelen's Embassy Hill had crashed into the crowd. Peterson finished fourth at Monaco and as the lack of success and the failure of Lotus to produce a new car continued, so Ickx became increasingly unhappy with the team. Earlier in the year he had been dropped from the team at the International Trophy (where Jim Crawford drove in his place), but by the British Grand Prix he was out for good. In this race Lotus entered three cars for Peterson, Brian Henton and Jim Crawford, but nothing was achieved. Both cars retired in Germany, where Peterson was partnered by John Watson. Subsequently Peterson finished fifth in the Austrian race, fourth in the non-Championship 'Swiss' Grand Prix held on the Dijon circuit in France, and fifth in the United States Grand Prix. Crawford had again driven for the team at Monza, while Henton was included at the Austrian race (where he non-started) and the United States Grand Prix.

Although the career of the 72 had spiralled into failure succeeding failure, it had proved one of the most successful racing cars ever built by Lotus, and it had won 20 World Championship races and gained three Formula 1 Constructors' Cups.

## Specification (72, 1970):

ENGINE: Cosworth DFV 2993cc.
GEARBOX: Hewland FG 5-speed combined gearbox and final drive.
CHASSIS: monocoque constructed from aluminium alloy with square steel tubular sub-frame integral with the forward part of the monocoque and locating the front suspension.
FRONT SUSPENSION: torsion bars operated by a link system connected to the upper of the unequal-length double wishbones.
REAR SUSPENSION: torsion bars with upper and lower reversed wishbones.
WHEELBASE: 8ft 4in.
FRONT AND REAR TRACK: 4ft 9in.
OVERALL LENGTH: 13ft 9in.
OVERALL WIDTH: 6ft 2in.
OVERALL HEIGHT: 2ft 11in.
WEIGHT: 10.45 cwt.

# 73

*Formula 3, 1972*

The origins of the 73 lay in a projected Formula 2 car that was proposed for the 1971 season and not proceeded with following the closure of Lotus Racing. Eventually the design appeared as a radical Formula 3 car, completely different from the opposition and to be built only as a works car raced in John Player Special colours and officially known as a John Player Special. Unlike other 'John Player Specials', it retained its original type number.

Much of the early design work was carried out by Maurice Phillippe prior to his departure to the Vels Parnelli team and it was completed by Martin Wade and Dave Baldwin. Many of the design features of the 72 Formula 1 car were

incorporated. There was a bath-tub monocoque running to the immediate rear of the cockpit with the engine forming a stressed member and attached via a tubular framework. At the front a tubular sub-frame carried the rack and pinion steering, the inboard disc brakes and mounted the rising rate front suspension which incorporated fabricated double wishbones and inboard coil spring/damper units. The rear suspension was formed by single upper links, twin parallel lower links, twin radius arms, anti-roll bar and outboard coil spring/damper units. The rear brakes were also mounted inboard, there were small side-mounted radiators, a Novamotor-developed Lotus twin-cam engine and a Hewland Mk 8 gearbox. The appearance of the car was very distinctive, with flat-top wedge-shaped nose and the curved sides of the monocoque bulging out round the cockpit.

With John Player backing and a highly sophisticated specification, the 73 Formula 3 had immense promise that was never fulfilled. Tony Trimmer is seen on the model's début at Mallory Park in March 1972 when he finished sixth. *(Nigel Snowdon)*

When the 73 apeared, Peter Warr of Lotus commented, 'It is complicated. There's as much work in the suspension of this F3 as there was in the whole 69 chassis.' Two cars were built for Tony Trimmer and Bernard Vermilio. Trimmer did much of the early testing with Vermilio's car and as he found the cockpit too cramped, his own car was built with a slightly longer monocoque.

Trimmer finished sixth on the car's début at Mallory Park in March 1972 and it was obvious that a great deal of development work was still needed. He took a superb second place at Monaco, despite tyre problems in his heat, to Patrick Depailler's Alpine and there were very real doubts about the legality of Depailler's Renault engine. Other good performances included a fourth by Trimmer at Brands in March, a win at Mallory Park in April, fifth at Mallory Park in May and sixth at Anderstorp in June. Vermilio finished fourth at Zandvort in April and sixth at the Paul Ricard circuit. The set-up of the cars varied substantially from race to race as Lotus struggled to keep them on the pace, but the works eventually lost interest in the project. Lotus disappeared from the Formula 3 scene altogether at the end of 1972, mainly because they were no longer involved in the commercial production of racing cars.

**Specification:**
ENGINE: Novamotor-Ford twin-cam.
GEARBOX: Hewland Mk 8 combined 5-speed gearbox and final drive.
CHASSIS: aluminium-alloy bath-tub monocoque.
FRONT SUSPENSION: double wishbones and inboard coil spring/damper units.
REAR SUSPENSION: single upper links, twin parallel lower links, twin radius arms and outboard coil spring/damper units.
WHEELBASE: 7ft 11in.
FRONT TRACK: 4ft 8in.
REAR TRACK: 4ft 8in.
WEIGHT: 7.90 cwt.

# 74

## *Formula 2, 1973*

There is some confusion over numbering, an ongoing problem, as 74 was also allotted to the twin-cam Europa. It seems that, just like most of the JPS cars, they were never oficially allotted numbers by Lotus who regarded the cars simply as 'Texaco Stars'.

Designed by Ralph Bellamy, the 74 featured a simple sheet-alloy monocoque, front and rear suspension by torsion bars (but incorporating coil spring/damper units at the rear), inboard disc brakes front and rear and side-mounted radiators almost flush with the sides of the monocoque, water radiator on the right side and oil radiator and tank on the left side. The most striking feature of the car was the wide, almost full-width 'shovel' nose. The power unit was the Lotus Type 906 twin overhead camshaft alloy-block 1973cc version of its production engine derived from the cast iron Vauxhall Victor block and extensively modified by Novamotor. There is no available figure for power output, but originally the engines were very unreliable, and when reliability was eventually achieved, it was believed to be at the expense of about 40 bhp and this made the cars hopelessly uncompetitive. They were also rather bulky by Formula 2 standards.

Because of the development delays, the cars were not revealed until the Belgian Grand Prix at Zolder in 1973 and eventually appeared in the Formula 2 race at Nivelles in Belgium on 10 June. Both Fittipaldi and Peterson retired in the first heat. The cars next appeared in much

The Texaco Star 74 shown on its début at the 1973 Belgian Grand Prix at Zolder, together with the crew and driver Emerson Fittipaldi in dark glasses. The 74s were over-complex, unreliable and, when reliability was found, underpowered. *(Nigel Snowdon)*

revised form, with engines rebuilt by Norvic Racing Engines in Norfolk at the Rouen race. Peterson crashed in his heat and retired in the final, but made fastest lap in his heat. Fittipaldi was running but unclassified at the finish. The Texaco Stars missed the Monza race and next appeared at Misano, where both retired with engine problems. The team missed Mantorp Park because of the Dutch Grand Prix and next appeared at Karlskoga. Fittipaldi had called 'enough' and the sole entry was driven by Peterson into an unspectacular fifth place, which was to prove the best result of the season.

By the Enna race in Sicily in late August Fittipaldi's place in the team had been taken by Dave Morgan. Peterson finished seventh, but Morgan retired. Texaco Stars missed the next two races and appeared on 16 September at Albi, where Chapman oversaw the 74's failure. Peterson kept switching from car to car in an effort to achieve a good time and as a result Morgan failed to qualify. After only 8 laps Peterson was out with engine failure. Both cars again failed at the Rome Grand Prix and the team missed the last race of the year at Estoril in Portugal. Lotus never again raced a Formula 2 car.

### Specification:
ENGINE: Novamotor-Lotus Type 906 1973cc (95.28 x 69.24mm).
GEARBOX: ZF combined 5-speed gearbox and final drive.
CHASSIS: sheet aluminium-alloy monocoque.
FRONT SUSPENSION: wishbones and torsion bars.
REAR SUSPENSION: wishbones and torsion bars.
WHEELBASE: 7ft 11in.
FRONT TRACK: 4ft 8in.
REAR TRACK. 4ft 8in.
WEIGHT: not known.

# 74 Europa Twin-Cam

*Production sports car, 1971–75*

Between 1966 and 1971 Lotus had been
manufacturing the Renault-powered Europa
(see 46), but in 1971 the decision was made to
change to the Lotus-Ford twin-cam 1558cc
engine developing 105 bhp at 5500 rpm. Lotus
continued to use the Renault 4-speed gearbox
with a special Lotus bellhousing which also
carried the alternator and mounted the inner
ends of the lower suspension links. Other

changes were twin fuel tanks (which together
held 12½ gallons and had separate fillers), a
spoiler at the front and the rear body sides were
cut down (which spoilt the aesthetics of the
styling without doing much to improve rear
vision). The price was £1995 (including
purchase tax for a completed car) and £1595 in
kit form. Lotus light alloy 'spider wheels' were
an optional extra. Maximum speed was around
120 mph and 0–60 mph acceleration took about
7.5 seconds.

In late 1972 the Europa Special was
introduced. This was powered by the Lotus 'Big

Two views of the twin-cam Europa with Lotus twin-cam engine and Renault gearbox built from 1971 to 1975. It could be
distinguished from the earlier cars by the cut-down sides of the rear body and the so-called 'spider' Lotus wheels.

Valve' engine developing 126 bhp and used the much stronger 5-speed gearbox developed by Renault for use in their higher performance 16TX model. Quite a number of these cars were finished in John Player Special black and gold colours. The price was £2471 (complete, including purchase tax) and £2044 (in component form). With the 'Big Valve' engine top speed was boosted slightly to 123 mph and 0–60 mph acceleration about 7 seconds. When production ceased in 1975, the total number of Europas built (both Renault and twin-cam versions) amounted to 9230.

**Specification (Europa Special):**
ENGINE: Lotus-Ford twin-cam 'Big Valve' developing 126 bhp at 6500 rpm.
GEARBOX: Renault 5-speed.
CHASSIS: central steel box-section backbone with fork extension at the rear, linked by light cross-member.
FRONT SUSPENSION: pressed steel wishbones (lower cranked) and coil spring/damper units.
REAR SUSPENSION: upper and lower links (upper formed by fixed-length drive-shafts), trailing radius arms, coil spring/damper units.
WHEELBASE: 7ft 8in.
FRONT TRACK: 4ft 5.5in.
REAR TRACK: 4ft 5in.
OVERALL LENGTH: 13ft 1.5in.
WIDTH: 5ft 4.5in.
WEIGHT: 14 cwt.

# 75 Elite (and 83)

*Production GT car, 1974–85*

## Lotus Engines

Before discussing the development of the Elite, a brief outline of the evolution of the Lotus engine, evolved from the slant-4 Vauxhall engine, must be stated. The various engines proposed by Lotus were as follows:

Type 904: Iron block 1995cc (95.25 x 69.24mm) with Lotus twin overhead camshaft 16-valve cylinder head with Tecalemit-Jackson fuel injection and a power output of about 220 bhp at 8000 rpm. Used to power the 62 Sports Prototypes during the 1969 season as part of the Lotus development programme. Also known as the LV220 (Lotus-Vauxhall, 220 bhp).

Type 905: Iron block 1995cc road car engine tested in 1969 in a Vauxhall Viva and a Bedford van.

Type 906: Sand-cast alloy block 1995cc racing engine as used in the 1973 Texaco Star Formula 2 cars. Also known as the LV240 (Lotus-Vauxhall, 240 bhp).

Type 907: Die-cast alloy block 1973cc (95.28 x 69.24mm) road car engine. Fitted with twin Dell'Orto carburettors (horizontal Zenith-Stromberg in 'Federal' form). Announced for fitment to the Jensen-Healey in 140 bhp form in 1971 and between 1972 and 1976 10,453 Jensen Healeys and 459 Jensen GTs were built with this engine. Powered in 155 bhp (soon increased to 160 bhp) form the Elite and Eclat until 1980 and in 160 bhp form the Esprit from 1976 to 1980.

Type 908: Alloy block 4-litre V8 race engine.

Type 909: Alloy block 4-litre V8 road car engine. Intended to power the proposed Etna V8 of which artists' impressions were released. This engine may conceivably still enter production.

Type 910: Die-cast alloy block 2174cc (95.28 x 76.2mm) engine with Garrett AiResearch T3 turbocharger, two twin-choke Dell'Orto DHLA carburettors and a power output of 210 bhp at 6000 rpm. This engine was used to power the Esprit Turbo, which

The Elite introduced in 1974 was the first Lotus to be powered by the 907 engine, developed by Lotus and used in the Jensen-Healey, and remained in production for six years in 2-litre form.

In 1980 Lotus introduced the S2.2 Elite with 2174cc engine and a Getrag 5-speed gearbox (in place of the original Lotus/British Leyland unit). Partly because of economic conditions, partly because the model had been in production so long with little change, very few were sold.

was manufactured by Lotus from 1980 onwards.

Type 911: Die-cast alloy block 2174cc (95.28 x 76.2mm) engine with two twin-choke Dell'Orto carburettors and developing 150 bhp at 5750 rpm and supplied to Peugeot Citroën (successor to Chrysler Great Britain) to power the Sunbeam-Lotus of which 2298 were built.

Type 912: Die-cast alloy block 2174cc (95.28 x 76.2mm) engine, with two twin-choke Dell'Orto carburettors and developing 160 bhp at 6500 rpm. Used to power the Elite S2.2, Eclat S2.2, Esprit S2.2 and Excel.

## Elite

Announced in May 1974 the launch had been planned for March, but was delayed because of the three-day working week (resulting from a miners' strike), the Elite marked very clearly a new direction in Lotus road cars, much more stylish, much more sophisticated and much more expensive than previous Lotus models. Once again there was the familiar Lotus steel backbone chassis frame (galvanized in later years) with two prongs at the front linked by a

cross-member. The engine was the 907 (see above) used with the 5-speed gearbox developed for the Elan Plus 2 130/5 – Austin Maxi gears in a Lotus casing manufactured by Beans Industries. The final drive was the Salisbury 7HA unit. At the front there were wishbones, coil spring/damper units and an anti-roll bar, with a layout at the rear not so dissimilar to that of the Europa; this consisted of fixed-length drive-shafts, lower transverse links, substantial pressed steel semi-trailing radius arms and coil spring/damper units. Rack and pinion steering was fitted, disc brakes at the front, inboard-mounted drum brakes at the rear and GKN die-cast light alloy wheels. The wedge-shaped lines, a combination of smoothly curved panels and squared edges, gave the Elite a distinctive appearance. Construction was in glass-fibre, with steel beams in the doors to comply with United States regulations, a very large windscreen with single wiper, large rear hatch panel, reasonable accommodation for four and a very luxurious interior style by Giugario's Ital Design.

The various Elite models can be summarized as follows:

501: Basic original production model priced in the UK at £5445. Delivery of this model did not start until January 1975.

502: Better-equipped version, more usually specified by customers, and priced in the UK at £5857. Delivery commenced immediately.

503: As for the 502, but fitted with power-assisted steering, air conditioning, stereo radio/cassette player, tinted glass and electric windows and available from the beginning of 1975. When tested by *Autocar* in January 1975 it achieved a maximum speed of 124 mph (mean), 0–60 in 7.8 seconds and overall fuel consumption of 20.9 mpg. The price was £7625.

504: As for the 503, but with Borg-Warner Model 65 3-speed automatic transmission. Launched in October 1975 and available from January 1976, when it was priced at £7970 (by which time the price of the 501 had risen to £6493). Road-tested by *Motor* in August 1978, the 504 was found to have a mean maximum speed of 119 mph, 0–60 acceleration of 10.4 secons and an overall fuel consumption of 19.1 mpg. Total production of all versions amounted to 2398 cars.

S2.2: Only the one model was offered from May 1980, the 83 (the '500' series numbering as above had been abandoned). Powered by the 912 engine, the other main changes were the adoption of the German Getrag 5-speed gearbox and galvanized chassis. Power-assisted steering, air conditioning and Borg-Warner automatic transmission were optional extras. The basic price was £16,142. By this stage the Elite was available to special order only and production ceased in 1982.

For much of the information contained in this section, the author relied on *The Third Generation Lotuses* by Graham Robson (Motor Racing Publications Ltd, 1983). Hopefully an update will appear shortly.

**Specification (503, 1975):**
ENGINE: Lotus Type 907 1973cc.
GEARBOX: 5-speed Lotus casing with Austin Maxi gears.
CHASSIS: steel backbone with two prongs at the front linked by box-section cross-member.
FRONT SUSPENSION: pressed steel double wishbones and coil spring/damper units.
REAR SUSPENSION: fixed length drive-shafts, lower wishbones, pressed steel semi-trailing radius arms and coil spring/damper units.
WHEELBASE: 8ft 1.8in.
FRONT TRACK: 4ft 10.5in.
REAR TRACK: 4ft 11in.
OVERALL LENGTH: 14ft 7.5in.
WIDTH: 5ft 11.5 in.
UNLADEN WEIGHT: 21.78 cwt.

# 76
# John Player Special Mark I

*Formula 1, 1974*

Whilst the Lotus team was sponsored by John Player, the Formula 1 cars were numbered as 'John Player Special' Mark 1 onwards and this explains the duplication of Type numbers.

Early in 1973 Chapman determined that the next Formula 1 car should be a lighter version of the 72 (the weight of which had crept up during its development), with new monocoque but similar suspension. Ralph Bellamy designed a monocoque fabricated in 16-gauge L72 alloy sheet of wedge shape with a stressed flat panel above the driver's legs and no separate subframe (as seen on the 72). The torsion bar suspension of the 72 was retained, but with fabricated double wishbones at the front and at the rear twin parallel upper links, single lower links and twin radius rods. The front suspension incorporated rising rate geometry and anti-dive. The 10.1in disc brakes were mounted inboard front and rear.

The Cosworth engine was used with a Hewland FG400 combined 5-speed gearbox and final drive. There was, however, a major innovation. The car featured four foot pedals and a gear-knob button to operate an electronic clutch. The pedal on the extreme left actuated

the clutch when the car left the line (and thereafter the clutch could be withdrawn by operation of the gear-knob button, which actuated an hydraulic system with a pump driven from the starter motor). The right foot was the throttle as usual. The two centre pedals (which were linked) gave alternative left- and right-foot braking. The 76, known as the John Player Special Mk 1, featured angular, so-called delta-form bodywork and a biplane rear wing.

Testing revealed the four-pedal system was not satisfactory. At the South African race the system had been removed from the car driven by Ickx and Peterson's car had the pedals rearranged right to left, throttle, brake, clutch, brake. Peterson's throttle jammed at the first corner and he collided with Ickx, putting both cars out of the race. Peterson led the International Trophy at Silverstone with the 76 in normal three pedal form, but, after a tyre problem, retired because of a seized engine. The auto-clutch was officially dropped 'for further development', but the cars were still far from right. Peterson led in the Spanish race, but retired because of brake trouble and engine failure.

Both cars retired in Belgium and the team now reverted to the 72, retaining the 76s purely as spares. Chapman, under pressure from Peterson, had concluded that the 76 was too heavy (the anticipated weight saving had not happened), the handling was unsatisfactory and

The press launch at the London Theatre of the 'John Player Special Mark 1' more familiarly known as the 76. However, because of the JPS nomenclature, the 76 appears in Lotus records as the Eclat 2-litre. *(Nigel Snowdon)*

Ronnie Peterson testing at Goodwood with the unsuccessful 76 or, more accurately, John Player Special Mark 1.
*(Nigel Snowdon)*

Peterson, despite the shortcomings of the 76, led the 1974 International Trophy at Silverstone until, first, a tyre blistered, and then the engine seized. *(Nigel Snowdon)*

it would be better to abandon the design and start again from scratch. After a crash in practice with his 72 at the German Grand Prix, however, the team built up overnight for Peterson a car that combined the monocoque and front suspension of the 76 with the engine and rear suspension of the 76 and he drove this into fourth place. Ickx drove a similar car without success in Austria and Italy and the final appearance of the 76 was in the United States Grand Prix in which Tim Schenken was at the wheel, but disqualified.

**Specification:**
ENGINE: Cosworth DFV 2993cc.
GEARBOX: Hewland FG400 combined 5-speed gearbox and final drive.
CHASSIS: monocoque fabricated in 16-gauge L72 alloy sheet.
FRONT SUSPENSION: fabricated double wishbones and torsion bars.
REAR SUSPENSION: twin parallel upper links, single lower links, twin radius rods and torsion bars.
WHEELBASE: 8ft 5in.
MAXIMUM TRACK: 5ft 2in.
WEIGHT: 11.32 cwt.

# 76 Eclat (and 84)

*Production coupé, 1975–82*

In almost all important respects the Eclat was identical to the Elite, built to sell at a lower price. The principal difference was that the upper mould of the body featured a roof line that sloped downwards, blending into a fastback tail with conventional boot lid. Many regarded the Eclat as a better-styled car overall than the Elite. A higher final drive ratio was fitted. The Eclat was announced in October 1975 and the variations were as follows:

520: The basic specification model with steel wheels and Ford Granada/Capri 4-speed all-synchromesh gearbox, which was the only variation built initially and priced at £5729. It was not a commercial success, as buyers preferred the better-equipped models. The 520 became available in 1977 in Eclat Sprint form with white paint, lower axle ratio, certain special equipment features, alloy road wheels and a price of £7842.

521: Mechanically the same as the Elite 501, with Lotus 5-speed gearbox and alloy wheels. Available as 520 above in Sprint form from 1977 at a price of £8372.

522: Better equipped version comparable with the Elite 502.

523: As for the 502/522, but with air conditioning, stereo radio/cassette player, tinted glass, electric windows and power-assisted steering. When road-tested by *Autocar*, it achieved a maximum speed of 129 mph, 0–60 mph in 7.9 seconds and an overall fuel consumption of 20.7 mpg.

S2.2: Built from May 1980 to 1982 and designated the 84, it was similar to the 521 apart from the Type 912 2174 cc engine and Getrag 5-speed all-synchromesh gearbox. The 1980 price was £15,842.

S2.2 Riviera: Limited edition car built in 1980–2 with styling changes that

The Eclat (the name perhaps took Lotus alliteration a little too far) was announced in October 1975. Originally intended to be known as the 'Elite Coupé', the Eclat represented an important part of Lotus marketing strategy: a more modestly priced car with style and flair.

Between 1980 and 1982 Lotus produced the Eclat S2.2 with the 2.2-litre engine and available only with the Getrag 5-speed gearbox.

included a lift-out roof panel, rear spoiler and 'Riviera' badge on the tail. The price was £15,842. Total Eclat production amounted to 1522 cars. See *The Third Generation Lotuses* by Graham Robson (Motor Racing Publications, 1983) for more information.

**Specification (S2.2):**
ENGINE: Lotus Type 912 2174cc.
GEARBOX: Getrag 5-speed.
CHASSIS: steel backbone with two prongs at the front linked by box-section cross-member.
FRONT SUSPENSION: pressed steel double wishbones and coil spring/damper units.
REAR SUSPENSION: fixed length drive-shafts, lower wishbones, pressed steel semi-trailing radius arms and coil spring/damper units.
WHEELBASE: 8ft 1.8in.
FRONT TRACK: 4ft 10.5in.
REAR TRACK: 4ft 11in.
OVERALL LENGTH: 14ft 7.5in.
WIDTH: 5ft 11.5in.
UNLADEN WEIGHT: 23.62 cwt.

# 77
# John Player Special Mark II

*Formula 1, 1976*

While the rest of the Formula 1 world moved on swiftly, Lotus had been static and falling behind other teams in terms of technical development. Accordingly for 1976 the team developed the 77, officially known as the John Player Special Mark II, very much an interim car while the team developed the 1977 78. At the same time as John Player Team Lotus raced the 77, a development team was experimenting with variations in wheelbase and track to exploit the theory of adjustability of a design to different circuits. It was known that cars with a shorter wheelbase performed better on shorter circuits with slow corners, whilst longer-wheelbase cars performed better on faster circuits with more gentle curves. Cars with a narrow track were often faster in a straight line, but for the ultimate cornering potential a wide track was required. Also in hand was the development of a new gearbox by Ralph Bellamy, but development on this proved slow and it was to prove unsatisfactory.

The basis of the 77 was a slim aluminium monocoque designed by Geoff Aldridge and this incorporated a structural pyramid top panel above the driver's legs, the fuel housed in two side and one central fuel cell and in a layout, designed by Martin Ogilvie, a structural calliper inboard brake system, whereby the calipers acted as pick-ups for the suspension links and wishbones. There were the usual side radiators neatly enclosed in pods, glass-fibre bodywork, fabricated double wishbones and outboard coil spring/damper units at the front and a rear suspension layout following that of the 76

Nilsson's 77 in the pits at the 1976 South African Grand Prix, with extinguishers in action on a fire caused by seized rear brakes. *(Nigel Snowdon)*

The late Gunnar Nilsson with the 77 in the 1976 Belgian Grand Prix in which he was eliminated very early on by an accident. *(Nigel Snowdon)*

incorporating single lower links, parallel upper links, twin radius rods and outboard coil spring/damper units. The Cosworth engine was used with the Hewland FG400 gearbox.

Ronnie Peterson remained with the team, but Lotus had difficulty engaging a second driver, and Mario Andretti agreed to drive for Lotus in the first round of the World Championship only, the Brazilian Grand Prix. During practice Peterson slid off because of coolant that had sprayed on to one of the rear tyres and in the race the two 76s collided. Peterson, lured by Robin Herd, and convinced that Lotus were to face another disastrous season, agreed to leave Lotus for March. At the South African Grand Prix, the Race of Champions and the United States Grand Prix West at Long Beach the cars were driven by Gunar Nilsson and Bob Evans, but no success was achieved.

By the International Trophy at Silverstone,

Nilsson, the sole entry, was driving a 77 with revised front suspension and brake layout hastily designed for the team by private consultant Len Terry. Ralt Formula 2 suspension uprights were substituted, there were new bottom wishbones, upper rocking arms and outboard 10.5in disc brakes (in fact Evans had failed to qualify a car in this trim at Long Beach.) That this was a very real improvement was only too clear at Silverstone where Nilsson was fourth fastest in practice and finished sixth in the race.

By the Spanish Grand Prix Andretti had agreed to join the team on a permanent basis. By this race both cars incorporated the new suspension layout and they also featured twin air-boxes either side of the rear engine 'hump', a feature dropped later in the year but then reintroduced. Although Andretti retired, Nilsson took a fine third place.

Immediately after the Spanish Grand Prix

Driving a skilfully judged race in the wet, Mario Andretti won the 1976 Japanese Grand Prix with his 77; it was the first Lotus World Championship victory since the 1974 Monaco race. *(Nigel Snowdon)*

Tony Southgate joined Team Lotus as chief engineer. Both cars retired in the Belgian Grand Prix, Nilsson (the only runner because Andretti was engaged at Indianapolis) retired at Monaco, and then in the Swedish Grand Prix Andretti, due to be penalized for jumping the flag, led the field until his engine blew up; Nilsson spun off. More failures followed in the French and British races but Nilsson was fifth at the Nürburgring. By the Austrian Grand Prix in mid-August a number of minor changes had been made to the cars and at the Österreichring Nilsson took third place and Andretti was classified fifth. Another third place, by Andretti, followed in the Dutch Grand Prix. For the Italian Grand Prix at Monza the cars appeared with modified front suspension geometry, but once again no success was gained. A third place for Andretti, followed in the Canadian Grand Prix at Mosport Park, where the cars had 4mm shorter wheelbases and were fitted with brush skirts. Both cars retired in the United States Grand Prix at Watkins Glen. However, in the last race of the season, the Japanese Grand Prix at Mount Fuji, Andretti proved that Lotus was on the way back to success. After taking pole position in practice, he held second place in this wet and misty race for many laps, falling back as he conserved his tyres, and coming through to take the lead and win the race when faster cars stopped for new tyres. Nilsson finished sixth.

**Specification:**
ENGINE: Cosworth DFV.
GEARBOX: Hewland FG400.
CHASSIS: aluminium monocoque.
FRONT SUSPENSION: double wishbones and outboard coil spring/damper units.
REAR SUSPENSION: single lower links, parallel upper links, twin radius rods and outboard coil spring/damper units.
WHEELBASE: 9ft 2in.
FRONT TRACK: 4ft 2in.
REAR TRACK: 5ft 1in.
WEIGHT: 11.60 cwt.

# 78
# John Player Special Mark III

*Formula 1, 1977–78*

Although the Ferrari 312T-2 and the Wolf (driven by Jody Scheckter) were to prove the two dominant marques, Lotus relying on the lessons learned in 1976 and on the basis of their research programme produced a car that was by any standards a winner, and brought the team back to the very forefront of international racing. Also known as the John Player Special Mark III, the 78 featured a slim monocoque, but with broad panniers, and forming a stressed section behind the driver's shoulders, with a structural top panel enclosing the driver's legs. For the front bulkhead and side skins Lotus used Cellite sandwich material (two thin dural sheets enclosing aluminium honeycomb) which strengthened the monocoque considerably. At the front suspension was by upper rocking arms

and lower fabricated wishbones, with inboard coil spring/damper units. The rear suspension was similar to that of the 77, save that lower wishbones were substituted for the lower links of the 77. Once again the Cosworth DFV engine was used with the Hewland FG400 gearbox.

However, the 78 had also brought a new concept to racing. Within the large panniers were the water radiators with leading edge intakes and with the hot air exhausted through top ducts. Behind the radiators were the wing fuel tanks, with undersides curved upwards, ending in line with the engine mounts and forming a wing section of inverted form so that an area of low pressure was generated and capable of sucking the car down on to the road. Cellite end-plates closed off the pannier wings and beneath the plates were bristle skirts extending down to road level. Whilst Peter Wright's development work had resulted in the first ground-effect Formula 1 car, the team relied on conventional wings and fins, which provided additional balance and trim. When the

Mario Andretti's 'John Player Special' (Lotus 78) in the pits at the 1977 South African Grand Prix. He retired with damaged front suspension after a collision with Reutemann's Ferrari. *(Nigel Snowdon)*

The turn-out of Lotus Formula 1 cars has been immaculate for many years (difficult to achieve with black-painted cars). The notion of 'Team Shambles' was thoroughly buried in the early 1960s. The 'wing' 78 enjoyed a good measure of success in 1977 and Mario Andretti is seen here on his way to a win on home territory in the United States Grand Prix West at Long Beach. He also won in Spain, France and Italy. *(Diana Burnett)*

The third Grand Prix win of the year was by Gunnar Nilsson in the Belgian Grand Prix at Zolder, a race run in torrentially wet conditions. *(Diana Burnett)*

cars first appeared they were fitted with the new Lotus lightweight gearbox built by Getrag, but this was soon abandoned because it was simply not strong enough.

The team drivers remained Andretti and Nilsson, and after fifth place by Andretti in the Argentine, fifth place by Nilsson in Brazil, followed by failures in South Africa and in the Race of Champions, Andretti scored a fine victory in the United States Grand Prix West at Long Beach. He followed this up with another win in the Spanish Grand Prix, where he had started from pole position, and Nilsson took fifth place. After a fifth by Andretti at Monaco, Nilsson won the Belgian Grand Prix at Zolder and set fastest lap. Other significant performances during the year were in the French Grand Prix, where Andretti took pole position, won the race and set fastest lap, while Nilsson finished fourth; third place by Nilsson in the British race followed and Andretti won the Italian Grand Prix and took second place in the United States Grand Prix at Watkins Glen. Andretti finished third in the World Championship and Lotus were second in the Constructors' Cup behind Ferrari.

For 1978 Ronnie Peterson rejoined Andretti in the team and in the early races the 78s continued to be raced. Andretti took pole position and won the Argentine Grand Prix (with Peterson fifth), Andretti finished fourth in Brazil, and Peterson won the South African

race. Andretti and Peterson were second and fourth in the United States Grand Prix West and whilst Andretti won the Belgian Grand Prix with a 79, Peterson finished second and took fastest lap with a 78. By the Spanish Grand Prix both drivers were at the wheel of 79s, but a 78 had been sold to Hector Rebaque, and he entered it at the remainder of the year's races without any success. Because of a crash during the warm-up Peterson drove a 78 in the Italian Grand Prix and it was at the wheel of this car that he received the injuries that proved fatal.

**Specification:**
ENGINE: Cosworth DFV.
GEARBOX: Hewland FG400.
CHASSIS: aluminium monocoque with Cellite (thin dural sheets enclosing aluminium honeycomb) incorporated in the front bulkhead and side skins.
FRONT SUSPENSION: upper rocking arms, lower wishbones and inboard coil spring/damper units.
REAR SUSPENSION; lower wishbones, parallel upper links, twin radius rods and outboard coil spring/damper units.
WHEELBASE: 8ft 11in.
FRONT TRACK: 5ft 7in.
REAR TRACK: 5ft 3in.
WEIGHT: 11.70 cwt.

# 79
# John Player Special Mark IV

*Formula 1, 1978–79*

By the 1978 season Tony Southgate had left Lotus to rejoin Shadow and Ralph Bellamy had left for Copersucar. The result was that Chapman was closely involved in the detail of the new car. It also meant that the design of the 79 was somewhat more reactionary than it would otherwise have been, for Chapman eschewed the extensive use of honeycomb and designed a very conventional sheet-aluminium monocoque. The monocoque was of the minimum possible width, strengthened at the front by a perforated stress-panel bulkhead around the dash-panel area (as on the 77 and 78), with an arched scuttle panel enclosing the driver's shins, a honeycomb-sandwich monocoque floor and with a single fuel cell behind the driver and engine. The basic layout of the front suspension was the same, upper rocking arms and lower wishbones, with inboard-mounted coil spring/damper units, but far less raked back than on the 78. At the rear there was new inboard coil spring/damper suspension. The Lotus double-calliper brake discs, outboard front and inboard rear, were reintroduced. On the right of the monocoque

there was a large water radiator within a side-pod and in the lefthand side-pod there was an oil cooler. Mated to the Cosworth DFV engine was the Lotus-Getrag gearbox, incorporating a limited slip differential, supplied by ZF, crown-wheel-and-pinion, cut by Oerlikon (a Swiss company) and with a gearbox featuring a sequential change (as on the old 'queerbox') but with an individual engagement mechanism for each ratio. Unfortunately the Lotus gearbox proved unreliable and was soon abandoned in favour of the traditional Hewland unit.

After early testing the monocoques of the 79s were made stiffer and various other changes were made, resulting in the final and definitive ground-effect bodywork. The bolt-on glass-fibre side-pods operated as venturis, with air entering at the front, accelerated to exit at the rear with skirts sealing the U-section air chamber against the road surface to enclose the low-pressure area and sucking the chassis down.

For 1978 Mario Andretti stayed with Lotus and the team was rejoined by Ronnie Peterson. The 79 made its début in the International Trophy at Silverstone in which one car was driven by Andretti and retired. Andretti had a 79 in practice only at Monaco and then drove the 79 in the Belgian Grand Prix at Zolder, taking pole position and winning the race. He followed this up with a victory in the Spanish Grand Prix

Mario Andretti on his way to a win with the 79 in the 1978 German Grand Prix. This photograph shows well the superb lines of the 'ground-effect' 79. Note the absence of 'John Player' signs in compliance with German law.

at Jarama, where Peterson was second with a 79, and then Peterson finished third in the Swedish Grand Prix at Anderstorp.

Andretti won again in the French Grand Prix at the Paul Ricard circuit, with Peterson second; both drivers retired in the British race, Andretti won the German Grand Prix at Hockenheim, and Peterson won in Austria. Another one-two followed in the Dutch Grand Prix, where Andretti won from Peterson, and then disaster followed in the Italian race at Monza. During warm-up on race morning Peterson crashed his 79 because of brake problems and took over his old 78 for the race. At the first corner, as the field accelerated from the wide starting area into the first fairly narrow corner, Hunt's McLaren hit the right rear wheel of Peterson's Lotus. It was shunted head-on into the guard-rail that blocked the entrance from the road circuit to the old banked circuit, and the impact crushed the front part of the monocoque of Peterson's car, breaking both the Swedish driver's legs. Peterson was quickly rescued from the car, and

although his injuries seemed severe, he did not appear to be in critical condition. He died overnight, however, because of surgical complications. When the race was restarted, Andretti finished first on the road, but lost a minute for jumping the start and was classified sixth. By now Andretti had scored sufficient points to clinch the World Championship.

For the United States Grand Prix at Watkins Glen, Jean-Pierre Jarier was brought into the Lotus team but was out of luck. Jarier led the Canadian race until eliminated by a leaking oil cooler and Andretti finished tenth after a collision early in the race with John Watson (Brabham). Andretti won the World Championship with 64 points to the posthumous second place of Peterson with 51 and Lotus also won the Constructors' Cup with 86 points to the 58 of Ferrari.

For most of the 1979 season, Lotus continued to rely on the 79 cars, now sponsored by Martini and painted British Racing Green with Martini red and blue stripes. Mario Andretti was now partnered in the team by Argentinian driver

A super view of Peterson's 79 in the pits at the Dutch Grand Prix at Zandvoort. Peterson took second place to team-mate Andretti. (Nigel Snowdon)

Ronnie Peterson in practice for his last race, the 1978 Italian Grand Prix. He was involved in a multi-car crash at the first corner, suffered severe leg injuries and died as the result of surgical complications. *(Nigel Snowdon)*

Jean-Pierre Jarier, who stepped into the team to replace Ronnie Peterson, so nearly won the 1978 Canadian Grand Prix with the 79, but was eliminated by a fractured brake pipe. *(Nigel Snowdon)*

Because of the failure of the 80, Team Lotus continued to race the 79s in 1979, but the leading car of 1978 had now been overtaken by developments from rivals. Following the loss of John Player sponsorship, the leading sponsor became Martini & Rossi with David Thieme's Essex company as number two. Because of the poor results Martini quit the team at the end of the year. This is Carlos Reutemann at Monaco, where he finished third. Reutemann showed no interest at all in the 80. *(Nigel Snowdon)*

Carlos Reutemann. Whilst Lotus concentrated on the development of the 80, which was to prove a failure, other constructors followed the lead set by Lotus and their ground-effect designs were to prove more effective during the year. A 79 was also sold to Hector Rebaque for him to enter privately.

Reutemann preferred to concentrate on the existing 79 during 1979 and never raced the new car, while Andretti made occasional appearances with the 80. In the face of Ligier domination earlier in the season, followed by the successes later of Ferrari and Williams, Lotus achieved little. Reutemann took second place in the Argentinian Grand Prix at the beginning of the season, he was third in Brazil, Andretti was fourth at Kyalami and Long Beach and finished third in the Race of Champions at Brands Hatch. Reutemann and Andretti took second and third places in the Spanish Grand Prix, Reutemann was fourth in Belgium and third at Monaco, but there followed a bad patch during which no further Championship points were scored until the Italian Grand Prix, where Andretti took fifth place. In the non-Championship Dino Ferrari Grand Prix at Imola, Reutemann took second place and the cars failed in the two remaining rounds of the Championship in Canada and the United States. By 1980 the team was running the new 81 cars.

**Specification:**
ENGINE: Cosworth DFV.
GEARBOX: Hewland FG400.
CHASSIS: aluminium monocoque with honeycomb sandwich floor, perforated stress-panel bulkhead and single fuel cell.
FRONT SUSPENSION: upper rocking arms, lower wishbones and inboard coil spring/damper units.
REAR SUSPENSION: lower wishbones, upper rocking arms and inboard coil spring/damper units.
WHEELBASE: 9ft 0in.
FRONT TRACK: 5ft 8in.
REAR TRACK: 5ft 4in.
WEIGHT: 11.32 cwt.

# 79 Esprit (and 85)

*Mid-engined production GT car, 1975 to date*

Developed under the project number M70, the Esprit was produced in close liaison with Giorgetto Giugario's Ital Design concern. At the Turin show in November 1972 Ital Design exhibited a car already known as the Esprit, but in fact based on a much modified Europa twin-cam chassis. Development took place over a period of almost two years, the first production prototype was completed in late 1974 and the model was finally announced in October 1975. Because, however, of the financial difficulties which Lotus was experiencing at the time, production did not get under way until well into 1976.

Based once again on a steel backbone chassis with a front cross-member and two prongs at the rear to accommodate the engine and gearbox and linked by a cross-member, the dimensions were larger than those of the Europa, as it was intended to be a much more spacious and roomy car. The engine was the Type 907 1973cc developing 160 bhp at 6200 rpm mounted ahead of the rear axle line and canted 45 degrees to the left. Transmission was by the Citroën SM combined 5-speed gearbox and final drive. At the front the suspension was similar to that of the Vauxhall Cavalier by double wishbones and coil spring/damper units with an anti-roll bar.

The independent rear suspension comprised fixed length drive-shafts doubling as upper transverse links, lower transverse links, box-section semi-trailing radius arms and coil spring/damper units. There was rack-and-pinion steering (without any power assistance option), solid disc brakes front and rear (inboard at the rear) without servo assistance and Wolfrace cast alloy wheels. The one-piece body, although still based on the 1972 Turin show car, was modified to facilitate mass production and in particular the very steep rake of the windscreen was reduced.

Although announced in October 1975 at a price of £5844, this had risen to £7883 by the time that deliveries started in the summer of 1976. In addition the performance of the Esprit proved disappointing. Lotus had made the claim that the Esprit had a maximum speed of 138 mph, but the road test published by *Autocar* in January 1977 revealed a mean maximum speed of 124 mph, 0–60 mph acceleration of 8.4 seconds and an overall fuel consumption of 23.3 mpg. Although 718 Esprits were built in 1976–77, with a substantial proportion, in 'Federalized' form with twin Zenith-Stromberg carburettors and 140 bhp, exported to the United States, the original Esprit was heavily criticized in the press for its high engine noise level in the cockpit and general harshness, in addition to the poor performance.

Styled by Giorgetto Giugario, the original mid-engined Esprit had superb well-balanced lines that retained a distinct family resemblance to the Elite and the Eclat. The Esprit has proved the longest-running of all Lotus production models.

Featuring the new chassis frame and modified suspension of the Esprit Turbo, the S3 Esprit entered production in 1981. In an effort to boost demand the price of the S3 was reduced and the 135mph performance helped to attract more buyers.

As a result of these criticisms Lotus produced the improved S2 car in December 1977. Most of the changes were under the skin, but there were now Speedline road wheels and, as a result of inflation, the price (in August 1988) of £11,124. At the first Motor Show at the NEC at Birmingham in 1978 Lotus announced a run of 100 cars finished in John Player Special black and gold colours to commemorate the victories of the Lotus 79 and Mario Andretti in the Constructors' Cup and the Drivers' World Championship.

In 1980 Lotus announced the Esprit S2.2 with the Type 912 2.2-litre engine, but apart from galvanizing of the chassis and a stainless steel exhaust system, there were few changes. The price of the S2.2 was £14,951. Given the Type number 85, in 1981 there appeared a further modified version, the S3, with the same chassis frame and suspension as the Turbo Esprit (see 82). Over the years the performance of the Esprit had improved and when the S3 was tested by *Autocar* in June 1981 it achieved a mean maximum speed of 134 mph, 0–60 mph acceleration in 6.7 seconds and an overall fuel consumption of

21 mpg. The price had been reduced to £13,461. Production of the non-turbo Esprit has continued and the current model is the HC.

For much of the material contained in this section the author was dependent on *The Third Generation Lotuses* by Graham Robson (Motor Racing Publications Ltd, 1983).

## Specification (1976):

ENGINE: Lotus Type 907 1973cc.
GEARBOX: Maserati SM 5-speed.
CHASSIS: steel backbone with two prongs at the rear linked by box-section cross-member.
FRONT SUSPENSION: double wishbones and coil spring/damper units.
REAR SUSPENSION: fixed-length drive-shafts, lower transverse links, box-section semi-trailing radius arms and coil spring/damper units.
WHEELBASE: 8ft 0in.
FRONT TRACK: 4ft 11.5in.
REAR TRACK: 4ft 11.5in.
OVERALL LENGTH: 13ft 9in.
WIDTH: 6ft 1.25in.
WEIGHT: 19.8 cwt.

# 80

## *Formula 1, 1979*

For 1979 Lotus developed the 80, a design which was intended to maximize underwing area so as to gain the utmost advantage from the download generated by ground-effect side-pods with sliding skirts. The car was based on an aluminium monocoque, with aluminium honeycomb sheet skin used inside and for much of the outside of the monocoque and with strengthening by titanium. At the front and rear upper rocking arm and lower wishbone suspension with inboard coil spring/damper units was used. Originally the upper rocking arms were fabricated in titanium, but at a very early stage problems with the welding were revealed (titanium has to be welded in an atmosphere in which oxygen is completely absent to prevent oxidization and component failure) and so fabricated steel rocking arms were soon substituted. The twin-calliper balanced brakes were mounted outboard at the front and inboard at the rear.

The Cosworth DFV engine was used with a new gearbox, the Hewland FGA with a Lotus casing which was split transversely as opposed to longitudinally, and this casing was shrouded in a moulded fairing with venturi tunnels each side. Many of the features of the 79 were incorporated, including driver-adjustable front and rear anti-roll bars and similar suspension geometry and weight distribution. The car featured a long nose-section with side skirts extending from the front of the nose back to the front suspension and a further main skirt system extending from behind the front suspension past the rear suspension to the tail. Originally the car was run without wings or fins of any kind. Because of the Martini sponsorship the cars were numbered in the 'ML' (Martini-Lotus) system and the first car was numbered ML23.

From the moment that testing started, there

Mario Andretti in the pits at the 1979 Spanish Grand Prix with the Lotus 80. Reutemann would have nothing to do with the 80, but Andretti persevered in the team's efforts to make it a race-winner. In Spain Andretti finished third, but the 80's handling problems were never resolved and it was abandoned in mid-season.

Andretti during practice with the 80 at Monaco in 1979. Because of poor handling he qualified only 13th and he retired in the race because of broken rear suspension. *(Nigel Snowdon)*

were constant problems with the skirts. Pitching of the nose damaged the under-nose skirts and early in the car's life they were removed and conventional nose fins were fitted. The curved main skirts would twist and jam their slides, so that suction was broken, and then they would free and the seal would be formed again when the driver was least expecting it. No solution to the problem could be found during the season and the cars were abandoned after the 1979 French Grand Prix. Three in all were built.

Andretti used an 80 during practice for the Race of Champions at Brands Hatch and he drove one of these cars into a very promising third place in the Spanish Grand Prix behind team-mate Reutemann. At the Belgian Grand Prix at Zolder, he crashed his 80 during practice and drove a 79 in the race. He retired his 80 both

at Monaco and in the French Grand Prix. Thereafter the 80 made only one more appearance, in qualifying at the British Grand Prix at Brands Hatch.

### Specification:
ENGINE: Cosworth DFV.
GEARBOX: Lotus/Hewland FGA.
CHASSIS: aluminium monocoque with internal and exterior aluminium honeycomb sheet skinning and titanium strengthening.
FRONT SUSPENSION: upper rocking arms, lower wishbones and inboard coil spring/damper units.
REAR SUSPENSION: upper rocking arms, lower wishbones and inboard coil spring/damper units.
WHEELBASE: 9ft 0in.
FRONT TRACK: 5ft 10in.
REAR TRACK: 5ft 4in.
WEIGHT: 11.41 cwt.

# 81

## *Formula 1, 1980–81*

Following the failure of the team's cars in 1979, Chapman contented himself, perhaps not very imaginatively, with the development of a new car for 1980 that was merely in most respects an improved version of the 80. There was a very similar aluminium honeycomb monocoque, but with new suspension; at both the front and rear there were upper rocking arms, lower wishbones and inboard coil spring/damper units. The upper part of the body was moulded in one piece, with straight-sided side-pods and straight skirts. The Cosworth DFV engine was used once again with the Lotus/Hewland gearbox as on the 80.

Following the poor showing in 1979, Martini withdrew their sponsorship and the cars were now sponsored by David Thieme's Essex Petroleum Company, although Tissot remained as a minor sponsor. Mario Andretti stayed with the team and he was joined by young Italian driver Elio de Angelis, formerly with Shadow.

The 1980 season was largely dominated by the Williams team, with Ligier and Brabham as also-rans. Lotus failed to win a single race in 1981. After a complete failure in the Argentine, de Angelis finished second in Brazil, but thereafter no success was gained until the Spanish race, where he took third place. In the paddock at the German race, Lotus had completed the 81B, with longer wheelbase, and this was driven by the team's tester, Nigel Mansell, in the Austrian race. At the Österreichring de Angelis finished sixth, but the other two drivers retired. During the remainder of the year the only finishes in the points were fourth places by de Angelis at Imola (scene of that year's Italian Grand Prix) and the United States Grand Prix at Watkins Glen. Despite all the glitter that had surrounded the launch of the 81 in December 1979 at a night club in Paris, despite the ebullience of David Thieme and despite the garish Essex colours of blue, red and grey with chromium stripes, it had been one of the most hopeless seasons experienced by the Lotus team.

For 1981 Chapman was planning to use his new and innovative twin-chassis car, but

In 1980 Lotus raced the 81 with Essex sponsorship. It was a much simpler car than its predecessor, but failed to win a single race. Here newcomer to the team Elio de Angelis is seen in the Italian Grand Prix in which he finished fourth. *(Nigel Snowdon)*

Essex sponsorship continued in the early part of 1981 and after the banning of the 88 Lotus continued to race the 1980 81 cars. Elio de Angelis is seen during qualifying for the 1981 South African Grand Prix in which he finished third. It was eventually decided that the race would not have Championship status. *(Nigel Snowdon)*

because of problems over its legality, the team continued to race the 81s. Andretti, weary of Lotus's continuing failures, moved to Alfa Romeo, and the team consisted of de Angelis and Mansell. In the South African Grand Prix, which was organized by FOCA as a non-Championship race, de Angelis took third place. Subsequently the cars failed in the United States Grand Prix West at Long Beach, de Angelis was fifth in the Brazilian Grand Prix and sixth in the Argentine. The team withdrew from the San Marino Grand Prix and Mansell finished third in the Belgian race at Zolder. Thereafter the team had available the 87, based on the twin-chassis 88, and the 81s were retained purely as spares.

**Specification:**
ENGINE: Cosworth DFV.
GEARBOX: Lotus/Hewland FGA.
CHASSIS: aluminium honeycomb monocoque.
FRONT SUSPENSION: upper rocking arms, lower wishbones and inboard coil spring/damper units.
REAR SUSPENSION: upper rocking arms, lower wishbones and inboard coil spring/damper units.
WHEELBASE: 9ft 0in.
FRONT TRACK: 5ft 10in.
REAR TRACK: 5ft 4in.
WEIGHT: 11.32 cwt.

# 82 Turbo Esprit

*Production GT car, 1983 to date*

Given the Project number M72 and the Type number 82 (which applied to the Series 1 cars only), the Turbo Esprit represented a radical redesign of the original mid-engined Esprit. Development work commenced late in 1977, was substantially delayed by the company's involvement with the De Lorean project and was eventually announced at a very costly launch, hosted by Team Lotus' Formula 1 sponsors, Essex Petroleum, at the Albert Hall in February 1980.

The Type 910 2174cc engine represented a major redesign of the 1973cc Type 907 unit used in earlier cars and it differed equally substantially from the Type 912 2174cc normally aspirated engines used in the S2.2 Elite and Eclat. The most significant changes were the installation of the Garrett AiResearch turbocharger mounted behind the cylinder block and above the clutch bellhousing and the adoption of dry sump lubrication. With nominal compression reduced to 7.5:1, the turbocharger boosting inlet air into the twin Dell'Orto carburettors at 8 psi above atmospheric pressure and modified cam profile, the maximum power was 210 bhp at 6250 rpm.

Lotus redesigned the backbone frame so that there was a much roomier engine bay (it was planned that the car would also take the V8 4-litre engine under development and the project number for this car was M71). Front suspension and steering remained unchanged, but at the rear there were now drive-shafts with sliding joints and the suspension consisted of wide-based lower wishbones, upper transverse links and coil spring/damper units. This eliminated much of the vibration and harshness of the rear end of earlier Esprits caused by the use of fixed length drive-shafts as upper suspension members.

Body changes included a larger wrap-round front bumper and new spoiler, skirts along the side with NACA-type ducts, larger rear bumper and black louvring over the engine bay.

The interior trim was much improved. Although a few cars were sold with three-piece Compomotive wheels, the majority of Turbo Esprits were fitted with BBS wheels. The first 100 cars were built as the Essex Esprit Turbo. These were finished in the startling Essex blue, silver and red colours, fitted with air conditioning and a Panasonic radio/cassette player mounted in the centre of the roof panel as standard and priced at a hefty £20,950.

Production of the Turbo Esprit did not start until August 1980 and once the first 100 cars with Essex colours had been completed, a 'normal'

Introduced in 1980, the Esprit Turbo featured a Garrett AiResearch turbocharger, 2174cc engine and a power output of 210 bhp. This is one of the first batch of 100 cars in dramatic Essex colours.

The current 1990 production Esprit Turbo.

production model with air conditioning as an optional extra was offered at £16,917. Only 57 cars were completed in 1980, 116 were sold in 1981 and 205 in 1982. Dry sump lubrication was dropped in favour of conventional wet sump in 1983. That year Lotus introduced a 'Federal' Turbo Esprit for export to the United States. When tested by *Autocar* in May 1981 the Esprit Turbo achieved a maximum speed of 148 mph, 0–60 mph acceleration in 6.1 seconds and overall fuel consumption of 18 mpg.

The Esprit Turbo remained in production in 1990 with the Lotus 'green' 910S engine (catalyst-equipped exhaust and unleaded fuel). Because of this 16-valve engine with what Lotus called 'chargecooler' (a compact and highly efficient water-cooled intercooler), power output was boosted to 264 bhp at 6500 rpm. The result was an immense improvement in performance with figures obtained by *Autocar and Motor* that encompassed a maximum speed of 159 mph (mean), 0–60 mph in 4.9 sec, 0–100 mph in 12.4 sec and an overall fuel consumption of 23–5 mpg. The standard version was priced at £35,900 and the SE with all-leather cockpit and other 'de-luxe' features cost £43,800. The Esprit Turbo had become a true 'supercar'.

**Specification (1980):**
ENGINE: Lotus Type 910 2174 cc Garrett AiResearch turbocharged.
GEARBOX: Maserati SM 5-speed.
CHASSIS: Steel backbone with two prongs at the rear and tubular structure.
FRONT SUSPENSION: double wishbones and coil spring/damper units.
REAR SUSPENSION: wide-based lower wishbones, upper transverse links and coil spring/damper units.
WHEELBASE. 8ft 0in.
FRONT TRACK: 4ft 11.5in.
REAR TRACK 5ft 0.5in.
OVERALL LENGTH: 13ft 9in.
WIDTH: 6ft 1.25in.
WEIGHT: 21 cwt.

# 83

Elite Series 2 2.2-litre. See 75.

# 84

Eclat Series 2 2.2-litre. See 76.

# 85

Esprit Series 3. See 79.

# 86

*Formula 1, 1980*

Technical developments by other teams had left Team Lotus sadly lacking and uncompetitive. Because of the use of sliding skirts, lap times had been much reduced, and cornering speeds were considerably higher, and as a result FISA banned sliding skirts for 1981 and introduced a minimum ground clearance of 6cm. Team Lotus devised a design that would circumvent the ban on sliding skirts and at the same time insulate the driver and the primary structure of the car from the immense downloads. Very stiff suspensions and ground effect were giving drivers an appalling time and if a skirt failed, then the immediate loss of downforce and grip could result in a serious accident.

So there came about the twin-chassis Lotus, built in prototype form as the 86, and incorporating many 81 components. The 81 aluminium honeycomb monocoque with its conventional suspension formed the primary chassis, but there was a secondary chassis constructed in moulded carbon-composite, supported by its own framework and itself carrying the bodywork, side-pods, wings and radiators. The primary monocoque carried the engine gearbox and front and rear suspensions, and the driver had a comparatively softly suspended ride in the primary moncoque structure. The secondary structure, insulated from the driver, transmitted the aerodynamic loads directly to the tyre contact areas. The 86 was used to test the team's basic ideas and once they were satisfied that things would work, the 86 was put into store and the team concentrated on the cars intended to be raced during the 1981 season.

**Specification:**
ENGINE: Cosworth DFV.
GEARBOX: Lotus/Hewland FGA.
CHASSIS: twin chassis, with inner aluminium monocoque and outer moulded carbon-composite body.
FRONT SUSPENSION: upper rocking arms, lower wishbones and inboard coil spring/damper units.
REAR SUSPENSION: upper rocking arms, lower wishbones and inboard coil spring/damper units.
WHEELBASE: 9ft 3in.
FRONT TRACK: 5ft 6in.
REAR TRACK: 5ft 4in.
WEIGHT: 11.52 cwt.

The experimental 86 'twin-chassis' Formula 1 car outside Ketteringham Hall. It was in this form that the car was tested at Jarama, but mainly with Nigel Mansell at the wheel.

# 87

*Formula 1, 1981*

Parallel with the development of the 88, which is described next, Lotus developed the conventional 87 with carbon-composite monocoque and with many features in common with the 81. Team Lotus used 81s at the first four races of the season, withdrew from the San Marino Grand Prix and used the 81s for the final time (save as for training cars) in Belgium.

It soon emerged that the 87s were hopelessly uncompetitive, both cars retired at Monaco, de Angelis and Mansell finished fifth and sixth in Spain, and sixth and seventh at Dijon. De Angelis retired in the British Grand Prix, whilst Mansell failed to qualify because of the problems with the 88B cars. In Germany and Austria de Angelis finished seventh, he took fifth place in the Dutch Grand Prix, fourth in the Italian and sixth in the Canadian. Mansell retired in all these races, but finished fourth in the Caesars Palace race at Las Vegas at the end of the season.

Although the new 91 appeared at the Brazilian Grand Prix in 1982, the team still relied on the 87, in modified 87B form in South Africa; in this form the wheelbase was increased by 3in. by a spacer between the engine and gearbox and there were wider side-pods. De Angelis finished eighth, whilst Mansell retired. The 87B was used as a training car in Brazil and at Long Beach, but thereafter disappeared from the scene.

Specification:
ENGINE: Cosworth DFV.
GEARBOX: Lotus/Hewland FGA.
CHASSIS: aluminium honeycomb monocoque.
FRONT SUSPENSION: upper rocking arms, lower wishbones and inboard coil spring/damper units.
REAR SUSPENSION: upper rocking arms, lower wishbones and inboard coil spring/damper units.
WHEELBASE: 8ft 11in.
FRONT TRACK: 5ft 10in.
REAR TRACK: 5ft 3in.
WEIGHT: 11.52 cwt.

By the middle of the 1981 season Chapman had accepted that he would have to race the conventional 87 cars. Here Mansell is practising with his 87 for the Dutch Grand Prix. He retired on the second lap because of electrical trouble. *(Nigel Snowdon)*

Elio de Angelis with the 87 in the wet Canadian Grand Prix in 1981. He finished sixth. *(Nigel Snowdon)*

Lotus was still using the 87 in lengthened 87B form at the 1982 South African Grand Prix. This is Nigel Mansell who retired on the first lap because of electrical problems. *(Nigel Snowdon)*

# 88

## *Formula 1, 1981*

For 1981 Team Lotus took the twin-chassis concept of the 86 forward in more sophisticated form. Chapman was well aware that there would be problems over the acceptability of the twin-chassis concept and parallel with the 88 Chapman developed the 87 conventional monocoque car. Lotus and McLaren were the pioneers of the use of carbon-composites in Formula 1, and whilst McLaren, under the direction of John Barnard, chose a moulded monocoque using carbon-composite built for the company by the Hercules Corporation in America, Lotus also went their own way and used a carbon-composite incorporating Kevlar developed by Du Pont Chemicals. The monocoque, later referred to as the 'secondary chassis', was formed from sheet carbon Kevlar-skinned sandwich with Nomex paper-foil honeycomb filling. This monocoque incorporated machined aluminium bulkheads bolted into position, which provided rigidity and mounting points for the suspension and engine, and carried the driver, fuel and the Cosworth engine.

The 'primary chassis' as referred to by Chapman was also constructed in carbon Kevlar with three cross-members of which two passed through the monocoque/engine assembly and the rear cross-member passed over the gearbox. This 'primary chassis' mounted the radiators and the underwing side-pod structures and fixed skirts and was suspended on very short, very stiff coil spring units acting through the wheel uprights on to the tyres. The result was that the aerodynamic download created by the bodywork was compressed directly on to the wheel uprights and tyres, whilst the secondary chassis, with conventional upper rocking arm and lower wishbone suspension, was comparatively softly sprung. As usual the Cosworth engine was used with the Lotus/Hewland FGA gearbox.

In 1981 Lotus retained its sponsorship from David Thieme's Essex company, with additional sponsorship from Tissot and Courage. The drivers were de Angelis and Mansell.

Then the wrangles started. After the press début the first 88 was flown to Long Beach for the United States Grand Prix West to be driven by de Angelis. It passed scrutineering and was driven by de Angelis in Friday's practice, but as a result of protests from other entrants, the stewards announced on the Friday evening that the protests would be upheld, the 88 would be banned from the race, and times taken during Friday's practice would not count. Chapman immediately appealed and the stewards then agreed that the car should be allowed to run in the remainder of the practice and the race, but on the basis that any points scored would be forfeited if the protests were confirmed. However, there was a further change of mind and during Saturday's practice the 88 was black-flagged and excluded from the race. The result of Chapman's appeal was that in March the car was approved by the American racing authorities. Accordingly Lotus took the 88 to Rio de Janeiro for de Angelis to drive in the Brazilian Grand Prix. Before the race, however, FISA had announced that the American decision carried authority only on American territory. The 88 was approved in scrutineering at Rio, but a number of teams immediately protested. During the Friday practice stewards requested to to examine the car again, and it was again black-flagged during the Friday afternoon practice session. De Angelis switched to the 81 for the race.

Next came the Argentine Grand Prix, where de Angelis again appeared with the 88, but the stewards immediately rejected the car at scrutineering. Chapman left the circuit before the race, arranging for a long statement to be made to the press. FISA imposed a US$100,000 fine on Team Lotus because of the outspoken nature of Chapman's statement, but 10 days later this was cancelled. An appeal by Lotus to the FIA court held in Paris was rejected. While these protests were going on, David Thieme, the team's sponsor, was arrested in Zurich in connection with various alleged offences concerning the Credit Suisse Bank, but was released after two weeks without charges. The team had not received the due sponsorship payment from Essex and in the absence of any competitive cars to race, Lotus withdrew from the San Marino Grand Prix. This was only the second Grand Prix which the team had missed since it first entered Formula 1 in 1958. After racing 81s in the Belgian Grand Prix, the simpler 87s appeared at Monaco.

Team Lotus now produced the revised 88B car, with mainly bodywork differences, in the hope of persuading organizers that the

During 1981 Chapman was plagued by the refusal of the scrutineers to accept the eligibility of the twin-chassis 88 and 88B cars. This is de Angelis in practice with the 88B for the British Grand Prix. The team was forced to use the conventional 87s in the race. *(Nigel Snowdon)*

bodywork constituted the main component of the car, and these included the gearbox, oil cooler and the brake ducts forming part of the 'primary structure'. Prior to the British Grand Prix at Silverstone, the 88B was offered for examination to the RAC and Chapman, now talking of 'two sprung structures', persuaded the RAC that the 88B should be acceptable for the British race. Despite a threat from FISA that the 88 and all versions of it were in breach of the regulations, that any organization allowing the cars to run would be in breach of what was known as the Concord Agreement and that the British race would lose its World Championship status, the RAC, after consulting other teams, allowed the cars to appear in practice. However, further protests were received from Alfa Romeo Ligier and Ferrari, and under further threats that the race would lose its Championship status, the cars were disqualified and the Thursday practice times were declared to be void. Overnight one of the 88Bs was rebuilt as an 87

for Mansell, but he failed to qualify, which was hardly surprising in all the circumstances, whilst an 87 was brought from the team headquarters for de Angelis, who qualified. No attempt was again made to race the 88 and the innovative twin-chassis concept with all its inherent safety features, was never fully developed.

**Specification:**
ENGINE: Cosworth DFV.
GEARBOX: Lotus/Hewland FGA.
CHASSIS: twin chassis, with inner carbon Kevlar monocoque, and outer carbon/Kevlar body.
FRONT SUSPENSION: upper rocking arms, lower wishbones and inboard coil spring/damper units.
REAR SUSPENSION: upper rocking arms, lower wishbones and inboard coil spring/damper units.
WHEELBASE: 8ft 11in.
FRONT TRACK: 5ft 10in.
REAR TRACK: 5ft 3in.
WEIGHT: 11.52 cwt.

During 1983 Gérard Ducarouge joined the Lotus team and his efforts resulted in the much improved 94T that appeared at the British Grand Prix that year. This is de Angelis's car. He retired on the second lap of the race because of a mysterious engine malady. *(Nigel Snowdon)*

Elio de Angelis with the 94T in the wet during the second qualifying session at the 1983 German Grand Prix. He retired in the race because of engine overheating. *(Nigel Snowdon)*

Development work on the turbocharged cars continued steadily and in 1984 Lotus ran the 95T. Elio de Angelis leads away at the start of the German Grand Prix, but he retired early in the race because of turbocharger failure. De Angelis finished third in that year's World Championship. *(Nigel Snowdon)*

By 1985 John Player Special Team Lotus was racing the 97T and in the very wet Portuguese race Ayrton Senna, who had joined the team that year, scored his first Grand Prix victory. Here he waves to the crowd on his slowing-down lap. Senna finished fourth in that year's World Championship. *(Nigel Snowdon)*

At Imola in 1985 de Angelis was the winner with the 97T leading home Boutsen (Arrows) and Tambay (Renault). De Angelis won no other races that year, but he was always a consistent performer. *(Nigel Snowdon)*

In 1986 Lotus were still using the Renault engine and that year's car was the 98T. Here Senna is seen in the Brazilian Grand Prix in which he finished second to fellow countryman Nelson Piquet (Williams). Senna won the Spanish and Detroit races that year and again finished fourth in the World Championship. *(Nigel Snowdon)*

By 1987 the Team had become known as Camel Team Lotus Honda and was using the Honda V6 turbocharged engine. Here Senna is seen at Detroit, where he won from Piquet (Williams) and Prost (McLaren). Senna finished third in the World Championship. *(Nigel Snowdon)*

Senna's team-mate in 1987 was Satoru Nakajima, seen here in the Japanese Grand Prix at Suzuka, where he finished sixth. *(Nigel Snowdon)*

Two views of Nelson Piquet with the V6 Honda-powered
100T in the 1988 Brazilian Grand Prix. At this time the
Lotus team was still competitive and Piquet finished third.
*(Nigel Snowdon)*

1989 proved a disastrous year for Camel Team Lotus, now using Judd engines, and at the Belgian race neither Piquet nor Nakajima qualified as a starter. Here in the Portuguese race Piquet retired after a collision with Caffi's Dallara. *(Nigel Snowdon)*

In the impossibly wet 1989 Australian Grand Prix Satoru Nakajima, on his last appearance for Lotus, drove the best race of his career and finished fourth. *(Diana Burnett)*

The 1990 Lotus Formula 1 car was the 102 with Lamborghini V12 power seen with drivers Derek Warwick and Martin Donnelly on its press launch at Ketteringham Hall. Sadly, the cars showed little promise in the early part of 1990. *(Nigel Snowdon)*

Derek Warwick was Lotus team-leader in 1990. He is seen in the Brazilian race. *(Nigel Snowdon)*

# 89 Excel

*Production GT, 1982 to date*

Since the introduction of the Elite and its successors from 1974 onwards, development had largely stultified at Hethel, prices had risen substantially and sales had steadily dropped. By 1981 Lotus was in a very difficult situation and a tie-up with Toyota offered the company a much-needed lifeline. The first result of this tie-up (which eventually proved abortive because of the take-over by General Motors) was the Excel which was announced in October 1982. The Excel, originally to be known as the Eclat 3, then as the Eclat Excel, was also confusingly given the project number M55.

There were subtle changes to the bodywork styling to give an updated appearance, but the main changes were under the glass-fibre skin.

The adoption of the name Excel for the new coupé introduced in 1982 was a change very much for the better. Changes included modified nose treatment, modified rear suspension and Toyota Supra transmission. A number of other Toyota components were incorporated and Lotus were able to effect a price reduction. The name Excel on the side rear and Eclat on the nose and tail was the definitive badging.

The 1990 production Excel with external changes that included rear spoiler, new wheels, 'flares' behind the rear wheels and new badging.

There was a Toyota 5-speed gearbox with overdrive fifth gear (similar to that fitted to the Celica Supra coupé), Toyota chassis-mounted final drive (again as used on the Supra) and the rear suspension was modified so as to incorporate transverse top links and wide-based lower wishbones. Other features were Toyota drive-shafts with plunging universal joints and Toyota ventilated disc brakes front and rear (outboard at the rear and superseding the previous inboard-mounted drum brakes). The bodywork was modified to give greater rear headroom, there was a modified nose-line and modified waistline. Power steering remained an optional extra. Compared with the S2.2, there was a substantial price reduction to £13,787. Maximum speed, according to *Autocar*'s road test in April 1983, was 130 mph, with 0–60 mph acceleration in 7.1 seconds and an overall fuel consumption of 19.5 mpg.

The Excel remains in production, now with Porsche 944-style wheel arches in standard (160 bhp/£20,900), SA (automatic/£27,900) and SE (180 bhp/£24,900) forms.

**Specification (1982):**
ENGINE: Lotus Type 910 2174cc.
GEARBOX: Toyota 5-speed all-synchromesh.
CHASSIS: steel backbone with two prongs at the front linked by box-section cross-member.
FRONT SUSPENSION: pressed steel double wishbones and coil spring/damper units.
REAR SUSPENSION: upper links, lower wishbones and coil spring/damper units.
WHEELBASE: 8ft 1.8in.
FRONT TRACK: 4ft 9.5in.
REAR TRACK: 4ft 9.5in.
OVERALL LENGTH: 14ft 4.3in.
WIDTH: 5ft 11.5in.
WEIGHT: 2503 lb.

# 90

Proposed successor to the original Elan, which was not produced. It would have been Toyota-powered and was developed during the period when there were strong links between Lotus and Toyota. Also known later as X100.

# 91

*Formula 1, 1982*

For 1982 Peter Wright was appointed chief engineer of Team Lotus and he was eventually to become a director. By this stage Chapman was too heavily involved in the problems of Group Lotus and De Lorean to be fully committed to the Formula 1 team.

The 91 represented an improved version of the 87B, retaining a carbon Kevlar monocoque, and in accordance with the latest change in the regulations, fixed skirts with protective rubbing strips on the bottom edges (these rubbing strips had been prohibited the previous year). There were now much stiffer front suspension uprights cast in magnesium and strengthened rear suspension and gearbox casing and the car had been designed so that there could be variations in wheelbase and track if required. The body, designed by Martin Ogilvie, featured smoothly curving lines and the aerodynamics were much improved compared with the 87.

De Angelis and Mansell remained with the team. Sponsorship was once again from John Player. The 1982 season was strongly contested by Williams, still using Cosworth engines, Ferrari, McLaren and Renault, whilst the turbocharged Brabhams were still finding their feet in racing. For much of the season the Lotus 91 was to prove an also-ran.

After a disappointing outing in the South African race, Mansell was classified third in the Brazilian Grand Prix after the two leading drivers, Piquet and Rosberg, were disqualified. After a fifth by de Angelis and seventh place by Mansell in the United States Grand Prix West at Long Beach, the team withdrew from the San Marino Grand Prix, along with all the other FOCA teams, and next appeared in the Belgian Grand Prix at Zolder. Here de Angelis finished fifth on the road, but was elevated to fourth place after Lauda (McLaren) was disqualified. Fourth and fifth places for Mansell and de Angelis followed in the Monaco Grand Prix, whilst both cars retired at Detroit, and de Angelis was the sole finisher in fourth place in the Canadian Grand Prix.

Mansell had badly injured an arm in a collision with Giacomelli's Alfa Romeo in Canada and missed the Dutch Grand Prix, where his place

Elio de Angelis with the 91 on his way to fourth place in the 1982 Belgian Grand Prix at Zolder. *(Nigel Snowdon)*

The 91 had very gently, smoothly curved lines, the work of Martin Ogilvie, and these are shown off to good advantage in this photograph of Nigel Mansell's car in the 1982 Detroit Grand Prix. In this race Mansell was eliminated by engine problems. This photograph was taken during qualifying when the cars ran without engine covers to improve cooling. *(Nigel Snowdon)*

was taken by Roberto Moreno, who failed to qualify. De Angelis retired. In the British race de Angelis took fourth place, but Mansell was forced to retire because of the pain from the arm. At this race one of the 91s was fitted with pull-rod front suspension in place of the rocking-arm layout. Mansell was still not fit to drive by the French Grand Prix and here his place in the team was taken by Geoff Lees, who finished 12th. De Angelis retired. Another failure followed at Hockenheim, where Mansell was ninth, but de Angelis retired. In the Austrian Grand Prix de Angelis scored his only win of the season, entirely unexpected, as other cars fell by the wayside. It was the first win by Team Lotus in four seasons of racing. During the remaining three races of the season the only finish in the points was a sixth place by de Angelis in the so-called Swiss Grand Prix at Dijon.

The 91s lacked sufficient speed to be truly competitive. On slower circuits they suffered from bad understeering problems and they porpoised badly on bumpy circuits. For 1983 the 91s were rebuilt as 92s for Nigel Mansell to drive, until Renault were able to deliver sufficient engines for Lotus to field two turbocharged cars.

**Specification:**
ENGINE: Cosworth DFV.
GEARBOX: Lotus/Hewland FGA.
CHASSIS: carbon/Kevlar monocoque.
FRONT SUSPENSION: upper rocking arms, lower wishbones and inboard coil spring/damper units.
REAR SUSPENSION: upper rocking arms, lower wishbones and inboard coil spring/damper units.
WHEELBASE: 9ft 2in.
FRONT TRACK: 5ft 8.89in.
REAR TRACK 5ft 3.8in.
WEIGHT: 11.42 cwt.

# 92

## *Formula 1, 1983*

For 1983 Team Lotus had entered into an arrangement with Renault whereby they would use the Renault turbocharged engines, and it soon became evident that there would only be sufficient engines to power one car during the early part of the season. Accordingly the Renault engines were reserved for Elio de Angelis and it would be necessary for the team to provide a Cosworth-powered car for Nigel Mansell. The decision was made to update the 1982 91 cars to comply with the latest regulations and, hopefully, make some sort of impact among the few remaining users of Cosworth engines, who were trailing at the tail end of the field.

Changes in the 91s included the adoption of flat bottoms to the cars extending the full width and running from a point in line with the trailing edge of the front tyres to the leading edge of the rear tyres to comply with the 1983 Regulations. Chapman decided to incorporate into the 92s the long under development computer-controlled 'Active' suspension system. This system incorporated hydraulic rams at each wheel, piped to reservoirs which were pressurized by a pump driven by a small engine. The rams replaced conventional springs, dampers and anti-roll bars and were controlled by a central computer. The 92 in this form was being tested at Snetterton on 16 December,

1982, with test driver Dave Scott at the wheel when the news broke that Colin Chapman had died during the early hours of that day.

Following Chapman's death, Peter Warr took over effective control of Team Lotus. In the first race of the season in Brazil, Mansell, struggling with the 'Active' suspension, qualified well down the grid and was classified 12th. He again drove the car in this form at Long Beach, where he was again 12th. After this the active suspension was abandoned and the 92 ran in conventional form. Mansell retired in the French Grand Prix on the Paul Ricard circuit, finished 12th in the San Marino Grand Prix and was eliminated at Monaco in a first-lap accident with Alboreto. In Belgium he was eliminated by gearbox problems, he finished sixth at Detroit, retired with handling problems in Canada and by the British Grand Prix both Lotus drivers were at the wheel of the new 94T cars. The 92 was not raced again.

**Specification:**
ENGINE: Cosworth DFY Mark 1.
GEARBOX: Lotus/Hewland FGA.
CHASSIS: carbon/Kevlar monocoque.
FRONT SUSPENSION: double wishbones, pull-rods and inboard coil spring/damper units.
REAR SUSPENSION: upper rocking arms, lower wishbones and inboard coil spring/damper units.
WHEELBASE: 9ft 2in.
FRONT TRACK: 5ft 8.89in.
REAR TRACK: 5ft 2.36in.
WEIGHT: 10.63 cwt.

In the first eight Championship races of 1983 Lotus number two, Nigel Mansell, drove the last of the Cosworth-Ford cars, the 92. This photograph was taken at the Brazilian race in which Mansell finished 12th. *(Nigel Snowdon)*

# 93T

*Formula 1, 1983*

For 1983 Colin Chapman, not long before his death, had negotiated a deal with Renault for the French company to supply to Lotus the Renault V6 90-degree 1492cc EFl engine with twin belt-driven overhead camshafts per bank of cylinders, four valves per cylinder, KKK turbochargers and Renix (Renault Electronics) Management System and at a time when Renault were changing from cast iron to lighter aluminium blocks. The power output of the Renault engine in 1983 was around 650 bhp at 12,000 rpm.

The new 93T Lotus designed to take this engine was the work of Martin Ogilvie and was again a carbon/Kevlar monocoque built from folded sheet, with a flat sloping scuttle section. The Renault engine was mounted at the rear of the monocoque and was fully stressed apart from needing tubular braces. There were full length side-pods (most teams had now adopted shorter side-pods), the front suspension now incorporated pull-rods, whilst the rear suspension was largely unchanged. Lotus also continued to use the Hewland FGA gearbox in their own casing. The car was built to comply with the 1983 flat-bottom rules. Apart from the fact that the 93T was bulky and heavy, one of the problems faced by Lotus was that they had entered into a contract with Pirelli to use their radial ply tyres during the year and these were to cause immense problems.

It was known initially that there would be a shortage of Renault engines and so only two 93Ts were built, both primarily for the use of Elio de Angelis. Mansell drove a 93T only once, in the Race of Champions at Brands Hatch, a non-Championship event, in which he retired after six laps with handling problems. From the beginning of the season de Angelis found the 93T to be a complete disaster. Before he even started racing he was reconciled to failure and his only finish with the car in eight races was in the Belgian Grand Prix, in which he was classified ninth. By the British Grand Prix Gérard Ducarouge had joined the team and the new 94T was raced.

The turbocharged Renault-powered 93T at the press launch held not long after Colin Chapman's death. *(Nigel Snowdon)*

**Specification:**
ENGINE: Renault EFl 1492cc (86 x 42.8mm) V6 turbocharged developing 650 bhp at 12,000 rpm.
GEARBOX: Lotus/Hewland FGB.
CHASSIS: carbon/Kevlar monocoque.
FRONT SUSPENSION: double wishbones, pull-rods and inboard coil spring/damper units.
REAR SUSPENSION: upper rocking arms, lower wishbones and inboard coil spring/damper units.
WHEELBASE: 8ft 10in.
FRONT TRACK : 5ft 10 9in.
REAR TRACK: 5ft 3in.
WEIGHT: 11.16 cwt.

This view of the 93T, also taken at the press launch, shows clearly the construction of the carbon/Kevlar monocoque and the pull-rod suspension. *(Nigel Snowdon)*

The installation of the 90-degree V6 Renault engine in the Lotus 93T monocoque. Note that Renault continued to use the name 'Gordini' on their engines as a tribute to the great designer. *(Nigel Snowdon)*

# 94T

## Formula 1, 1983

Following the 1983 Belgian Grand Prix, Team Lotus was joined by Gérard Ducarouge, with vast experience at Matra, Ligier, and Alfa Romeo with the brief of taking over complete technical control of the team and evolving as speedily as possible a car that would be competitive. Ducarouge had no alternative but to act from sheer expediency rather than any concept of perfection. He resolved to adapt the 91 cars, which were small and compact by modern standards for use with the Renault turbocharged engines. Because of the basic design of the 91, the original bulkheads could be removed and replaced by new bulkheads which would be suitable for the new suspension geometry. The rear bulkheads were adapted to provide mountings for the Renault turbocharged engine and the fuel cell was modified to suit the latest mid-race refuelling stops, which meant incorporating a new filler-neck and breather. The old upper rocking arm suspension of the 91 was retained, and there was new bodywork sketched out by Ducarouge himself.

There was a frantic rush to get the cars ready in time for the British Grand Prix at Brands Hatch. De Angelis was fourth fastest in qualifying but Mansell was plagued by misfiring caused by electrical problems. He qualified in the spare 93T on the Friday afternoon and in the race finished fourth, whilst de Angelis retired very early on because of engine failure. There were more problems in the German race at Hockenheim, where Mansell took his grid position with the 93T and both drivers retired their 94Ts in the race. In Austria Mansell qualified third and eventually took fifth place, whilst de Angelis was eliminated on the first lap, when he spun into the guard-rail. Both 94Ts retired in the Dutch Grand Prix at Zandvoort, but de Angelis finished fifth in the Italian Grand Prix and Mansell was eighth. In the European Grand Prix at Bands Hatch de Angelis took pole position in practice, but spun off early in the race while scrapping for the lead with Patrese (Brabham) and subsequently retired with engine problems. Mansell, however, finished third, which was to be the best Lotus performance of the season. The final round.of the Championship was the South African Grand Prix, in which neither Lotus driver qualified as a finisher. The 94T certainly was not a particularly competitive car, but it did mark the return of Lotus to the forefront of international racing.

Following the failure of the 93T in 1983, French engineer Gérard Ducarouge, vastly experienced and previously with Matra, Ligier and Alfa Romeo, designed the 94T which incorporated the old 91 chassis. The new car is seen in the British Grand Prix driven by de Angelis, who was eliminated by engine failure. (Nigel Snowdon)

The team's best performance of the year was in the European Grand Prix at Brands Hatch where Mansell took third place. *(Nigel Snowdon)*

## Specification:
ENGINE: Renault EFl turbocharged.
GEARBOX: Lotus/Hewland FGB.
CHASSIS: carbon/Kevlar monocoque.
FRONT SUSPENSION: upper rocking arms, lower wishbones and inboard coil spring/damper units.
REAR SUSPENSION: pull-rods, double wishbones and coil spring/damper units.
WHEELBASE: 8ft 10in.
FRONT TRACK: 5ft 10.9in.
REAR TRACK: 5ft 8.1in.
WEIGHT: 11.16 cwt approx.

# 95T

*Formula 1, 1984*

For 1984 Ducarouge developed the 95T, with an all-new carbon/Kevlar monocoque, front and rear suspension by pull-rods, double wishbones and inboard coil spring/damper units and a choice of aerodynamic set-ups for slow and fast circuits. The Renault EFl engine was still used, but it was less powerful than some of its rivals, and although the 95T was probably the best-handling chassis of the 1984 season, the team's prospects were somewhat restricted by the lack of power.

For 1984 Lotus switched to Goodyear tyres. The team was still sponsored by John Player, although, when the contract had come up for renewal in July 1983, there had been very real doubts as to whether the sponsorship would continue. Both de Angelis and Mansell remained with the team, but Mansell and Lotus were rapidly becoming disenchanted with each other. In 1984 the fuel allowance was restricted to 220 litres and refuelling during the race was now banned.

Throughout 1984 Lotus was pushing at the door, so close to success, but never actually winning a race. De Angelis finished third in Brazil (Mansell retired) and then after a seventh place in South Africa (Mansell again retired), finished fifth in Belgium and third at Imola. Mansell took third place in the French race with de Angelis fifth. Mansell was leading in the wet at Monaco when he lost control on a white line and crashed. In this race de Angelis finished fourth.

Thereafter de Angelis took fourth place in the Canadian Grand Prix (Mansell sixth), third at Detroit (Mansell retired), third at Dallas (Mansell sixth but not running at the finish) and fourth in the British Grand Prix (Mansell retired). In the German Grand Prix Mansell finish fourth (de Angelis retired) and both entries retired in the Austrian race. Mansell

For 1984 Ducarouge developed the completely new 95T, still with Renault engine. Mansell built up a good lead in the rain-soaked Monaco Grand Prix only to lose control on a white line, slamming into the armco and out of the race. *(Nigel Snowdon)*

In the British Grand Prix at Brands Hatch de Angelis finished third. His consistently good placings with the 95T earned him third place in the World Championship behind McLaren drivers Prost and Lauda. *(Nigel Snowdon)*

was third in the Dutch Grand Prix, with de Angelis fourth, but both the cars retired in the Italian Grand Prix and in the European Grand Prix at the Nürburgring.

In the final race of the season, the Portuguese Grand Prix, de Angelis finished fifth and Mansell retired. The 95T, of which four were built, could be described as one of the best of the also-rans.

**Specification:**
ENGINE: Renault EFl developing 750 bhp at 11,500 rpm.
GEARBOX: Lotus/Hewland FGB.
CHASSIS: carbon/Kevlar monocoque.
FRONT SUSPENSION: pull-rods, double wishbones and coil spring/damper units.
REAR SUSPENSION: pull-rods, double wishbones and coil spring/damper units.
WHEELBASE: 8ft 1in.
FRONT TRACK: 5ft 10.9in.
REAR TRACK: 5ft 3in.
WEIGHT: 10.63 cwt approx.

# 96

## CART, 1984

In 1984 Team Lotus was asked by Roy Winkelmann to build cars for American Indycar 'CART' racing. Winkelmann, who had run a very successful Formula 2 team during the 1960s, was now resident in the United States, very successful in business and keen to return to his old love and believed that there were good prospects of winning in CART racing with a team run on well organized lines like European teams. Team Lotus International and Winkelmann agreed on a three-year programme with a new Lotus car to be powered by Cosworth DFX 2.65-litre engines prepared by Cosworth themselves, and to be entered under the name Winkelmann Team Lotus.

Gérard Ducarouge designed a monocoque based on carbon/Kevlar sandwich skins, in accordance with the now usual practice, but with aluminium honeycomb filling between the skins and stronger and heavier than a Formula 1 monocoque. Suspension front and rear was similar to that of the 95T, but suitably strengthened.

Only the first prototype was built and before it was completed it became evident that Winkelmann's scheme would not work. The CART organization was hostile to the entry into this category of racing by a works team using works engines, and Winkelmann found it impossible to raise sponsorship. Reluctantly the project was abandoned and Winkelmann withdrew with badly burnt fingers.

**Specification:**
ENGINE: Cosworth DFX V8 turbocharged 2643cc.
GEARBOX: Lotus/Hewland FGB.
CHASSIS: carbon/Kevlar monocoque.
FRONT SUSPENSION: pull-rods, double wishbones and inboard coil spring/damper units.
REAR SUSPENSION: pull-rods, double wishbones and inboard coil spring/damper units.
WHEELBASE: 9ft 2in.
FRONT TRACK: 5ft 7in.
REAR TRACK: 5ft 4in.
WEIGHT: 13.42 cwt.

The carbon/Kevlar turbocharged Cosworth-powered 96 looking resplendent in British Racing Green paintwork. The model was to be run in CART racing by Roy Winkelmann's Winkelmann Team Lotus, but for political reasons he was unable to raise sponsorship and the project was abandoned.

# 97T

*Formula 1, 1985*

For 1985 Gérard Ducarouge continued the progressive development which he had commenced in 1983 and the new year's car was an improved version of the 95T. The monocoque incorporated aluminium foil as a sandwich between the composite skins. To comply with new regulations the car incorporated a deformable structure crash-protective nose-box and the winglets seen on the rear wings in 1984 had to be abandoned. There were now small winglets on the rear of the side-pods and vertical vanes at the front. The team was still using the Renault engines, in two forms, the EF4B, which was run in qualifying-boost tune, and the EF15, which was used in races. Both types of Renault engine were now fitted with Garrett AiResearch turbochargers in place of the KKKs.

Mansell had now left to drive for the Williams team and Lotus had signed on Ayrton Senna to drive alongside de Angelis. Although McLaren was to prove the dominant marque in 1985, Ferrari was very much in the running for the Drivers World Championship and Constructors' Cup for much of the season, and both the Williams FW10s with Honda power and the Lotus 97Ts were in strong contention for outright race victories for much of the year.

In all Senna was to take seven pole positions during the year and such was his skilful and forceful driving that he soon overshadowed his team-mate de Angelis, who, frustrated and despairing, slipped down the grid and further down the results as the season progressed. De Angelis finished third in the first race of the season in Brazil (Senna retired with electrical problems) and then Senna took his first ever pole position and won the Portuguese Grand Prix at Estoril in the wet. It was the first Team Lotus victory since Chapman's death. In this race de Angelis finished fourth. Senna was seventh after running out of fuel in the San Marino Grand Prix, but de Angelis scored his last and unexpected race victory after the winner on the road, Prost (McLaren), was disqualified because his car was found to be below the minimum weight limit at post-race

John Player Special Team Lotus raced the 97T in 1985, still with Renault power, and Ayrton Senna had joined the team in place of Nigel Mansell. Here Senna is seen at Detroit where he took pole position and led briefly. He retired because of engine trouble. *(Nigel Snowdon)*

Work on the 97Ts in the Lotus garage at Detroit. *(Nigel Snowdon)*

scrutineering. Another third place for de Angelis followed in the Monaco Grand Prix, but Senna, who had taken pole position, retired early with engine failure.

De Angelis and Senna took the first two places on the grid in Canada, but de Angelis could manage no better than fifth in the race, whilst Senna was classified 16th, after losing five laps in the pits, while lost turbo boost pressure was investigated and rectified. De Angelis finished fifth at Detroit, but Senna was eliminated; he crashed into a wall whilst trying to pass Alboreto's Ferrari. A fifth place for de Angelis followed in the French Grand Prix, but Senna was eliminated by engine failure. Senna completely dominated the British race until close to the finish, when he ran out of fuel, the result of a broken sensor in the Renault engine's electronic management system. Both Lotus drivers retired in the German Grand Prix, but then Senna finished second in Austria (with de Angelis fifth), third in Holland (de Angelis again fifth), third in Italy (de Angelis sixth), scored a brilliant victory at Spa-Francorchamps (de Angelis retired with engine trouble) and finished second in the European Grand Prix at Brands Hatch (de Angelis fifth). Both Lotus entries retired in the last two races of the season. Early in the year de Angelis had briefly led the World Championship, but Senna finally finished fourth in the Championship with de Angelis fifth and Lotus took fourth place in the Constructors' Cup. It was the best Lotus year for a very long time.

**Specification:**
ENGINE: Renault EF4B and EF15 (810 bhp).
GEARBOX: Lotus/Hewland DGB.
CHASSIS: carbon/Kevlar monocoque.
FRONT SUSPENSION: pull-rods, double wishbones and inboard coil spring/damper units.
REAR SUSPENSION: pull-rods, double wishbones and inboard coil spring/damper units.
WIDTH: 8ft 11in.
FRONT TRACK: 5ft 10.9in.
REAR TRACK: 5ft 3.7in.
WEIGHT: 10.63 cwt.

# 98T

## *Formula 1, 1986*

The 1986 Formula 1 Lotus featured a new method of construction for the monocoque. Whilst the carbon/Kevlar composite constructional method was retained, the monocoques were now integral mouldings (the system used by McLaren, Williams and Ferrari) instead of being based on flat sheet. As on the 96 and 97T, aluminium foil was used as a sandwich between the moulded composite skins. FISA had now introduced a 195-litre fuel restriction and so a smaller fuel tank was fitted, which reduced the height of the monocoque behind the cockpit. Pull-rod-operated suspension was retained front and rear, but the geometry was much revised.

Although Renault had withdrawn from racing themselves, they continued to supply and develop their turbocharged engines and the engines supplied to Lotus were built and prepared at Renault's research and development premises at Viry-Châtillon, whilst both Ligier and Tyrrell, also users of Renault engines, still had them supplied by the Mecachrome company at Bourges. Renault had now developed a much revised engine known as the EF15B or *Bis*. Apart from revised cylinder dimensions of 80.1mm x 49.4mm, this engine had been developed for economy with the new fuel restrictions very much in mind. The standard EF15B incorporated the usual valve springs, but the version known as the DP (*Distribution Pneumatique*) featured desmodromic mechanically closed valve gear, with gas closure of the valves from a compressed gas reservoir within the vee of the engine. This new system worked very well and throughout the season many of the EF15 *Bis* engines were converted to this form. The EF15 *Bis* engine was used for both qualifying and in the race, but for qualifying it ran with water injection and no wastegate.

Ayrton Senna with the 1986 98T at Monaco. He finished third behind the McLarens of Prost and Rosberg. He led the Championship in the early part of the year and eventually took fourth place behind Prost, Mansell and Piquet. *(Nigel Snowdon)*

Elio de Angelis left the team to drive for Brabham (and sadly was killed in a testing accident at the Paul Ricard circuit in May) and so the team leader was now Ayrton Senna, with Johnny Dumfries as number two. The year was to prove a battle for outright supremacy between the McLaren and Williams teams, and the Lotus 98T lacked sufficient speed in race trim and good enough fuel consumption to compete on even terms with the leading two teams. Nevertheless Senna turned in some stirring performances during the year and took pole position eight times, aided by a low ground clearance, high download qualifying device conceived by Ducarouge.

Senna finished second in Brazil, perilously low on fuel, but then sored a magnificent victory in the Spanish race from Mansell (Williams) and the two McLarens. At Imola Senna retired because of wheel bearing failure, he was third at Monaco, second in Belgium, fifth in Canada and brilliantly won the Detroit race on a street circuit which he disliked intensely. In the French race at the Paul Ricard circuit Senna slid off into a tyre barrier early in the race, he retired with gearbox problems at Brands Hatch, but bounced back to finish second in the German Grand Prix. Another second place followed in the latest addition to the Championship series,

the Hungarian Grand Prix, but he was eliminated by engine trouble in Austria and transmission failure in Italy. A fourth place by Senna followed in Portugal, he was third in Mexico and he retired in the last round of the Championship at Adelaide because of engine problems. He took fourth place in the World Championship.

Johnny Dumfries was too inexperienced in Formula 1 to achieve anything worthwhile during the year and his sole finish in the points was in the Australian Grand Prix, in which he took sixth place.

## Specification:
ENGINE: Renault EF15B or EF15C.
GEARBOX: Lotus/Hewland DGB.
CHASSIS: carbon/Kevlar monocoque.
FRONT SUSPENSION: pull-rods, double wishbones and coil spring/damper units.
REAR SUSPENSION: pull-rods, double wishbones and coil spring/damper units.
WHEELBASE: 8ft 11in.
FRONT TRACK: 5ft 10.9in.
REAR TRACK: 5ft 3.7in.
WEIGHT: 10.63cwt.

# 99T

## *Formula 1, 1987*

Although the 1987 Formula 1 Lotus was a development of the previous year's car, it was dramatically different. Lotus, whilst retaining the carbon/composite construction with aluminium honycomb filling, had now reverted to a much more refined form of the method of construction used prior to 1986 in that the monocoque was again made up from a folded single-sheet. Lotus had abandoned the Renault engine and the cars were now powered by the Honda turbocharged 80-degree V6, which was substantially more powerful than the French unit, but at the price of a serious and very harsh vibration which meant that the whole car had to be strengthened so it would withstand the shaking from the engine. Because of the very wide rev range of the Honda engine, Lotus developed a new 6-speed gearbox and final drive to fully exploit this.

Perhaps the most important change was the adoption of computer-controlled 'Active' suspension, which had long been under development at Lotus. The system was powered by an hydraulic pressure pump driven from a mechanical coupling at the rear of the left exhaust camshaft of the engine. The pressure fluid was distributed through pipes to each suspension corner. Electronically operated pressure-controlling valves controlled hydraulic actuators. Whilst a suspension system of pull-rods and double wishbones was used, the actuators were the sole suspension medium and there were no additional coil springs.

For 1987 John Player sponsorship was replaced by Camel and Ayrton Senna was joined in the team by Honda's nominee Satoru Nakajima. Although Lotus were well satisfied with the way that the new car performed, it never proved quite a match for the Williams team, whose cars were also Honda-powered.

After retiring in Brazil, Senna took pole position in practice for the San Marino Grand Prix and, worried by fuel consumption problems, was forced to settle for second place in the race behind Mansell's Williams. In the Belgian race Senna was eliminated in a collision with Mansell, but he scored another brilliant victory at Monaco, won again at Detroit and finished fourth in the French Grand Prix. The Brazilian finished third in the British Grand Prix, third again in the German race, and second in

For 1987 Lotus obtained the use of Honda V6 turbocharged engines and with new sponsorship became known as Camel Team Lotus Honda. Senna is seen at Monaco, where he had a fine – and unexpected – win with the improved 99T fitted with 'Active' suspension. *(Nigel Snowdon)*

In 1987 number two in the Lotus team, thanks to Honda money, was Japanese driver Satoru Nakajima. He is seen in the British Grand Prix in which he finished fourth, his best performance of the year. This photograph shows off the superb lines of the 99T. *(Nigel Snowdon)*

Hungary. At this last race the 99Ts appeared with much modified bodywork, incorporating a narrow and lower cockpit surround, together with lower side-pods. Senna finished fifth in Austria, a fine second in the Italian race, seventh in Portugal (after losing three laps in the pits because of a faulty throttle sensor), fifth in Spain, but retired in Mexico when he spun off after the clutch had failed and could not restart. In Japan Senna finished second and he again finished second on the road in the Australian Grand Prix, but he was disqualified at post-race scrutineering when his 99T was discovered to have brake ducts bigger than permitted under the regulations. In the World Championship Senna finished third with 57 points and Lotus were also third in the Constructors' Cup.

Nakajima held down his place in the Lotus team with reasonable competence, finishing sixth at Imola, fifth at Spa-Francorchamps, fourth at Silverstone and sixth in Japan.

In all six 99T chassis were built, three retained by the Works team, two retained by Team Lotus Research and Development and one which was despatched to Honda in Japan.

**Specification:**
ENGINE: Honda RA166-E and RA167-G 80-degree V6 turbocharged.
GEARBOX: Lotus/Hewland 6-speed.
CHASSIS: carbon/Kevlar monocoque.
FRONT SUSPENSION: computer-controlled, hydraulic pressure pump-powered 'Active', pull-rods and double wishbones.
REAR SUSPENSION: 'Active', pull-rods and double wishbones.
WHEELBASE: 8ft 11.5in.
FRONT TRACK: 5ft 10.5in.
REAR TRACK: 5ft 4.6in.
WEIGHT: 10.63 cwt.

# 100T

### *Formula 1, 1988*

After so much promise and success in 1987, Camel Team Lotus, now with World Champion Nelson Piquet leading the team, partnered by Nakajima, believed that they would be able to race on even terms with McLaren (also now using the Honda engine). However the year proved to be a complete disaster. Ducarouge had produced a development of the 1987 car, but with conventional suspension incorporating push-rods (Lotus wished to concentrate upon development of the 'Active' suspension for production cars); in other respects the 100T was very similar to its predecessor. Quite why the 100T should have been such an abysmal failure is far from clear, but it seems that the team may have been relying on wind tunnel data that was misleading and erroneous. As the year progressed, so Piquet's performances became increasingly lacklustre and dispirited.

At the start of the season Piquet and Nakajima finished third and sixth in the Brazilian Grand Prix, Piquet was third in the San Marino race, but Nakajima failed to qualify at Monaco, both cars retired in Mexico, Piquet was fourth in Canada and Nakajima again failed to qualify at Detroit, where Piquet was eliminated in an accident. A fifth for Piquet followed at the French race, fifth again in the British Grand Prix, sixth in the Belgian race and at the end of the year third place in Australia. It did not seem that Lotus fortunes could deteriorate further, but that was in fact to be the case in 1989.

### Specification:
ENGINE: Honda RA168-E turbocharged.
GEARBOX: Lotus/Hewland 6-speed.
CHASSIS: carbon/Kevlar monocoque.
FRONT SUSPENSION: push-rods, double wishbones and coil spring/damper units.
REAR SUSPENSION: push-rods, double wishbones and coil spring/damper units.
WHEELBASE: 9ft 1.3in.
FRONT TRACK: 5ft 10.8in.
REAR TRACK: 5ft 5in.
WEIGHT: 10.62 cwt.

Lotus continued to use Honda turbocharged engines in 1988, but with little success. Neither Nelson Piquet nor Nakajima could achieve much in the way of worthwhile results. Here in the Portuguese Grand Prix, Piquet, who retired because of clutch failure, leads Alboreto's Ferrari. *(Nigel Snowdon)*

# M100 Elan

*Production sports car, 1989 onwards*

As a result of the takeover of Lotus by General Motors, plans for a successor to the original Elan with Toyota engine were abandoned and work was put in hand on a completely new sports car to which the name Elan and project number M100 were given. To put the new car in production at the rate of 5000 units a year Lotus expended £35 million and the justification was that when the latest Elan appeared it gave the concept of the sports car a new dimension.

Powering the new car is the Lotus-developed Isuzu 1588cc unit available in normally aspirated or turbocharged forms. Front-wheel drive has been adopted, through a 5-speed trans-axle. There is a separate zinc-coated steel chassis with the body built up in mixed steel tube and box-sections with reinforced glass-fibre panels. At the front there is a patented suspension using an alloy sub-frame interwoven to the upper and lower wishbone mountings which provides very accurate wheel control and does much to eliminate road noise and vibration. Lotus use a more conventional system of wide-based lower wishbones, upper suspension arms, separate links down to the wishbones and coil spring/damper units at the rear. The styling is based on a smoothly curving wedge-shape with cut-off tail and more than a suggestion of the lines of the original Elan.

The basic model of the Elan with normally aspirated engine is priced at £17,850, while the SE version with turbocharged engine and power-assisted steering is priced at £19,850. Options include air conditioning (£980), metallic paint (£620) and leather trim (£780), whilst a detachable hard top was planned for the autumn of 1990. The claimed performance is: Maximum speed, 137 mph; 0–60 mph, 6.7 sec; standing quarter-mile, 15.4 sec. These figures of course relate to the turbocharged SE.

**Specification:**
ENGINE: Isuzu Lotus 4-cylinder, cast iron block, alloy head, 1588cc (80 x 79mm) turbocharged, electronic fuel injection and a power output of 165 bhp at 6600 rpm.
GEARBOX: 5-speed, front-wheel drive.
CHASSIS: zinc-coated steel with body built up in multiple sections of mixed steel tube and box-sections with reinforced glass-fibre panels and VARI moulding floor.
FRONT SUSPENSION: raft alloy sub-frames, double wishbones and coil spring/damper units.
REAR SUSPENSION: wide-based lower wishbones, single upper suspension arms, separate links to wishbones and coil spring/damper units.
WHEELBASE: 7ft 4.6in.
FRONT TRACK: 4ft 10.5in.
REAR TRACK: 4ft 10.5in.
LENGTH (Europe): 12ft 5.7in.
HEIGHT (hood up): 4ft 0.5in.
WEIGHT: 20.08 cwt.

The new Isuzu-powered Elan that Lotus announced in 1989 brought the company back into the sports car market and looks set to sell all that Lotus can make.

# 101

## *Formula 1, 1989*

With the departure of Gérard Ducarouge, at the end of 1988, Frank Dernie, formerly aerodynamacist at Williams, joined Lotus and had very little time indeed to prepare a new car for the 1989 season. With the end of the 1500cc turbocharged category, Honda withdrew its supply of engines from Lotus and so Lotus decided to use the Judd CV 90-degree V8 on a customer basis (Judd's main efforts were concentrated on his EV V8 for the March team). There were plans to use the Tickford cylinder heads with 5 valves per cylinder, but these proved disappointing in testing and were not raced. Dernie followed the usual Lotus principles, but produced a longer-wheelbase car, with 'waisted' front monocoque, widening out towards the cockpit, tall cockpit and apparently good aerodynamics. The drivers remained Piquet and Nakajima.

In the early races of the season the 101s were appallingly unsuccessful and Piquet was even more dispirited than in 1988. It was not until the Canadian race, the sixth round of the Championship, that Lotus managed to finish in the points and on the Île Notre Dame circuit Piquet finished fourth. Another fourth by Piquet

followed in the British Grand Prix. A week after that it was announced by Team Lotus International that Team director Peter Warr was leaving. Chairman Fred Bushell also left, facing fraud charges arising from the De Lorean programme and Tony Rudd joined the team from Group Lotus to act as Executive Chairman. In the German Grand Prix Piquet finished fifth, he was sixth in Hungary and then absolute disaster for the team followed at the Belgian Grand Prix, where neither Piquet nor Nakajima was able to qualify. During the remainder of the season's races the only finishes in the points were a fourth by Piquet in Japan and fourth by Nakajima in the rain-soaked Australian race.

**Specification:**
ENGINE: Judd CV 90-degree V8 3496cc developing 610 bhp at 11,000 rpm.
GEARBOX: Lotus/Hewland 6-speed.
CHASSIS: carbon/Kevlar monocoque.
FRONT SUSPENSION: pull-rods, double wishbones and coil spring/damper units.
REAR SUSPENSION: pull-rods, double wishbones and coil spring/damper units.
WHEELBASE: 9ft 6in.
FRONT TRACK: 5ft 11in.
REAR TRACK: 5ft 6in.
WEIGHT: 9.84 cwt approx.

Camel continued to support Lotus in 1989, but it was a hopeless year. The 1989 car was the 101 powered by the Judd CV8 engine. Piquet is seen in the British Grand Prix in which he finished fourth. *(Nigel Snowdon)*

# 102

*Formula 1, 1990*

Announced to the press in February 1990, the latest Formula 1 contender from Team Lotus, the 102, was in the words of the team's technical director, Frank Dernie, '...to a large exent an evolutionary progression on last year's car. We've tried to keep the strong points of the 101 and delete the weak ones.' The most important change was the adoption of the Lamborghini V12 80-degree 3493cc (85 x 51.3mm) Tipo 3512 engine. In 1989 claimed power output was 600 plus bhp at 13,000 rpm, but no updated figures for the 1990 engine were available at the time of going to press.

Although power output of the Lamborghini engine was higher than that of the Judd V8 used in 1989, it was also heavier, longer, less economical and needed more efficient aerodynamic arrangements. Accordingly the engine was set lower in the chassis, and there were improved aerodynamics with improved air flow to the rear wing. Another important change was a new 6-speed gearbox with Lamborghini gears in a Lotus casing.

There were larger fuel tanks, extending outwards behind the driver to the full width permitted by the regulations. Front and rear suspension, pull-rod at the front and push-rod at the rear, were developed from the 1989 101. Because both 1990 drivers, Derek Warwick and Martin Donnelly, were taller than their 1989 predecessors, the car was slightly higher and the driver sat more upright.

Still retaining Camel sponsorship, Team Lotus were hoping to finish not lower than fourth in the 1990 World Championship, but with such major opposition to face and without top-line drivers, Lotus's prospects of real success were slim.

For 1990 Lotus switched to Lamborghini V12 power, but in the early races of the season they showed little sign of being competitive. This is Derek Warwick, who retired early in the Phoenix Grand Prix because of suspension failure. *(Nigel Snowdon)*

# M104 Lotus Carlton/Omega

*Production saloon, 1990 onwards*

Lotus-developed and finished version of the Vauxhall Carlton and Opel Omega 4-door saloons with 3.6-litre, 24-valve twin turbo straight-six engine based on General Motor's 3-litre engine with cast iron block. Power output is 360 bhp at 5800 rpm. There is a 6-speed gearbox (as used in Chevrolet Corvettes) and much-modified suspension. The performance is believed to encompass a maximum speed of 165 mph with acceleration from 0–60 mph in under 6 seconds. The price is estimated at £35,000 and it was planned that Lotus would build a run of 1100 at Hethel in 1990.

# Appendix ▬▬▬▬▬▬▬▬▬

## Lotus Formula 1 Results, 1958–89

NC indicates non-World Championship race

### 1958

**International Trophy Race, Silverstone, 3 May, 146 miles NC**
8th, G. Hill (12-Climax 1.96-litre, 353), 1 lap in arrears

**Monaco Grand Prix, Monte Carlo, 18 May, 195 miles**
Not classified, C. Allison (12-Climax l.9-litre, 357), 13 laps in arrears
Retired, G. Hill (12-Climax l.9-litre, 353), engine failure

**Dutch Grand Prix, Zandvoort, 26 May, 195 miles**
6th, C. Allison (12-Climax 2.2-litre, 357), 2 laps in arrears
Retired, G. Hill (12-Climax 1.9-litre,353), gasket failure

**Belgian Grand Prix, Spa-Francorchamps, 15 June, 210 miles**
4th, C. Allison (12-Climax 2.2-litre, 357)
Retired, G. Hill (12-Climax 1.9-litre, 353), engine

**French Grand Prix, Reims, 7 July, 258 miles**
Retired, C. Allison (12-Climax 2.2-litre, 357), engine
Retired, G. Hill (16-Climax, 1.9-litre, 363), engine

**British Grand Prix, Silverstone, 20 July, 220 miles**
Retired, G. Hill (16-Climax 1.9-litre, 362), overheating
Retired, A. Stacey (16-Climax 1.9-litre, 363), overheating
Retired, C. Allison (12-Climax 2.2-litre, 357), engine bearings

**German Grand Prix, Nürburgring, 3 August, 212 miles**
10th (5th in Formula 1 category), C. Allison (16-Climax 1.9-litre), 2 laps in arrears

**Portuguese Grand Prix, Oporto, 24 August, 230 miles**
Retired, G. Hill (16-Climax 2.2-litre, 363), accident
Did Not Start, C. Allison (16-Climax l.9-litre, 362), practice accident

**Italian Grand Prix, Monza, 7 September, 250 miles**
Not classified, G. Hill (16-Climax 2.2-litre), 8 laps in arrears
Not classified, C. Allison (12-Climax 1.5-litre), 9 laps in arrears

**Moroccan Grand Prix, Ain-Diab, 19 October, 262 miles**
10th, C. Allison (12-Climax l.9-litre, 357), 4 laps in arrears
Not classified, G. Hill (16-Climax l.9-litre, 363), 8 laps in arrears

Drivers' World Championship:    13th=, C. Allison, 3 points
    16th=, G. Hill, 2 points

Manufacturers' World Championship: 6th, Lotus, 5 points

### 1959

**Richmond Tropy, Goodwood, 30 March, 101 miles NC**
Retired, G. Hill (16-Climax*, 363), brakes

**Aintree 200 race, Aintree, 18 April, 201 miles NC**
11th (5th in Formula 1 category), G. Hill (16-Climax, 368) 6 laps in arrears

**International Trophy race, Silverstone, 2 May, 146 miles NC**
Not classified, P. Lovely (16-Climax 2.2-litre, 368), 6 laps in arrears
Retired, G. Hill (16-Climax, 364), broken brake pipe

**Monaco Grand Prix, Monte Carlo, 10 May, 195 miles**
Retired, G. Hill (16-Climax, 368), fire
Did Not Qualify, P. Lovely (16-Climax, 364)

**Dutch Grand Prix, Zandvoort, 31 May, 195 miles**
4th, I. Ireland (16-Climax, 364), 1 lap in arrears
7th, G. Hill (16-Climax, 368), 2 laps in arrears

**French Grand Prix, Reims, 5 July, 258 miles**
Retired, G. Hill (16-Climax, 364), holed radiator
Retired, I. Ireland (16-Climax, 365), wheel bearing failure

**British Grand Prix, Aintree, 18 July, 225 miles**
8th, A. Stacey (16-Climax, 364), 4 laps in arrears
9th, G. Hill (16-Climax, 365), 5 laps in arrears

**German Grand Prix, Avus, 2 August, 309 miles (aggregate of two heats)**
Retired, G. Hill (16-Climax, 365), oil radiator
Retired, I. Ireland (16-Climax, 364), gear selectors

**Portuguese Grand Prix, Monsanto, 23 August, 207 miles**
Retired, I. Ireland (16-Climax, 364), gearbox
Retired, G. Hill (16-Climax, 365), accident

**Italian Grand Prix, Monza, 13 September, 257 miles**
Retired, G. Hill (16-Climax, 368), engine failure
Retired, I. Ireland (16-Climax, 364), brakes

**International Gold Cup, Oulton Park, 26 September, 152 miles NC**
5th, G. Hill (16-Climax, 368), 3 laps in arrears

**Silver City Trophy, Snetterton, 10 October, 68 miles NC**
Retired, G. Hill (16-Climax, 368), drive-shaft
Retired, I. Ireland (16-Climax, 364), anti-roll bar

**United States Grand Prix, Sebring, 12 December, 218 miles**
5th, I. Ireland (16-Climax, 365), 3 laps in arrears
Retired, A. Stacey (16-Climax, 364), clutch

* 2.5-litre unless otherwise indicated.

Drivers' World Championship:    10th=, I. Ireland, 5 points

Manufacturers' World Championship: 4th, Lotus, 5 points

# 1960

**Argentine Grand Prix, Buenos Aires Autodrome, 7 February, 194 miles**
6th, I. Ireland (18-Climax, 369), 1 lap in arrears
9th, R. Larreta (16-Climax, 365), 3 laps in arrears
Retired, A. Stacey (16-Climax, 364), engine

**Buenos Aires City Grand Prix, Cordoba, 14 February, 149 miles NC**
Retired, I. Ireland (16-Climax, 364), transmission
Retired, A. Stacey/I. Ireland (16-Climax, 365), transmission

**Richmond Trophy, Goodwood, 18 April, 101 miles NC**
1st, I. Ireland (18-Climax, 371), 100.39 mph
Retired, A. Stacey (18-Climax, 369), reason not known

**International Trophy, Silverstone, 14 May, 146 miles NC**
1st, I. Ireland (18-Climax, 371), 108.82 mph
4th, A. Stacey (18-Climax, 370), 1 lap in arrears

**Monaco Grand Prix, Monte Carlo, 29 May, 195 miles**
1st, S. Moss (18-Climax, 376), 67.46 mph*
Not classified, I. Ireland (18-Climax, 371), 44 laps in arrears
Retired, A. Stacey (18-Climax, 370), damaged suspension
Retired, J. Surtees (18-Climax, 373), gearbox

**Dutch Grand Prix, Zandvoort, 6 June, 195 miles**
2nd, Ireland (18-Climax, 371)
4th, S. Moss (18-Climax, 376)
Retired, A. Stacey (18-Climax, 370), final drive

**Belgian Grand Prix, Spa-Francorchamps, 19 June, 315 miles**
5th, J. Clark (18-Climax, 373), 2 laps in arrears
Retired, Ireland (18-Climax, 371), spun off
Retired, A. Stacey (18-Climax, 370), fatal crash

**French Grand Prix, Reims, 3 July, 258 miles**
5th, J. Clark (18-Climax, 373), 1 lap in arrears
6th, R. Flockhart (18-Climax, 374), 1 lap in arrears
7th, I. Ireland (18-Climax, 371), 7 laps in arrears

**British Grand Prix, Silverstone, 16 July, 225 miles**
2nd, J. Surtees (18-Climax, 373)
3rd, I. Ireland (18-Climax, 371)
16th, J. Clark (18-Climax, 374), 7 laps in arrears

**Silver City Trophy, Brands Hatch, 1 August, 133 miles NC**
6th, J. Surtees (18-Climax, 373), 1 lap in arrears
Retired, J. Clark (18-Climax, 374), gearbox
Retired, I. Ireland (18-Climax, 371), oil pressure/handling

**Portuguese Grand Prix, Oporto, 14 August, 253 miles**
3rd, J. Clark (18-Climax, 374)
6th, I. Ireland (18-Climax, 371), 2 laps in arrears
Retired, J. Surtees (18-Climax, 373), split radiator
Disqualified, S. Moss (18-Climax, 376)*

**Lombank Trophy, Snetterton, 17 September, 100 miles NC**
1st, I. Ireland (18-Climax, 372), 102.73 mph
2nd, J. Clark (18-Climax, 374)
Retired, J. Surtees (18-Climax, 373), engine

**Gold Cup, Oulton Park, 24 September, 166 miles NC**
1st, S. Moss (18-Climax, 376), 91.11 mph*
Retired, I. Ireland (18-Climax, 372), gearbox
Retired, J. Clark (18-Climax, 374), accident
Retired, J. Surtees (18-Climax, 373), fuel pump failure

**Watkins Glen Formule Libre Grand Prix, 9 October, 230 miles NC**
1st, S. Moss (18-Climax, 376), 105.80 mph*

**United States Grand Prix, Riverside Raceway, 20 November, 246 miles**
1st, S. Moss (18-Climax, 376), 103.17 mph*
2nd, I. Ireland (18-Climax, 372)
16th, J. Clark (18-Climax, 371), 14 laps in arrears
Retired, J. Surtees (18-Climax, 373), accident

*R.R.C. Walker entry

| | |
|---|---|
| Drivers' World Championship: | 3rd S. Moss, 19 points |
| | 4th, I. Ireland, 18 points |
| | 7th=, J. Clark, 8 points |
| | 9th=, J. Surtees, 6 points |
| | 13th=, R. Flockhart, 1 point |
| Constructors' Cup: | 2nd Lotus-Climax, 32 points |

# 1961 (Formula 1, except where indicated)

**Lombank Trophy, Snetterton, 26 March, 100 miles (Formula 1 and InterContinental) NC**
6th, J. Clark (18-Climax Fl, 371), 2 laps in arrears
Retired, I. Ireland (18-Climax, IC, 374), gearbox

**Richmond Trophy, Goodwood, 3 April, 100 miles NC**
4th, S. Moss (18-Climax, 912)*
5th, I. Ireland (18-Climax, 372), 1 lap in arrears

**Pau Grand Prix, Pau, 3 April, 171 miles NC**
1st, J. Clark (18-Climax, 371), 63.50 mph
9th, T. Taylor (18-Climax, 374), 9 laps in arrears, not running at the finish

**Brussels Grand Prix, Heysel, 9 April, 3 heats totalling 187 miles NC**
6th, I. Ireland (18-Climax, 371)
7th, S. Moss (18-Climax, 906)*
Retired, J. Clark (18-Climax, 374), gearbox

**Vienna Grand Prix, Aspern, 16 April, 100 miles NC**
1st, S. Moss (18-Climax, 906), 85.67 mph*

**Aintree 200, Aintree, 22 April, 150 miles NC**
9th, J. Clark (18-Climax, 372), 2 laps in arrears
10th, I. Ireland (18-Climax, 371), 2 laps in arrears
19th, T. Taylor (18-Climax, 374), 9 laps in arrears

**Syracuse Grand Prix, Siracusa, 25 April, 195 miles NC**
6th, J. Clark (18-Climax, 374), 3 laps in arrears
8th, S. Moss (18-Climax, 906), 4 laps in arrears*
Retired, I. Ireland (18-Climax, 371), accident

**International Trophy, Silverstone, 6 May,
234 (InterContinental) NC**
12th, I. Ireland (18-Climax, 371), 20 laps in arrears
Retired, J. Clark (18-Climax, 374), engine

**Monaco Grand Prix, Monte Carlo, 14 May,
195 miles**
1st, S. Moss (18-Climax, 912), 70.70 mph*
10th, J. Clark (21-Climax, 930), 11 laps in arrears

**Dutch Grand Prix, Zandvoort, 22 May, 197 miles**
3rd, J. Clark (21-Climax, 930)
4th, S. Moss (18-Climax, 912)*
13th, T. Taylor (18-Climax, 371), 2 laps in arrears

**Silver City Trophy, Brands Hatch, 3 June,
201 miles NC**
1st, S. Moss (18/21-Climax, 918), 91.78 mph+
2nd, J. Clark (21-Climax, 930)
9th, T. Taylor (18-Climax, 371), 7 laps in arrears

**Belgian Grand Prix, Spa-Francorchamps,
18 June, 263 miles**
8th, S. Moss (18/21-Climax, 912)*
12th, J. Clark (21-Climax, 932), 6 laps in arrears
Retired, I. Ireland (21-Climax, 933), engine

**French Grand Prix, Reims, 2 July, 268 miles**
3rd, J. Clark (21-Climax, 932)
4th, I. Ireland (21-Climax, 933)
Retired, S. Moss (18/21-Climax, 912), brake pipe*

**British Empire Trophy, Silverstone, 8 July,
152 miles (InterContinental) NC**
5th, J. Clark (18-Climax, 372), 2 laps in arrears
9th, I. Ireland (18-Climax, 371), 2 laps in arrears

**British Grand Prix, Aintree, 15 July, 225 miles**
10th, I. Ireland (21-Climax, 933), 3 laps in arrears
Retired, J. Clark (21-Climax, 932), oil gauge pipe
Retired, S. Moss (18/21-Climax, 912), brake pipe*

**Solitude Grand Prix, Solitude, 23 July, 177 miles
NC**
1st, I. Ireland (21-Climax, 933), 105.20 mph
7th, J. Clark (21-Climax, 932)
9th, T. Taylor (21-Climax, 930)
Retired, S. Moss (18/21-Climax, 917), gearbox+

**German Grand Prix, Nürburgring, 6 August,
213 miles**
1st, S. Moss (18/21-Climax, 912), 92.34 mph*
4th, J. Clark (21-Climax, 930)
Retired, I. Ireland (21-Climax, 933), fire

**Guards Trophy, Brands Hatch, 7 August, 201 miles
NC**
2nd, J. Clark (18-Climax, 372)
Retired, I. Ireland (18-Climax, 371), gearbox

**Kanonloppet, Karlskoga, 20 August, 56 miles NC**
1st, S. Moss (18/21-Climax, 918), 69.26 mph+
Retired, I. Ireland (18-Climax, 371), engine mountings
Retired, J. Clark (21-Climax, 930), wishbone and oil tank

**Danish Grand Prix, Roskildering, 26/27 August,
3 heats totalling 59 miles**
1st, S. Moss (18/21-Climax, 916), 60.18 mph+
2nd, I. Ireland (21-Climax, 930)
7th, J. Clark (18-Climax, 371), 10 laps in arrears

**Modena Grand Prix, Modena, 3 September,
147 miles NC**
1st, S. Moss (18/21-Climax, 912), 88.08 mph*
4th, J. Clark (21-Climax, 933), 1 lap in arrears

**Italian Grand Prix, Monza, 10 September,
267 miles**
Retired, J. Clark (21-Climax, 934), collision with von Trips
Retired, I. Ireland (18/21-Climax, 912), chassis frame
Retired, S. Moss (21-Climax, 933), wheel bearings*

**Flugplatzrennen, Zeltweg, 17 September,
159 miles NC**
1st, I. Ireland (21-Climax, 933), 91.45 mph
4th, J. Clark (21-Climax, 930), 3 laps in arrears

**Gold Cup, Oulton Park, 23 September,
166 miles NC**
Retired, I. Ireland (21-Climax, 933), engine
Retired, J. Clark (21-Climax, 930), rear suspension
Retired, T. Taylor (18-Climax, 371), exhaust pipe

**United States Grand Prix, Watkins Glen,
8 October, 230 miles**
1st, I. Ireland (21-Climax, 933), 103.22 mph
7th, J. Clark (21-Climax, 930), 4 laps in arrears
Retired, S. Moss (18/21-Climax, 912), engine*

**Rand Grand Prix, Kyalami, 9 December,
191 miles NC**
1st, J. Clark (21-Climax, 937), 90.551 mph
2nd, T. Taylor (21-Climax, 933)

**Natal Grand Prix, Westmead, 17 December,
200 miles NC**
1st, J. Clark (21-Climax, 937), 89.59 mph
2nd, S. Moss (18/21-Climax, 918)+
Retired, T. Taylor (21-Climax, 933), accident

**South African Grand Prix, East London,
26 December, 195 miles NC**
1st, J. Clark (21-Climax, 937), 92.20 mph
2nd, S. Moss (18/21-Climax, 918)+
Retired, T. Taylor (21-Climax, 933), radiator

*R.R.C. Walker entry
+U.D.T.-Laystall entry

Drivers' World Championship:   3rd=, S. Moss, 21 points
6th, I. Ireland, 12 points
7th=, J. Clark, 11 points

Constructors' Cup: 2nd, Lotus-Climax, 32 points

# 1962

**Cape Grand Prix, Killarney, 2 January, 123 miles NC**
1st, T. Taylor 21-Climax, 933), 81.50 mph
2nd, J. Clark (21-Climax, 937)

**Lombank Trophy, Snetterton, 14 April, 136 miles NC**
1st, J. Clark, (24-Climax, 948), 101.09 mph
Retired, T. Taylor (21-Climax, 938), engine

**Pau Grand Prix, Pau, 23 April, 171 miles NC**
1st, M. Trintignant (18/21-Climax, 918), 64.48 mph*
11th, T. Taylor (24-Climax, 950), 8 laps in arrears
Retired, J. Clark (24-Climax, 948), gearchange linkage

**Aintree 200, Aintree, 28 April, 150 miles NC**
1st, J. Clark (24-Climax, 948), 92.65 mph
5th, T. Taylor (24-Climax, 950), 1 lap in arrears

**International Trophy, Silverstone, 12 May, 152 miles NC**
2nd, J. Clark (24-Climax, 948)
10th, T. Taylor (24-Climax, 950), 2 laps in arrears

**Dutch Grand Prix, Zandvoort, 20 May, 208 miles**
2nd, T. Taylor (24-Climax, 948)
9th, J. Clark (25-Climax, R1), 10 laps in arrears

**Monaco Grand Prix, Monte Carlo, 3 June, 195 miles**
Retired, J. Clark (25-Climax, R1), clutch
Retired, T. Taylor (24-Climax, 948), oil leak

**International 2000 Guineas, Mallory Park, 11 June, 101 miles NC**
Retired, J. Clark (25-Climax, Rl), oil pressure

**Belgian Grand Prix, Spa-Francorchamps, 17 June, 280 miles**
1st, J. Clark (25-Climax, Rl), 131.89 mph
Retired, T. Taylor (24-Climax, 948), accident

**Reims Grand Prix, Reims, 1 July, 258 miles NC**
Retired, T. Taylor (24-Climax, 949), accident
Retired, J. Clark (25-Climax, Rl), header tank
Retired, P. Arundell/J. Clark (24-BRM, 950), ran out of fuel

**French Grand Prix, Rouen-les-Essarts, 8 July, 221 miles**
8th, T. Taylor (25-Climax, Rl), 6 laps in arrears
Retired, J. Clark (25-Climax, R2), front suspension

**Solitude Grand Prix, Solitude, 15 July, 177 miles NC**
3rd, T. Taylor (24-Climax, 949)
Retired, J. Clark (25-Climax, R1), accident

**British Grand Prix, Aintree, 21 July, 225 miles**
1st, J. Clark (25-Climax, R2), 92.25 mph
8th, T. Taylor (24-Climax, 949), 1 lap in arrears

**German Grand Prix, Nürburgring, 5 August, 213 miles**
4th, J. Clark (25-Climax, R2)
Retired, T. Taylor (24-Climax, 949), accident

**Gold Cup, Oulton Park, 1 September, 201 miles NC**
1st, J. Clark (25-Climax, R2), 97.70 mph
Retired, T. Taylor (25-Climax, R3), gear selectors

**Italian Grand Prix, Monza, 16 September, 307 miles**
Retired, J. Clark (25-Climax, R3), gearbox
Retired, T. Taylor (25-Climax, R2), gearbox

**United States Grand Prix, Watkins Glen, 7 October, 230 miles**
1st, J. Clark (25-Climax, R3), 108.61 mph
12th, T. Taylor (25-Climax, R2), 15 laps in arrears

**Mexican Grand Prix, Magdalena Mixhuca, 4 November, 186 miles NC**
1st, T. Taylor/J. Clark (25-Climax, R2), 90.31 mph
Disqualified, J. Clark (25-Climax, R3), push-start

**Rand Grand Prix, Kyalami, 15 December, 127 miles NC**
1st, J. Clark (25-Climax, R3), 95.70 mph
2nd, T. Taylor (25-Climax, R2)

**Natal Grand Prix, Westmead, 22 December, two 50-mile heats and 75-mile final NC**
1st, T. Taylor (25-Climax, R2), 92.47 mph (speed in final)
2nd, J. Clark (25-Climax, R3)

**South African Grand Prix, East London, 29 December, 200 miles**
Retired, J. Clark (25-Climax, R5), oil leak
Retired, T. Taylor (25-Climax, R2), gearbox

*R.R.C. Walker entry

Drivers' World Championship: 2nd, J. Clark 30 points
10th, T. Taylor 6 points

Constructors' Cup: 2nd, Lotus-Climax, 36 points

# 1963

**Lombank Trophy, Snetterton, 30 March, 136 miles NC**
2nd, J. Clark (25-Climax, R3)

**Pau Grand Prix, Pau, 15 April, 171 miles NC**
1st, J. Clark (25-Climax, R5), 61.62 mph
2nd, T. Taylor (25-Climax, R3)

**Imola Grand Prix, Castellaccis, 21 April, 156 miles NC**
1st, J. Clark (25-Climax, R5), 99.36 mph
9th, T. Taylor (25-Climax, R3), 14 laps in arrears

**Syracuse Grand Prix, Siracusa, 25 April, 195 miles NC**
1st, J. Siffert (24-BRM, 950), 90.77 mph*

**Aintree 200, Aintree, 27 April, 150 miles NC**
3rd, T. Taylor/J. Clark (25-Climax, R3)
7th, J. Clark/T. Taylor (25-Climax, R5), 3 laps in arrears

**International Trophy, Silverstone, 11 May, 152 miles NC**
1st, J. Clark (25-Climax, R5), 108.12 mph
3rd, T. Taylor (25-Climax, R3)

**Monaco Grand Prix, Monte Carlo, 26 May,
195 miles**
6th, T. Taylor (25-Climax, R5) 2 laps in arrears
8th, J. Clark (25-Climax, R4), 12 laps in arrears, not running
at the finish, gear-selectors

**Belgian Grand Prix, Spa-Francorchamps, 9 June,
280 miles**
1st, J. Clark (25-Climax, R4), 114.11 mph
Retired, T. Taylor (25-Climax, R3), driver unwell following
practice accident

**Dutch Grand Prix, Zandvoort, 23 June, 208 miles**
1st, J. Clark (25-Climax, R4), 97.53 mph
10th, T. Taylor (25-Climax, R2), 14 laps in arrears

**French Grand Prix, Reims, 30 June, 273 miles**
1st, J. Clark (25-Climax, R4), 125.01 mph
13th, T. Taylor (25-Climax, R2), 12 laps in arrears, not
running at the finish, rear axle

**British Grand Prix, Silverstone, 20 July, 240 miles**
1st, J. Clark (25-Climax, R4), 107.75 mph
Retired, T. Taylor (25-Climax, R2), fuel pump

**Solitude Grand Prix, Solitude, 28 July,
177 miles NC**
2nd, P. Arundell (25-Climax, R2)
Not classified, J. Clark (25-Climax, R4), 17 laps completed out
of 25 after drive-shafts changed at start
Retired, T. Taylor (25-Climax, R3), final drive

**German Grand Prix, Nürburgring, 4 August,
213 miles**
2nd, J. Clark (25-Climax, R4)
8th, T. Taylor (25-Climax, R2)

**Kanonloppet, Karlskoga, 11 August,
aggregate of two heats, 75 miles NC**
1st, J. Clark (25-Climax, R3), 68.80 mph
2nd, T. Taylor (25-Climax, R2)

**Mediterranean Grand Prix, Pergusa, 18 August,
179 miles NC**
2nd, P. Arundell (25-Climax, R3)
Retired, T. Taylor (25-Climax, R2), accident

**Austrian Grand Prix, Zeltweg, 1 September,
158 miles NC**

Retired, J. Clark (25-Climax, R6), oil pipe

**Italian Grand Prix, Monza, 8 September,
307 miles**
1st, J. Clark (25-Climax, R4), 127.74 mph
13th, M. Spence (25-Climax, R3), 13 laps in arrears, not
running at the finish, oil pressure

**Gold Cup, Oulton Park, 21 September,
201 miles NC**
1st, J. Clark (25-Climax, R4), 98.34 mph
Retired, T. Taylor (25-Climax, R6), final drive

**United States Grand Prix, Watkins Glen,
6 October, 253 miles**
3rd, J. Clark (25-Climax, R4), 1 lap in arrears
Retired, T. Taylor (25-Climax, R6), electrics
Retired, P. Rodriguez (25-Climax, R3), engine

**Mexican Grand Prix, Magdalena Mixhuca,
27 October, 202 miles**
1st, J. Clark (25-Climax, R4), 93.28 mph
Retired, T. Taylor (25-Climax, R6), engine
Retired, P. Rodriguez (25-Climax, R3), rear suspension

**Rand Grand Prix, Kyalami, 14 December,
aggregate of two heats, 127 miles NC**
10th, T. Taylor (25-Climax, R7), 4 laps in arrears
16th, J. Clark (25-Climax, R4), 7 laps in arrears

**South African Grand Prix, East London,
28 December, 207 miles**
1st, J. Clark (25-Climax, R4), 95.10 mph
8th, T. Taylor (25-Climax, R7), 4 laps in arrears

*Entered by Scuderia Filipinetti

Drivers' World Championship:      1st, J. Clark, 54 points
     16th, T. Taylor, 1 point

Constructors' Cup:      1st, Lotus-Climax, 54 points

# 1964

***Daily Mirror* Trophy, Snetterton, 14 March,
95 miles NC**
Retired, J. Clark, (25-Climax, R6), ignition
Retired, P. Arundell (25-Climax, R4), gearbox

***News of the World* Trophy, Goodwood, 30 March,
101 miles NC**
1st, J. Clark (25-Climax, R6), 104.91 mph
2nd, P. Arundell (25-Climax, R4)

**Syracuse Grand Prix, Siracusa, 12 April,
139 miles NC**
3rd, M. Spence/P. Arundell (25-Climax, R4)
Retired, P. Arundell/M. Spence (25-Climax, R6), gearbox

**Aintree 200, Aintree, 18 April, 201 miles NC**
3rd, P. Arundell (25-Climax, R6)
Retired, J. Clark (33-Climax, R8), accident

**International Trophy, Silverstone, 2 May,
152 miles NC**
3rd, P. Arundell (25-Climax, R4)
Retired, J. Clark (25-Climax, R6), engine

**Monaco Grand Prix, Monte Carlo, 10 May,
195 miles**
3rd, P. Arundell (25-Climax, R4), 3 laps in arrears
4th, J. Clark (25-Climax, R6), 4 laps in arrears, not running at
the finish, seized engine

**Dutch Grand Prix, Zandvoort, 24 May, 208 miles**
1st, J. Clark (25-Climax, R6), 98.02 mph
3rd, P. Arundell (25-Climax, R4), 1 lap in arrears

**Belgian Grand Prix, Spa-Francorchamps,
14 June, 280 miles**
1st, J. Clark (25-Climax, R6), 132.79 mph
9th, P. Arundell (25-Climax, R4), 4 laps in arrears

**French Grand Prix, Rouen-les-Essarts, 28 June,
232 miles**
4th, P. Arundell (25-Climax, R4)
Retired, J. Clark (25-Climax, R6), piston failure

**British Grand Prix, Brands Hatch, 11 July, 212 miles**

1st, J. Clark (25-Climax, R6), 94.14 mph

9th, M. Spence (25-Climax, R4), 3 laps in arrears

**Solitude Grand Prix, Solitude, 19 July, 142 miles NC**

1st, J. Clark (33-Climax, R8), 91.50 mph
Retired, G. Mitter (24-Climax, R4), accident
Retired, M. Spence (24-Climax, R6), accident caused by broken steering arm

**German Grand Prix, Nürburgring, 2 August, 213 miles**

8th, M. Spence (33-Climax, R8), 1 lap in arrears
9th, G. Mitter (25-Climax, R6), 1 lap in arrears
Retired, J. Clark (33-Climax, R9), valve gear

**Mediterranean Grand Prix, Pergusa, 16 August, 179 miles NC**

2nd, J. Clark (25-Climax, R6)
5th, M. Spence (25-Climax, R4), 2 laps in arrears

**Austrian Grand Prix, Zeltweg, 23 August, 209 miles NC**

Retired, J. Clark (33-Climax, R9), drive-shaft failure
Retired, M. Spence (33-Climax, R8), drive-shaft failure

**Italian Grand Prix, Monza, 6 September, 279 miles**

6th, M. Spence (33-Climax, R8), 1 lap in arrears
Retired, J. Clark (25-Climax, R6), piston failure

**United States Grand Prix, Watkins Glen, 4 October, 253 miles**

5th, W. Hansgen (33-Climax, R8), 3 laps in arrears
7th, M. Spence/J. Clark (33-Climax, R9), 8 laps in arrears, not runnng at the finish, fuel starvation
Retired, J. Clark/M. Spence (25-Climax, R6), fuel injection

**Mexican Grand Prix, Magdalena Mixhuca, 25 October, 202 miles**

4th, M. Spence (25-Climax, R6)
5th, J. Clark (33-Climax, R9), 1 lap in arrears, not running, at the finish, seized engine
10th, M. Solana (33-Climax, R8), 2 laps in arrears

**Rand Grand Prix, Kyalami, 12 December, aggregate of two heats, 127 miles NC**

16th, M. Spence (33-Climax, R9), 24 laps in arrears, not running at the finish, rose-joint failure in heat 2
17th, J. Stewart (33-Climax, R10), 25 laps in arrears, drive-shaft failure at start of heat 1, won heat 2

Drivers' World Championship:  3rd, J. Clark, 32 points
8th=, P. Arundell, 11 points
12th=, M. Spence, 4 points
16th=, W. Hansgen, 2 points

Constructors' Cup:  3rd, Lotus-Climax, 37 points

# 1965

**South African Grand Prix, East London, 1 January, 207 miles**
1st, J. Clark (33-Climax, R10), 97.97 mph
4th, M. Spence (33-Climax, R9)

**Race of Champions, Brands Hatch, 13 March, aggregate of two heats, 212 miles NC**
1st, M. Spence (33-Climax, R9), 96.58 mph
Retired, J. Clark (33-Climax, R10), accident

**Syracuse Grand Prix, Siracusa, 4 April, 195 miles NC**
1st, J. Clark (33-Climax, R11), 110.60 mph
Retired, M. Spence (33-Climax, R9), accident

***Sunday Mirror* Trophy, Goodwood, 19 April, 101 miles NC**
1st, J. Clark (25-Climax, R6), 105.07 mph
Non-started, M. Spence (33-Climax, R9), fuel injection problems on the starting grid

**International Trophy, Silverstone, 15 May, 152 miles NC**
3rd, M. Spence (33-Climax, R9)
4th, P. Rodriguez (25-Climax, R6)

**Belgian Grand Prix, Spa-Francorchamps, 13 June, 280 miles**
1st, J. Clark (33-Climax, R11), 117.16 mph
7th, M. Spence (33-Climax, R9), 1 lap in arrears

**French Grand Prix, Clermont-Ferrand, 27 June, 200 miles**
1st, J. Clark (25-Climax, R6), 89.22 mph
7th, M. Spence (33-Climax, R9), 1 lap in arrears

**British Grand Prix, Silverstone, 10 July, 234 miles**
1st, J. Clark (33-Climax, R11), 112.02 mph
4th, M. Spence (33-Climax, R9)

**Dutch Grand Prix, Zandvoort, 18 July, 208 miles**
1st, J. Clark (33-Climax, R9), 100.87 mph
8th, M. Spence (25-Climax, R6), 1 lap in arrears

**German Grand Prix, Nürburgring, 1 August, 212 miles**
1st, J. Clark (33-Climax, R11), 99.80 mph
Retired, M. Spence (33-Climax, R9), drive-shaft failure
Retired, G. Mitter (33-Climax, R6), water hose failure

**Mediterranean Grand Prix, Pergusa, 15 August, 179 miles NC**
2nd, J. Clark (25-Climax, R6)
Retired, M. Spence (33-Climax, R9), accident

**Italian Grand Prix, Monza, 12 September, 272 miles**
10th, J. Clark (33-Climax, R11), 13 laps in arrears, not running at the finish, fuel pump
11th, M. Spence (33-Climax, R9), 14 laps in arrears, not running at the finish, alternator
Retired, G. Russo (25-Climax, R6), gearbox oil seal

**United States Grand Prix, Watkins Glen, 3 October, 253 miles**
12th, M. Solana (25-Climax, R6), 15 laps in arrears
Retired, M. Spence (33-Climax, R9), piston failure
Retired, J. Clark (33-Climax, R11), piston failure

**Mexican Grand Prix, Magdalena Mixhuca,
24 October, 202 miles**
3rd, M. Spence (33-Climax, R9)
Retired, J. Clark (33-Climax, R11), seized engine
Retired, M. Solana (25-Climax, R9), ignition

| Drivers' World Championship: | 1st, J. Clark, 54 points |
| | 8th=, M. Spence, 10 points |

| Constructors' Cup: | 1st, Lotus-Climax, 54 points |

# 1966

**South African Grand Prix, East London,
2 January, 146 miles NC**
1st, M. Spence (33-Climax, R11), 97.75 mph
3rd, P. Arundell (33-Climax, R9), 2 laps in arrears

**Monaco Grand Prix, Monte Carlo, 22 May,
195 miles**
Retired, J. Clark (33-Climax, R11), rear suspension

**Belgian Grand Prix, Spa-Francorchamps,
12 June, 245 miles**
Retired, J. Clark (33-Climax, R11), engine

**French Grand Prix, Reims, 3 July, 248 miles**
Retired, P. Arundell (43-BRM H16, 43/1), gear-change
Retired, P. Rodriguez (33-Climax, R11), broken oil pipe
NOTE: J. Clark non-started after being hit in face by bird
during practice

**British Grand Prix, Brands Hatch, 16 July,
202 miles**
4th, J. Clark (33-Climax, R14), 1 lap in arrears
Retired, P. Arundell (33-BRM, R11), gear change

**Dutch Grand Prix, Zandvoort, 24 July, 235 miles**
3rd, J. Clark (33-Climax, R14), 2 laps in arrears
Retired, P. Arundell (33-BRM, R11), ignition

**German Grand Prix, Nürburgring, 7 August,
213 miles**
12th, P. Arundell (33-BRM, R11), 2 laps in arrears
Retired, J. Clark (33-Climax, R14), accident

**Italian Grand Prix, Monza, 4 September,
243 miles**
8th, P. Arundell (33-BRM, R11), 5 laps in arrears, not running
at the finish, engine
9th, 'Geki' (33-Climax, R14), 5 laps in arrears
Retired, J. Clark (43-BRM H16, 43/1), gearbox

**Gold Cup, Oulton Park, 17 September,
110 Miles NC**
3rd, J. Clark (33-Climax, R14)

**United States Grand Prix, Watkins Glen,
2 October, 248 miles**
1st, J. Clark (43-BRM H16, 43/1), 114.94 mph
6th, P. Arundell (33-Climax, R14), 7 laps in arrears
Retired, P. Rodriguez (33-BRM, R11), overheating

**Mexican Grand Prix, Magdalena Mixhuca,
23 October, 202 miles**
7th, P. Arundell (33-BRM, R11), 4 laps in arrears
Retired, J. Clark (43-BRM H16, 43/1), gear linkage
Retired, P. Rodriguez (33-Climax, R14), final drive

| Drivers' World Championship: | 6th, J. Clark, 16 points |
| | 17th=, P. Arundell, 1 point |

| Constructors' Cup: | 5th, Lotus-BRM, 13 points |
| | 6th, Lotus-Climax, 8 points |

# 1967

**South African Grand Prix, Kyalami, 2 January,
204 miles**
Retired, G. Hill (43-BRM, 43/1), suspension
Retired, J. Clark (43-BRM, 43/2), fuel system

**International Trophy, Silverstone, 29 April,
150 miles NC**
4th, G. Hill (33-BRM, R11), 1 lap in arrears

**Monaco Grand Prix, Monte Carlo, 7 May,
195 miles**
2nd, G. Hill (33-BRM, R11), 1 lap in arrears
Retired, G. Clark (33-Climax, R14), broken damper mounting,
accident

**Dutch Grand Prix, Zandvoort, 4 June, 235 miles**
1st, J. Clark (49-Ford, 49/R2), 104.49 mph
Retired, G. Hill (49-Ford, 49/Rl), camshaft

**Belgian Grand Prix, Spa-Francorchamps,
18 June, 245 miles**
6th, J. Clark (49-Ford, 49/R2), 1 lap in arrears
Retired, G. Hill (49-Ford, 49/Rl), gearbox

**French Grand Prix, Bugatti Circuit, Le Mans,
2 July, 224 miles**
Retired, J. Clark (49-Ford, R2), final drive
Retired, G. Hill (49-Ford, Rl), gearbox

**British Grand Prix, Silverstone, 15 July, 240 miles**
1st, J. Clark (49-Ford, R2), 117.64 mph
Retired, G. Hill (49-Ford, R3), engine

**German Grand Prix, Nürburgring, 6 August,
213 miles**
Retired, J. Clark (49-Ford, 49/R2), suspension
Retired, G. Hill (49-Ford, 49/R3), suspension

**Canadian Grand Prix, Mosport Park, 27 August,
221 miles**
4th, G. Hill (49-Ford, 49/R3), 2 laps in arrears
Retired, J. Clark (49-Ford, 49/R2), ignition
Retired, E. Weitzes (49-Ford, 49/Rl), engine

**Italian Grand Prix, Monza, 10 September,
243 miles**
3rd, J. Clark (49-Ford, 49/R2)
Retired, G. Hill (49-Ford, 49/R3), con-rod
Retired, G. Baghetti (49-Ford, 49/Rl), engine

**United States Grand Prix, Watkins Glen,
1 October, 248 miles**
1st, J. Clark (49-Ford, 49/R2), 120.95 mph
2nd, G. Hill (49-Ford, 49/R3)
Retired, M. Solana (49-Ford, 49/Rl), stalled engine

**Mexican Grand Prix, Magdalena Mixhuca,
22 October, 202 miles**
1st, J. Clark (49-Ford, 49/Rl), 101.42 mph
Retired, G. Hill (49-Ford, R3), broken universal joint
Retired, M. Solana (49-Ford, R2), front suspension

**Madrid Grand Prix, Jarama, 12 November,
114 miles NC**
1st, J. Clark (49-Ford, 49/Rl), 81.71 mph
2nd, G. Hill (49-Ford, 49/R2)

| | |
|---|---|
| Drivers' World Championship: | 3rd, J. Clark, 41 points |
| | 6th=, G. Hill, 15 points |
| Constructors' Cup: | 2nd, Lotus-Ford, 44 points |
| | 8th, Lotus-BRM, 6 points |

# 1968

**South African Grand Prix, Kyalami, 1 January,
204 miles**
1st, J. Clark (49-Ford, 49/R4), 107.42 mph
2nd, G. Hill (49-Ford, 49/R3)

**Race of Champions, Brands Hatch, 17 March,
133 miles NC**
Retired, G. Hill (49-Ford, 49/R5), drive-shaft

**International Trophy, Silverstone, 27 April,
152 miles NC**
Retired, G. Hill (49-Ford, 49/Rl), fuel line

**Spanish Grand Prix, Jarama, 12 May, 190 miles**
1st, G. Hill (49-Ford, 49/Rl), 84.41 mph

**Monaco Grand Prix, Monte Carlo, 26 May,
156 miles**
1st, G. Hill (49B-Ford, 49B/R5), 77.82 mph
Retired, J. Oliver (49-Ford, 49/Rl), accident

**Belgian Grand Prix, Spa-Francorchamps, 9 June,
245 miles**
5th, J. Oliver (49B-Ford, 49B/R6), 2 laps in arrears
Retired, G. Hill (49B-Ford, 49B/R5), drive-shaft universal joint

**Dutch Grand Prix, Zandvoort, 23 June, 234 miles**
9th, G. Hill (49B-Ford, 49B/R5), 9 laps in arrears, not running
at the finish, accident
Not classified, J. Oliver (49B-Ford, 49B/R6), 10 laps in arrears

**French Grand Prix, Rouen-les-Essarts, 7 July,
244 miles**
Retired, G. Hill (49B-Ford, 49B/R5), drive-shaft
Did Not Start, J. Oliver (49B-Ford, 49B/R6), no spare car
following practice crash

**British Grand Prix, Brands Hatch, 20 July,
212 miles**
1st, J. Siffert (49B-Ford, 49B/R7), 104.83 mph*
Retired, G. Hill (49B-Ford, 49B/R5), universal joint
Retired, J. Oliver (49B-Ford, 49B/R2), final drive

**German Grand Prix, Nürburgring, 4 August,
199 miles**
2nd, G. Hill (49B-Ford, 49B/R5)
11th, J. Oliver (49B-Ford, 49B/R2), 1 lap in arrears

**Gold Cup, Oulton Park, 17 August, 110 miles NC**
3rd, J. Oliver (49B-Ford, 49B/R2)
Retired, G. Hill (49B-Ford, 49B/R5), final drive

**Italian Grand Prix, Monza, 8 September,
243 miles**
Retired, G. Hill (49B-Ford, 49B/R6), lost wheel, accident
Retired, J. Oliver (49B-Ford, 49B/R5), transmission

**Canadian Grand Prix, Mont Tremblant,
22 September, 239 miles**
4th, G. Hill (49B-Ford, 49B/R6), 4 laps in arrears
Retired, J. Oliver (49B-Ford, 49B/R2), transmission

**United States Grand Prix, Watkins Glen,
6 October, 248 miles**
2nd, G. Hill (49B-Ford, 49B/R6)
Retired, M. Andretti (49B-Ford, 49B/R5), clutch
Did Not Start, J. Oliver (49B-Ford, 49B/R2), no spare car
following practice crash

**Mexican Grand Prix, Magdalena Mixhuca,
3 November, 202 miles**
1st, G. Hill (49B-Ford, 49B/R6), 103.80 mph
3rd, J. Oliver (49B-Ford, 49B/R5)
Retired, M. Solana (49B-Ford, 49B/R2), collapsed rear wing

*R.R.C. Walker entry

| | |
|---|---|
| Drivers' World Championship: | 1st, G. Hill, 48 points |
| | 11th, J. Clark, 9 points+ |
| | 13th=, J. Oliver, 6 points |

+Deceased

| | |
|---|---|
| Constructors' Cup: | 1st, Lotus-Ford, 64 points |

# 1969

**South African Grand Prix, Kyalami, 1 March,
204 miles**
2nd, G. Hill (49B-Ford, 49B/R6)
Retired, M. Andretti (49B-Ford, 49B/R11), transmission
Retired, J. Rindt (49B-Ford, 49B/R9), fuel pump

**Race of Champions, Brands Hatch, 16 March,
133 miles NC**
2nd, G. Hill (49B-Ford, 49B/R6)
Retired, J. Rindt (49B-Ford, 49B/R9)

**International Trophy Silverstone, 30 March,
152 miles NC**
2nd, J. Rindt (49B-Ford, 49B/R9)
7th, G. Hill (49B-Ford, 49B/R6), 2 laps in arrears

**Spanish Grand Prix, Montjuich Park, Barcelona,
4 May, 212 miles**
Retired, G. Hill (49B-Ford, 49B/R6), accident
Retired, J. Rindt (49B-Ford, 49B/R9), aerofoil failure, accident

**Monaco Grand Prix, Monte Carlo, 18 May,
156 miles**
1st, G. Hill (49T/B-Ford, 49B/R10), 80.18 mph
3rd, J. Siffert (49B-Ford, 49B/R7)*
4th, R. Attwood (49T/B-Ford, 49B/R8)

**Dutch Grand Prix, Zandvoort, 21 June, 235 miles**
2nd, J. Siffert (49B-Ford, 49B/R7)*
7th, G. Hill (49B-Ford, 49B/R10), 2 laps in arrears
Retired, J. Rindt (49B-Ford, 49B/R6), drive-shaft joint

**French Grand Prix, Clermont-Ferrand, 6th July,
190 miles**
6th, G. Hill (49B-Ford, 49B/R10), 1 lap in arrears
Retired, J. Rindt (49B-Ford, 49B/R6), driver unwell
Retired, J. Miles (63-Ford, 63/2), fuel pump

**British Grand Prix, Silverstone, 19 July, 246 miles**
4th, J. Rindt (49B-Ford, 49B/R6), 1 lap in arrears
7th, G. Hill (49B-Ford, 49B/R8), 2 laps in arrears
10th, J. Miles (63-Ford, 63/2), 9 laps in arrears
Retired, J. Bonnier (63-Ford, 63/1), engine (car loaned to driver)

**German Grand Prix, Nürburgring, 3 August, 199 miles**
4th, G. Hill (49B-Ford, 49B/R10)
Retired, J. Rindt (49B-Ford, 49B/R6), ignition
Retired, M. Andretti (63-Ford, 63/2), accident

**Gold Cup, Oulton Park, 16 August, 110 miles NC**
2nd, J. Rindt (63-Ford, 63/1)

**Italian Grand Prix, Monza, 7 September, 243 miles**
2nd, J. Rindt (49B-Ford, 49B/R6)
9th, G. Hill (49B-Ford, 49B/R10), 5 laps in arrears, not running at the finish, drive-shaft
Retired, J. Miles (63-Ford, 63/1), engine

**Canadian Grand Prix, Mosport Park, 20 September, 221 miles**
3rd, J. Rindt (49B-Ford, 49B/R6)
Retired, G. Hill (49B-Ford, 49B/R10), camshaft
Retired, J. Miles (63-Ford, 63/2), gearbox

**United States Grand Prix, Watkins Glen, 5 October, 248 miles**
1st, J. Rindt (49B-Ford, 49B/R6), 126.36 mph
Retired, G. Hill (49B-Ford, 49B/R10), accident
Retired, M. Andretti (63-Ford, 63/2), rear suspension

**Mexican Grand Prix, Magdalena Mixhuca, 19 October, 202 miles**
Retired, J. Rindt (49B-Ford, 49B/R6), broken front wishbone
Retired, J. Miles (63-Ford, 63/2), fuel pump

*R.R.C. Walker entry

Drivers' World Championship:      4th, J. Rindt, 22 points
                                  7th, G. Hill, 19 points
                                  13th=, R. Attwood, 3 points

Constructors' Cup:                3rd, Lotus-Ford, 44 points

# 1970

**South African Grand Prix, Kyalami, 7 March, 204 miles**
5th, J. Miles (49C-Ford, 49B/R10), 1 lap in arrears
6th, G. Hill (49C-Ford, 49B/R7), 1 lap in arrears*
Retired, J. Rindt (49C-Ford, 49B/R6), engine

**Race of Champions, Brands Hatch, 22 March, 132 miles NC**
2nd, J. Rindt (49C-Ford, 49B/R6)

**Spanish Grand Prix, Jarama, 19 April, 190 miles**
4th, G. Hill (49C-Ford, 49B/R7), 1 lap in arrears*
Retired, J. Rindt (72-Ford, 72/2), ignition
Did Not Start, J. Miles (72-Ford, 72/1), failed to qualify

**International Trophy, Silverstone, 26 April, aggregate of two 76-mile heats NC**
Retired, J. Rindt (72-Ford, 72/2), ignition
Retired, J. Miles (72-Ford, 72/1), engine

**Monaco Grand Prix, Monte Carlo, 10 May, 156 miles**
1st, J. Rindt (49C-Ford, 49B/R6), 81.84 mph
Did Not Start, J. Miles (49C-Ford, 49B/R10), failed to qualify

**Belgian Grand Prix, Spa-Francorchamps, 7 June, 245 miles**
Retired, J. Rindt (49C-Ford, 49B/R6), piston failure
Retired, J. Miles (72-Ford, 72/1), fuel-feed trouble and deflated tyres
Did Not Start, A. Soler-Roig (72-Ford, 72/2), failed to qualify+

**Dutch Grand Prix, Zandvoort, 21 June, 209 miles**
1st, J. Rindt (72-Ford, 72/2), 112.95 mph
7th, J. Miles (72-Ford, 72/1), 2 laps in arrears

**French Grand Prix, Clermont-Ferrand, 5 July, 190 miles**
1st, J. Rindt (72-Ford, 72/2), 98.42 mph
8th, J. Miles (72-Ford, 72/1)
Did Not Start, A. Soler-Roig (49C-Ford, 49B/R6), failed to qualify+

**British Grand Prix, Brands Hatch, 19 July, 212 miles**
1st, J. Rindt (72-Ford, 72/2), 108.69 mph
6th, G. Hill (49C-Ford, 49B/R7), 1 lap in arrears*
8th, E. Fittipaldi (49C-Ford, 49B/R10), 2 laps in arrears
Retired, J. Miles (72-Ford, 72/1), engine

**German Grand Prix, Hockenheim, 2 August, 211 miles**
1st, J. Rindt (72-Ford, 72/2), 123.90 mph
4th, E. Fittipaldi (49C-Ford, 49B/R10)
Retired, J. Miles (72-Ford, 72/3), engine

**Austrian Grand Prix, Österreichring, 16 August, 220 miles**
15th, E. Fittipaldi (49C-Ford, 49B/R10), 5 laps in arrears
Retired, J. Miles (72-Ford, 72/3), front brake-shaft
Retired, J. Rindt (72-Ford, 72/2), suspected camshaft failure

**Gold Cup, Oulton Park, 22 August, aggregate of two 55-mile heats NC**
2nd, J. Rindt (72-Ford, 72/2)

**Italian Grand Prix, Monza, 6 September, 243 miles**
Did Not Start, J. Rindt (72-Ford, 72/2), fatal accident in practice
Did Not Start, J. Miles (72-Ford, 72/3), car withdrawn
Did Not Start, E. Fittipaldi (72-Ford, 72/5), car withdrawn

**United States Grand Prix, Watkins Glen, 4 October, 248 miles**
1st, E. Fittipaldi (72-Ford, 72/5), 126.79 mph
3rd, R. Wisell (72-Ford, 72/3)

**Mexican Grand Prix, Ricardo Rodriguez, 25 October, 202 miles**
Not classified, R. Wisell (72-Ford, 72/3), 9 laps in arrears
Retired, E. Fittipaldi (72-Ford, 72/5), engine

*R.R.C. Walker entry
+Entered in the name of Lotus subsidiary, World Wide Racing

Drivers' World Championship:      1st, J. Rindt, 45 points++
                                  10th, E. Fittipaldi, 12 points
                                  15th=, R. Wisell, 4 points
                                  19th=, J. Miles, 2 points

++ Deceased

Constructors' Cup:                1st, Lotus-Ford, 59 points

## 1971

**Argentine Grand Prix, Buenos Aires Autodrome, 24 January, aggregate of two 106-mile heats NC**
7th, R. Wisell (72-Ford, 72/3), 16 laps in arrears
9th, W. Fittipaldi (49C-Ford, 49B/R6), 19 laps in arrears
Not classified, E. Fittipaldi (72-Ford, 72/5), failed to start second heat because of loss of oil pressure

**South African Grand Prix, Kyalami, 6 March, 201 miles**
4th, R. Wisell (72-Ford, 72/3)
Retired, E. Fittipaldi (72-Ford, 72/5), engine

**Race of Champions, Brands Hatch, 21 March, 132 miles NC**
Retired, A. Trimmer (72-Ford, 72/5), fuel pump
Retired, R. Wisell (72-Ford, 72/3), engine
Retired, E. Fittipaldi (56B-Pratt & Whitney, 56B/l), suspension

**Questor Grand Prix, Ontario, California, 28 March, aggregate of two 102-mile heats NC**
21st, E. Fittipaldi (72-Ford, 72/5), failed to start second heat because of engine problems
27th, R. Wisell (72-Ford, 72/3), failed to start second heat because of seized engine

**Rothmans International Trophy, Oulton Park, 9 April, 110 miles NC**
6th, A. Trimmer (49C-Ford, 49B/R6), 4 laps in arrears
7th, E. Fittipaldi (72-Ford, 72/5), 13 laps in arrears
Retired, R. Wisell (56B-Pratt & Whitney, 56B/1), suspension

**Spanish Grand Prix, Montjuich Park, 18 April, 177 miles**
12th, R. Wisell (72-Ford, 72/3), 17 laps in arrears
Retired, E. Fittipaldi (72-Ford, 72/5), suspension

**International Trophy, Silverstone, 8 May, aggregate of two 75-mile heats NC**
13th, R. Wisell (72-Ford, 72/3), 4 laps in arrears, not running at the finish, engine failure in second heat
Not Classified, E. Fittipaldi (56B-Pratt & Whitney, 56B/1), retired in first heat because of suspension failure

**Monaco Grand Prix, Monte Carlo, 23 May, 156 miles**
5th, E. Fittipaldi (72-Ford, 72/5), 1 lap in arrears
Retired, R. Wisell (72-Ford, 72/3), rear hub bearing

**Jochen Rindt Memorial Race, Hockenheim, 13 June, 147 miles NC**
9th, D. Walker (72-Ford, 72/5), 1 lap in arrears
10th, R. Wisell (72-Ford, 72/3), 2 laps in arrears

**Dutch Grand Prix, Zandvoort, 20 June, 183 miles**
Retired, D. Walker (56B-Pratt & Whitney, 56B/l), accident
Disqualified, R. Wisell (72-Ford, 72/3), reversed into pits
Did Not Start, D. Charlton (72-Ford, 72/5), car crashed in practice by Walker

**French Grand Prix, Paul Ricard, 4 July, 198 miles**
3rd, E. Fittipaldi (72-Ford, 72/5)
6th, R. Wisell (72-Ford, 72/3)

**British Grand Prix, Silverstone, 17 July, 199 miles**
3rd, E. Fittipaldi (72-Ford, 72/5)
Not classified, R. Wisell (56B-Pratt & Whitney, 56B/1), 11 laps in arrears
Retired, D. Charlton (72-Ford), 72/3), engine

**German Grand Prix, Nürburgring, 1 August, 170 miles**
8th, R. Wisell (72-Ford, 72/6)
Retired, E. Fittipaldi (72-Ford, 72/5), loss of oil pressure

**Austrian Grand Prix, Österreichring, 15 August, 198 miles**
2nd, E. Fittipaldi (72-Ford, 72/5)
4th, R. Wisell (72-Ford, 72/6)

**Italian Grand Prix, Monza, 5 September, 196 miles**
8th, E. Fittipaldi (56B-Pratt & Whitney, 56B/l), 1 lap in arrears+

**Canadian Grand Prix, Mosport Park, 19 September, 157 miles (race stopped short because of weather conditions)**
5th, R. Wisell (72D-Ford, 72/6), 1 lap in arrears
7th, E. Fittipaldi (72D-Ford, 72/5), 2 laps in arrears

**United States Grand Prix, Watkins Glen, 3 October, 199 miles**
19th, E. Fittipaldi (72D-Ford, 72/5), 10 laps in arrears
Retired, R. Wisell (72D-Ford, 72/6), brake failure accident

**Rothmans World Championships Victory Race, Brands Hatch, 24 October, 31 miles (race stopped short following Siffert's fatal accident) NC**
2nd, E. Fittipaldi (72-Ford, 72/5)

+World Wide Racing entry

Drivers' World Chamionship: 6th, E Fittipaldi 16 points
9th=, R. Wisell, 9 points

Constructors' Cup: 5th, Lotus-Ford, 21 points

## 1972

**Argentine Grand Prix, Buenos Aires Autodrome, 23 January, 201 miles**
Retired, E. Fittipaldi (72D-Ford, 72D/5), broken radius rod
Disqualified, D. Walker (72D-Ford, 72D/6), use of tools not carried on car

**South African Grand Prix, Kyalami, 4 March, 201 miles**
2nd, E. Fittipaldi (72D-Ford, 72D/5)
10th, D. Walker (72D-Ford, 72D/6), 1 lap in arrears

**Race of Champions, Brands Hatch, 19 March, 106 miles NC**
1st, E. Fittipaldi (72D-Ford, 72D/5), 112.22 mph
9th, D. Walker (72D-Ford, 72D/6), 1 lap in arrears

**Brazilian Grand Prix, Interlagos, São Paulo, 30 March, 185 miles NC**
5th, D. Walker (72D-Ford, 72D/6), 1 lap in arrears
Retired, E. Fittipaldi (72D-Ford, 72D/7), suspension

**International Trophy, Silverstone, 23 April, 117 miles NC**
1st, E. Fittipaldi (72D-Ford, 72D/7), 131.81 mph
Did Not Start, D. Walker (72D-Ford, 72D/6), crashed in practice

**Spanish Grand Prix, Jarama, 1 May, 190 miles**
1st, E. Fittipaldi (72D-Ford, 72D/7), 92.35 mph
9th, D. Walker (72D-Ford, 72D/5), 5 laps in arrears, not
running at the finish, ran out of fuel

**Monaco Grand Prix, Monte Carlo, 14 May,
156 miles**
3rd, E. Fittipaldi (72D-Ford, 72D), 1 lap in arrears
14th, D. Walker (72D-Ford, 72D/5), 5 laps in arrears

**Gold Cup, Oulton Park, 29 May, 110 miles NC**
2nd, E. Fittipaldi (72D-Ford, 72D/5)
Retired, D. Walker (72D-Ford, 72D/6), gearbox

**Belgian Grand Prix, Nivelles, 4 June, 197 miles**
1st, E. Fittipaldi (72D-Ford, 72D/7), 113.35 mph
14th, D. Walker (72D-Ford, 72D/6), 6 laps in arrears

**Gran Premio Repubblica Italiana, Vallelunga,
158 miles NC**
1st, E. Fittipaldi (72D-Ford, 72D/5), 97.85 mph

**French Grand Prix, Clermont-Ferrand, 2 July,
190 miles**
2nd, E. Fittipaldi (72D-Ford, 72D/7), 101.56 mph
Retired, D. Walker (72D-Ford, 72D/6), transmission

**British Grand Prix, Brands Hatch, 15 July,
201 miles**
1st, E. Fittipaldi (72D-Ford, 72D/7), 112.06 mph
Retired, D. Walker (72D-Ford, 72D/6), suspension

**German Grand Prix, Nürburgring, 30 July,
199 miles**
Retired, D. Walker (72D-Ford, 72D/6), split oil tank
Retired, E. Fittipaldi (72D-Ford, 72D/7), transmission failure,
fire

**Austrian Grand Prix, Österreichring, 13 August,
198 miles**
1st, E. Fittipaldi (72D-Ford, 72D/7), 133.32 mph
Retired, D. Walker (72D-Ford, 72D/6), engine

**Rothmans 50,000 Race (Formule Libre),
Brands Hatch, 28 August, 312 miles NC**
1st, E. Fittipaldi (72D-Ford, 72D/5), 109.84 mph

**Italian Grand Prix, Monza, 10 September,
196 miles**
1st, E. Fittipaldi (72D-Ford, 72D/5), 131.61 mph+

**Canadian Grand Prix, Mosport Park,
24 September, 196 miles**
11th, E. Fittipaldi (72D-Ford, 72D/7), 2 laps in arrears
14th, R. Wisell (72D-Ford, 72D/6), 15 laps in arrears, not
running at the finish, broken fuel line

**United States Grand Prix, Watkins Glen,
8 October, 199 miles**
10th, R. Wisell (72D-Ford, 72D/6), 2 laps in arrears
Retired, E. Fittipaldi (72D-Ford, 72D/5), damaged rear
suspension
Retired, D.Walker (72D-Ford, 72D/7), loss of engine oil

+World Wide Racing entry

NOTE: all cars entered as 'John Player Specials' in 1972

Drivers' World Championship:  1st, E. Fittipaldi, 61 points

Constructors' Cup:  1st, John Player Special-
Ford, 61 points

# 1973

**Argentine Grand Prix, Autodromo Almirante
Brown, Buenos Aires, 28 January, 200 miles**
1st, E. Fittipaldi (72D-Ford, 72D/7), 102.95 mph
Retired, R. Peterson (72D-Ford, 72D/8), oil pressure

**Brazilian Grand Prix, Interlagos, 11 February,
198 miles**
1st, E. Fittipaldi (72D-Ford, 72D/7), 114.22 mph
Retired, R. Peterson (72-Ford, 72D/8), broken rear wheel

**South African Grand Prix, Kyalami, 3 March,
201 miles**
3rd, E. Fittipaldi (72D-Ford, 72D/7)
11th, R. Peterson (72D-Ford, 72D/8), 6 laps in arrears

**Race of Champions, Brands Hatch, 18 March,
106 miles NC**
Retired, E. Fittipaldi (72E-Ford, 72E/5), fuel metering unit
Retired, R. Peterson, (72E-Ford, 72E/6), gearbox

**International Trophy, Silverstone, 8 April,
117 miles NC**
2nd, R. Peterson (72E-Ford, 72E/8)
Retired, E. Fittipaldi (72E-Ford, 72E/5), flywheel

**Spanish Grand Prix, Montjuich Park, 29 April,
177 miles**
1st, E. Fittipaldi (72E-Ford, 72E/5), 97.86 mph
Retired, R. Peterson (72E-Ford, 72E/8), gearbox

**Belgian Grand Prix, Zolder, 20 May, 184 miles**
3rd, E. Fittipaldi (72E-Ford, 72E/7)
Retired, R. Peterson (72E-Ford, 72E/6), accident

**Monaco Grand Prix, Monte Carlo, 3 June,
159 miles**
2nd, E. Fittipaldi (72E-Ford, 72E/7)
3rd, R. Peterson (72E-Ford, 72E/6), 1 lap in arrears

**Swedish Grand Prix, Anderstorp, 17 June,
200 miles**
2nd, R. Peterson (72E-Ford, 72E/6)
Retired (E. Fittipaldi (72E-Ford, 72E/7), gearbox

**French Grand Prix, Paul Ricard, 1 July, 195 miles**
1st, R. Peterson (72E-Ford, 72E/6), 115.12 mph
Retired, E. Fittipaldi (72E-Ford, 72E/5), accident

**British Grand Prix, Silverstone, 14 July, 196 miles**
2nd, R. Peterson (72E-Ford, 72E/6)
Retired, E. Fittipaldi (72E-Ford, 72E/5), constant velocity joint

**Dutch Grand Prix, Zandvoort, 29 July, 189 miles**
11th, R. Peterson (72E-Ford, 72E/6), 6 laps in arrears, not
running at the finsh, engine and gearbox
Retired, E. Fittipaldi (72E-Ford, 72E/7), driver unwell
following practice accident

**German Grand Prix, Nürburgring, 5 August,
199 miles**
6th, E. Fittipaldi (72E-Ford, 72E/7)
Retired, R. Peterson (72E-Ford, 72E/6), distributor

**Austrian Grand Prix, Österreichring, 19 August,
198 miles**
1st, R. Peterson (72E-Ford, 72E/6), 133.99 mph
Retired, E. Fittipaldi (72E-Ford, 72E/7), fuel pipe

**Italian Grand Prix, Monza, 9 September, 197 miles**
1st, R. Peterson (72E-Ford, 72E/6), 132.63 mph
2nd, E. Fittipaldi (72E-Ford, 72E/7)

**Canadian Grand Prix, Mosport Park, 23 September, 197 miles**
2nd, E. Fittipaldi (72E-Ford, 72E/7)
Retired, R. Peterson (72E-Ford, 72E/6), puncture, accident

**United States Grand Prix, Watkins Glen, 7 October, 199 miles**
1st, R. Peterson (72E-Ford, 72E/7), 118.05 mph
6th, E. Fittipaldi (72E-Ford, 72E/6)

Drivers' World Championship:  2nd, E. Fittipaldi, 55 points
3rd, R. Peterson, 52 points

Constructors' Cup:  1st, John Player Special-Ford, 92 points

NOTE: The 72s were raced throughout 1973 as 'John Player Specials'

# 1974

**Argentine Grand Prix, Autodromo Almirante Brown, Buenos Aires, 13 January, 197 miles**
13th, R. Peterson (72E-Ford, 72E/8), 4 laps in arrears
Retired, J. Ickx (72E-Ford, 72E/5), transmission

**Brazilian Grand Prix, Interlagos, 27 January, 158 miles**
3rd, J. Ickx (72E-Ford, 72E/5), 1 lap in arrears
6th, R. Peterson (72E-Ford, 72E/8), 1 lap in arrears

**Race of Champions, Brands Hatch, 17 March, 106 miles NC**
1st, J. Ickx (72E-Ford, 72E/5), 99.96 mph

**South African Grand Prix, Kyalami, 30 March, 199 miles**
Retired, J. Ickx (76-Ford, JPS10), brakes
Retired, R. Peterson (76-Ford, JPS9), accident

**International Trophy, Silverstone, 7 April, 117 miles**
Retired, R. Peterson (76-Ford, JPS9), tyres, engine

**Spanish Grand Prix, Jarama, 28 April, 178 miles**
Retired, J. Ickx (76-Ford, JPS10), brake fluid leak
Retired, R. Peterson (76-Ford, JPS9), overheating, engine

**Belgian Grand Prix, Nivelles, 12 May, 197 miles**
Retired, J. Ickx (76-Ford, JPS10), brakes
Retired, R. Peterson (76-Ford, JPS9), fuel leak

**Monaco Grand Prix, Monte Carlo, 26 May, 159 miles**
1st, R. Peterson (72E-Ford, 72E/8), 80.74 mph
Retired, J. Ickx (72E-Ford, 72E/5), gearbox

**Swedish Grand Prix, Anderstorp, 9 June, 200 miles**
Retired, J. Ickx (72E-Ford, 72E/5), oil pressure
Retired, R. Peterson (72E-Ford, 72E/8), drive-shaft

**Dutch Grand Prix, Zandvoort, 23 June, 197 miles**
8th, R. Peterson (72E-Ford, 72E/8), 2 laps in arrears
11th, J. Ickx (72E-Ford, 72E/5), 4 laps in arrears

**French Grand Prix, Dijon-Prenois, 7 July, 163 miles**
1st, R. Peterson (72E-Ford, 72E/8), 119.75 mph
5th, J. Ickx (72E-Ford, 72E/5)

**British Grand Prix, Brands Hatch, 20 July, 199 miles**
3rd, J. Ickx (72E-Ford, 72E/5)
10th, R. Peterson (72E-Ford, 72E/8), 2 laps in arrears

**German Grand Prix, Nürburgring, 4 August, 199 miles**
4th, R. Peterson (76-Ford, JPS10)
5th, J. Ickx (72E-Ford, 72E/5)

**Austrian Grand Prix, Österreichring, 18 August, 198 miles**
Retired, R. Peterson (72E-Ford, 72E/8), universal joint
Retired, J. Ickx (76-Ford, JPS10), accident

**Italian Grand Prix, Monza, 8 September, 187 miles**
1st, R. Peterson (72E-Ford, 72E/8), 135.09 mph
Retired, J. Ickx (76-Ford, JPS10), throttle linkage

**Canadian Grand Prix, Mosport Park, 22 September, 197 miles**
3rd, R. Peterson (72E-Ford, 72E/8)
13th, J. Ickx (72E-Ford, 72E/5), 2 laps in arrears

**United States Grand Prix, Watkins Glen, 6 October, 199 miles**
Retired, R. Peterson (72E-Ford, 72E/8), engine
Retired, J. Ickx (72E-Ford, 72E/5), accident
Retired, T. Schenken (76-Ford, JPS9), disqualified for starting without authority.

Drivers' World Championship:  5th, R. Peterson, 35 points
10th=, J. Ickx, 12 points

Constructors' Cup:  4th, John Player Special-Ford, 42 points

NOTE: the 72s and 76s were raced throughout 1974 as 'John Player Specials'

# 1975

**Argentine Grand Prix, Autodromo Almirante Brown, 12 January, 197 miles**
8th, J. Ickx (72E-Ford, 72E/5), 1 lap in arrears
Retired, R. Peterson (72E/8), brakes and gearbox

**Brazilian Grand Prix, Interlagos, 26 January, 198 miles**
9th, J. Ickx (72E-Ford, 72E/5)
15th, R. Peterson (72E-Ford, 72E/8), 2 laps in arrears

**South African Grand Prix, Kyalami, 1 March, 199 miles**
10th, R. Peterson (72E-Ford, 72E/9), 1 lap in arrears
12th, J. Ickx (72E-Ford, 72E/5), 2 laps in arrears

**Race of Champions, Brands Hatch, 16 March, 106 miles NC**
3rd, R. Peterson (72E-Ford, 72E/9)
4th, J. Ick (72E-Ford, 72E/5)

**International Trophy, Silverstone, 13 April, 117 miles NC**
Did Not Start, R. Peterson (72E-Ford, 72E/9), engine failure during warm-up
Did Not Start, J. Crawford (72E-Ford, 72E/5), practice crash

**Spanish Grand Prix, Montuich Park, 28 April, 68 miles (race stopped short following Stommelen's crash)**
2nd, J. Ickx (72E-Ford, 72E/5)
Retired, R. Peterson (72E-Ford, 72E/9), accident

**Monaco Grand Prix, Monte Carlo, 11 May, 153 miles**
4th, R. Peterson (72E-Ford, 72E/9)
8th, J. Ickx (72E-Ford, 72E/5), 1 lap in arrears

**Belgian Grand Prix, Zolder, 25 May, 185 miles**
Retired, J. Ickx (72E-Ford, 72E/5), broken front brake-shaft
Retired, R. Peterson (72E-Ford, 72E/9), brakes, accident

**Swedish Grand Prix, Anderstorp, 8 June, 200 miles**
9th, R. Peterson (72E-Ford, 72E/9), 1 lap in arrears
15th, J. Ickx (72E-Ford, 72E/5), 3 laps in arrears

**Dutch Grand Prix, Zandvoort, 22 June, 197 miles**
15th, R. Peterson (72E-Ford, 72E/9), 1 lap in arrears, not running at the finish, out of fuel
Retired, J. Ickx (72E-Ford, 72E/5), engine

**French Grand Prix, Paul Ricard, 6 July, 195 miles**
10th, R. Peterson (72E-Ford, 72E/9)
Retired, J. Ickx (72E-Ford, 72E/5), front brake-shaft

**British Grand Prix, Silverstone, 19 July, 164 miles (race stopped short because of accidents in rain)**
16th, B. Henton (72E-Ford, 72E/5), 3 laps in arrears, not running at the finish, accident
Retired, J. Crawford (72E-Ford, 72E/8) accident
Retired, R. Peterson (72E-Ford, 72E/9), engine

**German Grand Prix, Nürburgring, 3 August, 199 miles**
Retired, J. Watson (72F-Ford, 72F/8), front suspension
Retired, R. Peterson (72E-Ford, 72E/9), clutch

**Austrian Grand Prix, Österreichring, 17 August, 106 miles (raced stopped short because of flooded circuit)**
5th, R. Peterson (72E-Ford, 72E/9)
Did Not Start, B. Henton (72F-Ford, 72F/5), practice crash

**Swiss Grand Prix, Dijon-Prenois, 24 August, 122 miles NC**
4th, R. Peterson (72E-Ford, 72E/9)

**Italian Grand Prix, Monza, 7 September, 187 miles**
13th, J. Crawford (72F-Ford, 72F/8), 6 laps in arrears
Retired, R. Peterson (72E-Ford, 72E/9), engine

**United States Grand Prix, Watkins Glen, 5 October, 199 miles**
5th, R. Peterson (72E-Ford, 72E/9)
Retired, B. Henton (72F-Ford, 72F/5)

| | |
|---|---|
| Drivers' World Championship: | 12th=, R. Peterson, 6 points |
| | 16th, J. Ickx, 3 points |
| Constructors' Cup: | 7th, John Player Special-Ford, 9 points |

NOTE: The 72s were raced throughout 1975 as 'John Player Specials'

# 1976

**Brazilian Grand Prix, Interlagos, 25 January, 198 miles**
Retired, R. Peterson (77-Ford, JPS12), accident with Andretti
Retired, M. Andretti (77-Ford, JPS11), accident with Peterson

**South African Grand Prix, Kyalami, 6 March, 199 miles**
10th, R. Evans (77-Ford, JPS12), 1 lap in arrears
Retired, G. Nilsson (77-Ford, JPS11), clutch

**Race of Champions, Brands Hatch, 14 March, 106 mile NC**
8th, G. Nilsson (77-Ford, JPS11), 2 laps in arrears
9th, R. Evans (77-Ford, JPS12), 4 laps in arrears

**United States Grand Prix West, Long Beach, 28 March, 162 miles**
Retired, G. Nilsson (77-Ford, JPS11), suspension failure, accident
Did Not Start, R. Evans (77-Ford, JPS12), failed to qualify

**International Trophy, Silverstone, 11 April, 117 miles NC**
6th, G. Nilsson (77-Ford, JPS12)

**Spanish Grand Prix, Jarama, 2 May, 159 miles**
3rd, G. Nilsson (77-Ford, JPS12)
Retired, M. Andretti (77-Ford, JPS11), gear selection

**Belgian Grand Prix, Zolder, 16 May, 185 miles**
Retired, M. Andretti (77-Ford, JPS11), drive-shaft
Retired, G. Nilsson (77-Ford, JPS12), accident

**Monaco Grand Prix, Monte Carlo, 30 May, 161 miles**
Retired, G. Nilsson (77-Ford, JPS12), engine

**Swedish Grand Prix, Anderstorp, 13 June, 180 miles**
Retired, M. Andretti (77-Ford, JPS11), engine
Retired, G. Nilsson (77-Ford, JPS12), accident

**French Grand Prix, Paul Ricard, 4 July, 195 miles**
5th, M. Andretti (77-Ford, JPS11)
Retired, G. Nilsson (77-Ford, JPS12), transmission

**British Grand Prix, Brands Hatch, 18 July, 199 miles**
Retired, G. Nilsson (77-Ford, JPS12), engine
Retired, M. Andretti (77-Ford, JPS11), engine

**German Grand Prix, Nürburgring, 1 August, 199 miles**
5th, G. Nilsson (77-Ford, JPS12)
12th, M. Andretti (77-Ford, JPS14)

**Austrian Grand Prix, Österreichring, 15 August, 198 miles**
3rd, G. Nilsson (77-Ford, JPS12)
5th, M. Andretti (77-Ford, JPS14)

**Dutch Grand Prix, Zandvoort, 29 August, 197 miles**
3rd, M. Andretti (77-Ford, JPS11)
Retired, G. Nilsson (77-Ford, JPS12), accident

**Italian Grand Prix, Monza, 12 September, 187 miles**
13th, G. Nilsson (77-Ford, JPS12), 1 lap in arrears
Retired, M. Andretti (77-Ford, JPS14), accident

**Canadian Grand Prix, Mosport Park, 3 October, 197 miles**
3rd, M. Andretti (77-Ford, JPS11)
12th, G. Nilsson (77-Ford, JPS12), 1 lap in arrears

**United States Grand Prix, Watkins Glen, 10 October, 199 miles**
Retired, M. Andretti (77-Ford, JPS11), damaged suspension
Retired, G. Nilsson (77-Ford, JPS12), engine

**Japanese Grand Prix, Fuji, 24 October, 198 miles**
1st, M. Andretti (77-Ford, JPS11), 114.09 mph
6th, G. Nilsson (77-Ford, JPS12)

| Drivers' World Championship: | 6th, M. Andretti, 22 points |
| | 10th, G. Nilsson, 11 points |
| Constructors' Cup: | 4th, John Player Special-Ford, 29 points |

NOTE: The 77s were raced throughout 1976 as 'John Player Specials'

# 1977

**Argentine Grand Prix, Buenos Aires Autodrome, 9 January, 197 miles**
5th, M. Andretti (78-Ford, JPS15), 2 laps in arrears
Did Not Start, G. Nilsson (78-Ford, JPS15), car taken over by Andretti after Andretti's car damaged by onboard extinguisher explosion

**Brazilian Grand Prix, Interlagos, 23 January, 198 miles**
5th, G. Nilsson (78-Ford, JPS15), 1 lap in arrears
Retired, M. Andretti (78-Ford, JPS16), ignition switch

**South African Grand Prix, Kyalami, 5 March, 199 miles**
12th, G. Nilsson (78-Ford, JPS15), 1 lap in arrears
Retired, M. Andretti (78-Ford, JPS16), accident

**Race of Champions, Brands Hatch, 20 March, 106 miles NC**
Retired, M. Andretti (78-Ford, JPS16), ignition switch

**United States Grand Prix West, Long Beach, 3 April, 162 miles**
1st, M. Andretti (78-Ford, JPS17), 86.89 mph
8th, G. Nilsson (78-Ford, JPS16), 1 lap in arrears

**Spanish Grand Prix, Jarama, 8 May, 159 miles**
1st, M. Andretti (78-Ford, JPS17), 92.53 mph
5th, G. Nilsson (78-Ford, JPS16)

**Monaco Grand Prix, Monte Carlo, 22 May, 156 miles**
5th, M. Andretti (78-Ford, JPS17)
Retired, G. Nilsson (78-Ford, JPS16), gearbox

**Belgian Grand Prix, Zolder, 5 June, 185 miles**
1st, G. Nilsson (78-Ford, JPS16), 96.64 mph
Retired, M. Andretti (78-Ford, JPS17), accident

**Swedish Grand Prix, Anderstorp, 19 June, 180 miles**
6th, M. Andretti (78-Ford, JPS17)
Retired, G. Nilsson (78-Ford, JPS16), wheel bearing

**French Grand Prix, Dijon-Prenois, 3 July, 189 miles**
1st, M. Andretti (78-Ford, JPS17), 113.71 mph
4th, G. Nilsson (78-Ford, JPS16)

**British Grand Prix, Silverstone, 16 July, 199 miles**
3rd, G. Nilsson (78-Ford, JPS16)
14th, M. Andretti (78-Ford, JPS17), 6 laps in arrears, not running at the finish, engine

**German Grand Prix, Hockenheim, 31 July, 198 miles**
Retired, M. Andretti (78-Ford, JPS17), engine
Retired, G. Nilsson (78-Ford, JPS18), engine

**Austrian Grand Prix, Österreichring, 14 August, 199 miles**
Retired, G. Nilsson (78-Ford, JPS16), engine
Retired, M. Andretti (78-Ford, JPS17), engine

**Dutch Grand Prix, Zandvoort, 28 August, 197 miles**
Retired, G. Nilsson (78-Ford, JPS18), accident
Retired, M. Andretti (78-Ford, JPS17), engine

**Italian Grand Prix, Monza, 11 September, 187 miles**
1st, M. Andretti (78-Ford, JPS17), 128.01 mph
Retired, G. Nilsson (78-Ford, JPS16), front suspension upright

**United States Grand Prix, Watkins Glen, 2 October, 199 miles**
2nd, M. Andretti (78-Ford, JPS17)
Retired, G. Nilsson (78-Ford, JPS18), accident

**Canadian Grand Prix, Mosport Park, 9 October, 197 miles**
9th, M. Andretti (78-Ford, JPS17), 3 laps in arrears, not running at the finish, engine
Retired, G. Nilsson (78-Ford, JPS18), stuck throttle, accident

**Japanese Grand Prix, Fuji, 23 October, 198 miles**
Retired, G. Nilsson (78-Ford, JPS18), gearbox
Retired, M. Andretti (78-Ford, JPS17), accident

| Drivers' World Championship: | 3rd, M. Andretti, 47 points |
| | 8th, G. Nilsson, 20 points |
| Constructors' Cup: | 2nd John Player Special-Ford, 62 points |

NOTE: The 78s were raced throughout 1977 as 'John Player Specials'

# 1978

**Argentine Grand Prix, Buenos Aires Autodrome, 15 January, 193 miles**
1st, M. Andretti (78-Ford, 78/3), 119.19 mph
5th, R. Peterson (78-Ford, 78/2)

**Brazilian Grand Prix, Jacarepagua, 29 January, 197 miles**
4th, M. Andretti (78-Ford, 78/3)
Retired, R. Peterson (78-Ford, 78/2), collision, damaged suspension

**South African Grand Prix, Kyalami, 4 March, 199 miles**
1st, R. Peterson (78-Ford, 78/2), 116.70 mph
7th, M. Andretti (78-Ford, 78/3), 1 lap in arrears

**International Trophy, Silverstone, 19 March, 117 miles NC**
Retired, M. Andretti (79-Ford, 79/2), accident
Retired, R. Peterson (78-Ford, 78/2), poor handling following accident in warm-up

**United States Grand Prix West, Long Beach, 2 April, 163 miles**
2nd, M. Andretti (78-Ford, 78/3)
4th, R. Peterson (78-Ford, 78/2)

**Monaco Grand Prix, Monte Carlo, 7 May, 154 miles**
11th, M. Andretti (78-Ford, 78/3), 6 laps in arrears
Retired, R. Peterson (78-Ford, 78/2), gearbox

**Belgian Grand Prix, Zolder, 21 May, 185 miles**
1st, M. Andretti (79-Ford, 79/2), 111.37 mph
2nd, R. Peterson (78-Ford, 78/2)

**Spanish Grand Prix, Jarama, 4 June, 159 miles**
1st, M. Andretti (79-Ford, 79/3), 93.50 mph
2nd, R. Peterson (79-Ford, 79/2)

**Swedish Grand Prix, Anderstorp, 17 June, 175 miles**
3rd, R. Peterson (79-Ford, 79/2)
Retired, M. Andretti (79-Ford, 79/3), engine

**French Grand Prix, Paul Ricard, 2 July, 195 miles**
1st, M. Andretti (79-Ford, 79/3), 118.31 mph
2nd, R. Peterson (79-Ford, 79/2)

**British Grand Prix, Brands Hatch, 16 July, 199 miles**
Retired, M. Andretti (79-Ford, 79/3), engine
Retired, R. Peterson (79-Ford, 79/2), fuel leak

**German Grand Prix, Hockenheim, 30 July, 190 miles**
1st, M. Andretti (79-Ford, 79/3), 129.41 mph
Retired, R. Peterson (79-Ford, 79/2), gearbox

**Austrian Grand Prix, Österreichring, 13 August, 199 miles**
1st, R. Peterson (79-Ford, 79/2), 118.03 mph
Retired, M. Andretti (79-Ford, 79/3), accident

**Dutch Grand Prix, Zandvoort, 27 August, 197 miles**
1st, M. Andretti (79-Ford, 79/4), 116.91 mph
2nd, R. Peterson (79-Ford, 79/2)

**Italian Grand Prix, Monza, 10 September, 144 miles**
6th, M. Andretti (79-Ford, 79/4), first on road, but penalized for jumping the start
Retired, R. Peterson (78-Ford, 78/3), used 78 after warm-up crash with 79, seriously injured in start-line crash (subsequently dying) and race restarted

**United States Grand Prix, Watkins Glen, 1 October, 199 miles**
15th, J.-P. Jarier (79-Ford, 79/1), 4 laps in arrears, not running at the finish, out of fuel
Retired, M. Andretti (79-Ford, 79/3), engine

**Canadian Grand Prix, Île Notre-Dame, Montreal, 8 October, 196 miles**
10th, M. Andretti (79-Ford, 79/4), 1 lap in arrears
Retired, J.-P. Jarier (79-Ford, 79/3), leaking oil cooler

Drivers' World Championship:  1st, M. Andretti, 64 points
2nd, R. Peterson, 51 points+

+Deceased

Constructors' Cup:  1st, Lotus-Ford, 86 points

# 1979

**Argentine Grand Prix, Buenos Aires Autodrome, 21 January, 197 miles**
2nd, C. Reutemann (79-Ford, 79/2)
5th, M. Andretti (79-Ford, 79/4), 1 lap in arrears

**Brazilian Grand Prix, Interlagos, 4 February, 198 miles**
3rd, C. Reutemann (79-Ford, 79/2)
Retired, M. Andretti (79-Ford, 79/4), misfire, fuel leak

**South African Grand Prix, Kyalami, 3 March, 199 miles**
4th, M. Andretti (79-Ford, 79/5)
5th, C. Reutemann (79-Ford, 79/2)

**United States Grand Prix West, Long Beach, 8 April, 163 miles**
4th, M. Andretti (79-Ford, 79/5)
Retired, C. Reutemann (79-Ford, 79/2), drive-shaft

**Race of Champions, Brands Hatch, 15 April, 106 miles NC**
3rd, M. Andretti (79-Ford, 79/3)

**Spanish Grand Prix, Jarama, 29 April, 159 miles**
2nd, C. Reutemann (79-Ford, 79/2)
3rd, M. Andretti (80-Ford, 80/1)

**Belgian Grand Prix, Zolder, 13 May, 185 miles**
4th, C. Reutemann (79-Ford, 79/2)
Retired, M. Andretti (79-Ford, 79/5), brakes

**Monaco Grand Prix, Monte Carlo, 27 May, 156 miles**
3rd, C. Reutemann (79-Ford, 79/4)
Retired, M. Andretti (80-Ford, 80/1), rear suspension

**French Grand Prix, Dijon-Prenois, 1 July, 189 miles**
13th, C. Reutemann (79-Ford, 79/4), 3 laps in arrears, not running at the finish, accident
Retired, M. Andretti (80-Ford, 80/1), brakes, suspension, puncture

**British Grand Prix, Silverstone, 14 July, 199 miles**
8th, C. Reutemann (79-Ford, 79/5), 2 laps in arrears
Retired, M. Andretti (79-Ford, 79/4), wheel bearing

**German Grand Prix, Hockenheim, 29 July, 190 miles**
Retired, M. Andretti (79-Ford, 79/5), constant-velocity joint
Retired, C. Reutemann (79-Ford, 79/3), accident

**Austrian Grand Prix, Österreichring, 12 August, 199 miles**
Retired, C. Reutemann (79-Ford, 79/4), handling
Retired, M. Andretti (79-Ford, 79/5), clutch

**Dutch Grand Prix, Zandvoort, 26 August, 197 miles**
Retired, M. Andretti (79-Ford, 79/2), rear suspension
Retired, C. Reutemann (79-Ford, 79/4), accident damage

**Italian Grand Prix, Monza, 9 September, 180 miles**
5th, M. Andretti (79-Ford, 79/5)
7th, C. Reutemann (79-Ford, 79/4)

**Dino Ferrari Grand Prix, Imola, 16 September, 125 miles NC**
2nd, C. Reutemann (79-Ford, 79/2)

**Canadian Grand Prix, Île Notre Dame, Montreal, 30 September, 197 miles**
10th, M. Andretti (79-Ford, 79/5), 6 laps in arrears, not running at the finish, out of fuel
Retired, C. Reutemann (79-Ford, 79/3), rear suspension

**United States Grand Prix, Watkins Glen, 7 October, 199 miles**
Retired, M. Andretti (79-Ford, 79/5), gearbox
Retired, C. Reutemann (79-Ford, 79/3), accident

Drivers' World Championship:    6th=, C. Reutemann, 20 points
                                10th=, M. Andretti, 14 points

Constructors' Cup:    4th, Lotus-Ford, 39 points

# 1980

**Argentine Grand Prix, Buenos Aires Autodrome, 13 January, 197 miles**
Retired, M. Andretti (81-Ford, 81/2), fuel metering unit
Retired, E. de Angelis (81-Ford, 81/1), suspension

**Brazilian Grand Prix, Interlagos, 27 January, 196 miles**
2nd, E. de Angelis (81-Ford, 81/1)
Retired, M. Andretti (81-Ford, 81/2), spun off

**South African Grand Prix, Kyalami, 1 March, 199 miles**
12th, M. Andretti (81-Ford, 81/2), 2 laps in arrears
Retired, E. de Angelis (81-Ford, 81/1), accident

**United States Grand Prix West, Long Beach, 30 March, 163 miles**
Retired, E. de Angelis (81-Ford, 81/3), accident
Retired, M. Andretti (81-Ford, 81/2), accident

**Belgian Grand Prix, Zolder, 4 May, 191 miles**
10th, E. de Angelis (81-Ford, 81/3), 3 laps in arrears, not running at the finish, accident
Retired, M. Andretti (81-Ford, 81/1), gear linkage

**Monaco Grand Prix, Monte Carlo, 18 May, 156 miles**
7th, M. Andretti (81-Ford, 81/2), 3 laps in arrears
9th, E. de Angelis (81-Ford, 81/3), 8 laps in arrears, not running at the finish, accident

**Spanish Grand Prix, Jarama, 1 June, 165 miles Note: Non-Championship as race declared illegal by FISA)**
3rd, E. de Angelis (81-Ford, 81/3)
Retired, M. Andretti (81-Ford, 81/2), engine

**French Grand Prix, Paul Ricard, 29 June, 195 miles**
Retired, M. Andretti (81-Ford, 81/1), gearbox
Retired, E. de Angelis (81-Ford, 81/3), clutch

**British Grand Prix, Brands Hatch, 13 July, 199 miles**
Retired, M. Andretti (81-Ford, 81/1), gearbox
Retired, E. de Angelis (81-Ford, 81/3), rear suspension

**German Grand Prix, Hockenheim, 10 August, 190 miles**
7th, M. Andretti (81-Ford, 81/1)
16th, E. de Angelis (81-Ford, 81/3), 1 lap in arrears, not running at the finish, wheel bearing

**Austrian Grand Prix, Österreichring, 17 August, 199 miles**
6th, E. de Angelis (81-Ford, 81/3)
Retired, M. Andretti (81-Ford, 81/1), engine

**Dutch Grand Prix, Zandvoort, 31 August, 190 miles**
8th, M. Andretti (81-Ford, 81/1), 2 laps in arrears, not running at the finish, out of fuel
Retired, N. Mansell (81B-Ford, 81B/l), brakes, accident
Retired, E. de Angelis (81-Ford, 81/3), accident

**Italian Grand Prix, Monza, 14 September, 186 miles**
4th, E. de Angelis (81-Ford, 81/3), 1 lap in arrears
Retired, M. Andretti (81-Ford, 81/1), engine
Did Not Start, N. Mansell (81-Ford, 81/2), failed to qualify

**Canadian Grand Prix, Île Notre Dame, Montreal, 28 September, 192 miles**
10th, E. de Angelis (81-Ford, 81/2), 2 laps in arrears
Retired, M. Andretti (81-Ford, 81/1), engine

**United States Grand Prix, Watkins Glen, 5 October, 199 miles**
4th, E. de Angelis (81-Ford, 81/2)
6th, M. Andretti (81-Ford, 81/3), 1 lap in arrears

Drivers' World Championship:    7th, E. de Angelis, 13 points
                                20th=, M. Andretti, 1 point

Constructors' Cup:    5th, Lotus-Ford, 14 points

# 1981

**South African Grand Prix, Kyalami, 7 February, 196 miles (NOTE: race organized by FOCA with skirts permitted and not part of the World Championship)**
3rd, E. de Angelis (81-Ford, 81/3)
10th, N. Mansell (81-Ford, 81/2), 3 laps in arrears

**United States Grand Prix West, Long Beach, 15 March, 163 miles**
Retired, N. Mansell (81-Ford, 81/2), accident
Retired, E. de Angelis (81-Ford, 81/3), accident

**Brazilian Grand Prix, Jacarepagua, 29 March, 194 miles (NOTE: race scheduled to run one more lap, but stopped after 2 hours (62 laps) in accordance with FIA rules)**
5th, E. de Angelis (81-Ford, 81/3)
11th, N. Mansell (81-Ford, 81/2), 1 lap in arrears

**Argentine Grand Prix, Buenos Aires Autodrome, 12 April, 197 miles**
6th, E. de Angelis (81-Ford, 81/3), 1 lap in arrears
Retired, N. Mansell (81-Ford, 81/2), engine

**San Marino Grand Prix, Imola, 3 May, 188 miles**
Lotus entries withdrawn in dispute over the eligibility of the twin-chassis 88

**Belgian Grand Prix, Zolder, 17 May, 143 miles (race stopped short because of rain)**
3rd, N. Mansell (81-Ford, 81/1)
5th, E. de Angelis (81-Ford, 81/3)

**Monaco Grand Prix, Monte Carlo, 31 May, 156 miles**
Retired, E. de Angelis (87-Ford, 87/2), engine
Retired, N. Mansell (87-Ford, 87/1), rear suspension

**Spanish Grand Prix, Jarama, 21 June, 165 miles**
5th, E. de Angelis (87-Ford, 87/2)
6th, N. Mansell (87-Ford, 87/1)

**French Grand Prix, Dijon-Prenois, 5 July, 189 miles (NOTE: race stopped during cloudburst and restarted as track dried out)**
6th, E. de Angelis (87-Ford, 87/2), 1 lap in arrears
7th, N. Mansell (87-Ford, 87/1), 1 lap in arrears

**British Grand Prix, Silverstone, 18 July, 199 miles**
Retired, E. de Angelis (87-Ford, 87/3), black-flagged for overtaking under yellow flag and failed to rejoin race mistakenly believing that he was disqualified
Did Not Start, N. Mansell (87-Ford, 87/2), failed to qualify.

NOTE: Lotus entered the 88B twin-chassis cars, which were banned after the first practice session had started. 87/2 had been converted to 88B/2 for Silverstone and converted back to 87 specification overnight.

**German Grand Prix, Hockenheim, 2 August, 190 miles**
7th, E. de Angelis (87-Ford, 87/3), 1 lap in arrears
Retired, N. Mansell (87-Ford, 87/4), fuel leak

**Austrian Grand Prix, Österreichring, 16 August, 196 miles**
7th, E. de Angelis (87-Ford, 87/3), 1 lap in arrears
Retired, N. Mansell (87-Ford, 87/4), engine

**Dutch Grand Prix, Zandvoort, 30 August, 190 miles**
5th, E. de Angelis (87-Ford, 87/3), 1 lap in arrears
Retired, N. Mansell (87-Ford, 87/4), electrics

**Italian Grand Prix, Monza, 13 September, 187 miles**
4th, E. de Angelis (87-Ford, 87/3)
Retired, N. Mansell (87-Ford, 87/4), handling problems

**Canadian Grand Prix, Île Notre Dame, Montreal, 27 September, 173 miles**
6th, E. de Angelis (87-Ford, 87/3), 1 lap in arrears
Retired, N. Mansell (87-Ford, 87/5), accident

**Caesars Palace Grand Prix, Las Vegas, 17 October, 170 miles**
4th, N. Mansell (87-Ford, 87/5)
Retired, E. de Angelis (87-Ford, 87/3), water leak

Drivers' World Championship:  8th, E. de Angelis, 14 points
14th, N. Mansell, 8 points

Constructors' Cup:  7th, Lotus-Ford, 22 points

# 1982

**South African Grand Prix, Kyalami, 23 January, 196 miles**
8th, E. de Angelis (87B-Ford, 87/6), 1 lap in arrears
Retired, N. Mansell (87B-Ford, 87/5), electrics

**Brazilian Grand Prix, Jacarepagua, 21 March, 197 miles**
3rd, N. Mansell (91-Ford, 91/7)
Retired, E. de Angelis (91-Ford, 91/6), accident

**United States Grand Prix (Long Beach), 4 April, 161 miles**
5th, E. de Angelis (91-Ford, 91/6), 1 lap in arrears
7th, N. Mansell (9l-Ford, 91/7), 3 laps in arrears

**San Marino Grand Prix, Imola, 25 April, 188 miles**
FOCA supporting teams boycotted the race and Lotus did not run.

**Belgian Grand Prix, Zolder, 9 May, 185 miles**
4th, E. de Angelis (91-Ford, 91/6), 2 laps in arrears
Retired, N. Mansell (91-Ford, 91/7), clutch

**Monaco Grand Prix, Monte Carlo, 23 May, 156 miles**
4th, N. Mansell 91-Ford, 91/7), 1 lap in arrears
5th, E. de Angelis (91-Ford, 91/6), 1 lap in arrears

**United States Grand Prix (Detroit), 6 June, 155 miles**
Retired, N. Mansell (91-Ford, 91/7), engine
Retired, E. de Angelis (91-Ford, 91/9), gearbox

**Canadian Grand Prix, Circuit Gilles Villeneuve, Montreal, 13 June, 192 miles**
4th, E. de Angelis (91-Ford, 91/6), 1 lap in arrears
Retired, N. Mansell (91-Ford, 91/7), accident

**Dutch Grand Prix, Zandvoort, 3 July, 190 miles**
Retired, E. de Angelis (91-Ford, 91/6), handling problems
Did Not Start, R. Moreno (91-Ford, 91/7), failed to qualify

**British Grand Prix, Brands Hatch, 18 July, 199 miles**
4th, E. de Angelis (91-Ford, 91/8)
Retired, N. Mansell (91-Ford, 91/7), handling problems, driver unwell

**French Grand Prix, Paul Ricard, 25 July, 195 miles**
12th, G. Lees (91-Ford, 91/6), 2 laps in arrears
Retired, E. de Angelis (91-Ford, 91/8), fuel pressure

**German Grand Prix, Hockenheim, 8 August, 190 miles**
9th, N. Mansell (91-Ford, 91/7), 2 laps in arrears
Retired, E. de Angelis (91-Ford, 91/8), transmission

**Austrian Grand Prix, Österreichring, 15 August, 196 miles**
1st, E. de Angelis (91-Ford, 91/8), 138.068 mph
Retired, N. Mansell (91-Ford, 91/7), engine

**Swiss Grand Prix, Dijon-Prenois, 29 August, 189 miles**
6th, E. de Angelis (91-Ford, 91/8), 1 lap in arrears
8th, N. Mansell (91-Ford, 91/7), 1 lap in arrears

**Italian Grand Prix, Monza, 12 September,
187 miles**
7th, N. Mansell (91-Ford, 91/7), 1 lap in arrears
Retired, E. de Angelis (91-Ford, 91/8), broken side-pod

**Caesars Palace Grand Prix, Las Vegas,
25 September, 170 miles**
Retired, E. de Angelis (91-Ford, 91/9), engine
Retired, N. Mansell (91-Ford, 91/8), accident, damaged
suspension

Drivers' World Championship:  9th, E. de Angelis, 23 points
14th, N. Mansell, 7 points

Constructors Cup:  6th, Lotus-Ford, 30 points

# 1983

**Brazilian Grand Prix, Jacarepagua, 13 March,
197 miles**
12th, N. Mansell (92-Ford, 92/10), 2 laps in arrears
Disqualified, E. de Angelis (93T-Renault, 93T/l), changing
from 92

**United States Grand Prix (Long Beach),
27 March, 153 miles**
12th, N. Mansell (92-Ford, 92/10), 3 laps in arrears
Retired, E. de Angelis (93T-Renault, 93T/1), tyres

**Race of Champions, Brands Hatch, 10 April,
106 miles NC**
Retired, N. Mansell (93T-Renault, 93T/2), handling problems

**French Grand Prix, Paul Ricard, 17 April,
195 miles**
Retired, E. de Angelis (93T-Renault, 93T/l), electrics
Retired, N. Mansell (92-Ford, 92/10), injured foot in pre-race
accident

**San Marino Grand Prix, Imola, 1 May, 188 miles**
12th, N. Mansell (92-Ford, 92/10), 4 laps in arrears, not
running at the finish, rear wing failure, accident
Retired, E. de Angelis (93T-Renault, 93T/1), handling
problems

**Monaco Grand Prix, Monte Carlo, 15 May,
156 miles**
Retired, E. de Angelis (93T-Renault, 93T/l), drive-shaft
Retired, N. Mansell (92-Ford, 92/10), accident

**Belgian Grand Prix, Spa-Francorchamps, 22 May,
173 miles**
9th, E. de Angelis (93T-Renault, 93T/1), 1 lap in arrears
Retired, N. Mansell (92-Ford, 92/10), gearbox

**United States Grand Prix (Detroit), 5 June,
150 miles**
6th, N. Mansell (92-Ford, 92/10), 1 lap in arrears
Retired, E. de Angelis (93T-Renault, 93T/1), transmission

**Canadian Grand Prix, Circuit Gilles Villeneuve,
Montreal, 12 June, 192 miles**
Retired, N. Mansell (92-Ford, 92/10), handling, tyres
Retired, E. de Angelis (93T-Renault, 93T/l), throttle linkage

**British Grand Prix, Silverstone, 16 July, 196 miles**
4th, N. Mansell (94T-Renault, 94T/2)
Retired, E. de Angelis (94T-Renault, 94T/l), engine flame-out

**German Grand Prix, Hockenheim, 17 August,
190 miles**
Retired, E. de Angelis (94T-Renault, 94T/l), overheating
Retired, N. Mansell (93T-Renault, 93T/l), engine

**Austrian Grand Prix, Österreichring, 14 August,
196 miles**
5th, N. Mansell (94T-Renault, 94T/2), 1 lap in arrears
Retired, E. de Angelis (94T-Renault, 94T/l), accident

**Dutch Grand Prix, Zandvoort, 28 August,
190 miles**
Retired, N. Mansell (94T-Renault, 94T/2), spun off
Retired, E. de Angelis (94T-Renault, 94T/3), fuel metering unit

**Italian Grand Prix, Monza, 11 September,
187 miles**
5th, E. de Angelis (94T-Renault, 94T/1)
8th, N. Mansell (94T-Renault, 94T/3)

**European Grand Prix, Brands Hatch,
25 September, 199 miles**
3rd, N. Mansell (94T-Renault, 94T/2)
Retired, E. de Angelis (94T-Renault, 94T/1), engine

**South African Grand Prix, Kyalami, 15 October,
196 miles**
Not classified, N. Mansell (94T-Renault, 94T/2), 9 laps in
arrears
Retired, E. de Angelis (94T-Renault, 94T/3), engine

Drivers' World Championship:  12th=, N. Mansell, 10 points
17th=, E. de Angelis, 2 points

Constructors' Cup:  7th=, Lotus, 12 points

# 1984

**Brazilian Grand Prix, Jacarepagua, 25 March,
191 miles**
3rd, E. de Angelis (95T-Renault, 95T/3)
Retired, N. Mansell (95T-Renault, 95T/2), accident

**South African Grand Prix, Kyalami, 7 April,
191 miles**
7th, E. de Angelis (95T-Renault, 95T/3), 4 laps in arrears
Retired, N. Mansell (95T-Renault, 95T/2), collapsed turbo inlet
duct

**Belgian Grand Prix, Zolder, 29 April, 185 miles**
5th, E. de Angelis (95T-Renault, 95T/3), 1 lap in arrears
Retired, N. Mansell (95T-Renault, 95T/2), clutch

**San Marino Grand Prix, Imola, 6 May, 188 miles**
3rd, E. de Angelis (95T-Renault, 95T/3), 1 lap in arrears
Retired, N. Mansell (95T-Renault, 95T/l), brakes, spun off

**French Grand Prix, Dijon-Prenois, 20 May,
187 miles**
3rd, N. Mansell (95T-Renault, 95T/2)
5th, E. de Angelis (95T-Renault, 95T/3)

**Monaco Grand Prix, Monte Carlo, 3 June,
64 miles (race stopped short because of rain)**
6th, E. de Angelis (95T-Renault, 95T/3)
Retired, N. Mansell (95T-Renault, 95T/2), accident

**Canadian Grand Prix, Circuit Gilles Villeneuve,
Montreal, 192 miles**
4th, E. de Angelis (95T-Renault, 95T/4) 1 lap in arrears
6th, N. Mansell (95T-Renault, 95T/2), 2 laps in arrears

**United States Grand Prix (Detroit), 24 June,
158 miles**
3rd, E. de Angelis (95T-Renault, 95T/4)
Retired, N. Mansell (95T-Renault, 95T/2), gearbox

**United States Grand Prix (Dallas), 8 July,
162 miles**
3rd, E. de Angelis (95T-Renault, 95T/3), 1 lap in arrears
6th, N. Mansell (95T-Renault, 95T/2), not running at the
finish, gearbox

**British Grand Prix, Brands Hatch, 22 July,
185 miles**
4th, E. de Angelis (95T-Renault, 95T/3), 1 lap in arrears
Retired, N. Mansell (95T-Renault, 95T/2), gearbox

**German Grand Prix, Hockenheim, 5 August,
186 miles**
4th, N. Mansell (95T-Renault, 95T/2)
Retired, E. de Angelis (95T-Renault, 95T/3), turbocharger

**Austrian Grand Prix, Österreichring, 19 August,
188 miles**
Retired, N. Mansell (95T-Renault, 95T/2), engine
Retired, E. de Angelis (95T-Renault, 95T/3), engine

**Dutch Grand Prix, Zandvoort, 26 August,
188 miles**
3rd, N. Mansell (95T-Renault, 95T/2)
4th, E. de Angelis (95T-Renault, 95T/3), 1 lap in arrears

**Italian Grand Prix, Monza, 9 September, 184 miles**
Retired, E. de Angelis (95T-Renault, 95T/3), gearbox
Retired, N. Mansell (95T-Renault, 95T/2), spun off

**European Grand Prix, Nürburgring, 7 October,
189 miles**
Retired, N. Mansell (95T-Renault, 95T/2), engine
Retired, E. de Angelis (95T-Renault, 95T/3), turbocharger

**Portuguese Grand Prix, Estoril, 21 October,
189 miles**
5th, E. de Angelis (95T-Renault, 95T/4)
Retired, N. Mansell (95T-Renault, 95T/2), brake fluid loss,
spun off

| Drivers' World Championship: | 3rd, E. de Angelis, 34 points |
| | 9th=, N. Mansell, 13 points |
| Constructors' Championship: | 3rd, Lotus-Renault, 47 points |

# 1985

**Brazilian Grand Prix, Jacarepagua, 7 April,
191 miles**
3rd, E. de Angelis (97T-Renault, 97T/3), 1 lap in arrears
Retired, A. Senna (97T-Renault, 97T/2), electrics

**Portuguese Grand Prix, Estoril, 21 April,
181 miles**
1st, A. Senna (97T-Renault, 97T/2), 90.20 mph
4th, E. de Angelis (97T-Renault, 97T/3), 1 lap in arrears

**San Marino Grand Prix, Imola, 5 May, 188 miles**
1st, E. de Angelis (97T-Renault, 97T/3), 119.18 mph
7th, A. Senna (97T-Renault, 97T/2), 3 laps in arrears, not
running at the finish, out of fuel

**Monaco Grand Prix, Monte Carlo, 19 May,
161 miles**
3rd, E. de Angelis (97T-Renault, 97T/1)
Retired, A. Senna (97T-Renault, 97T/2), engine

**Canadian Grand Prix, Circuit Gilles Villeneuve,
Montreal, 16 June, 192 miles**
5th, E. de Angelis (97T-Renault, 97T/3)
16th, A. Senna (97T-Renault, 97T/2), 5 laps in arrears

**United States Grand Prix, (Detroit), 23 June,
158 miles**
5th, E. de Angelis (97T-Renault, 97T/3)
Retired, A. Senna (97T-Renault, 97T/2), accident

**French Grand Prix, Paul Ricard, 7 July, 191 miles**
5th, E. de Angelis (97T-Renault, 97T/3)
Retired, A. Senna (97T-Renault, 97T/4), engine failure,
accident

**British Grand Prix, Silverstone, 21 July, 191 miles
(race due to run 66 laps, but stopped at 65 laps in
error)**
10th, A. Senna (97T-Renault, 97T/4), 5 laps in arrears, not
running at the finish, fuel injection, electronics
Not classified, E. de Angelis (97T-Renault, 97T/3), 28 laps in
arrears

**German Grand Prix, Nürburgring, 4 August,
189 miles**
Retired, E. de Angelis (97T-Renault, 97T/3), engine
Retired, A. Senna (97T-Renault, 97T/4), constant-velocity joint

**Austrian Grand Prix, Österreichring, 18 August,
192 miles**
2nd, A. Senna (97T-Renault, 97T/4)
5th, E. de Angelis (97T-Renault, 97T/2)

**Dutch Grand Prix, Zandvoort, 25 August,
185 miles**
3rd, A. Senna (97T-Renault, 97T/4)
5th, E. de Angelis (97T-Renault, 97T/3), 1 lap in arrears

**Italian Grand Prix, Monza, 8 September, 184 miles**
3rd, A. Senna (97T-Renault, 97T/4)
6th, E. de Angelis (97T-Renault, 97T/3), 1 lap in arrears

**Belgian Grand Prix, Spa-Francorchamps,
15 September, 186 miles**
1st, A. Senna (97T-Renault, 97T/4), 117.94 mph
Retired, E. de Angelis (97T-Renault, 97T/3), turbocharger

**European Grand Prix, Brands Hatch, 6 October,
196 miles**
2nd, A. Senna (97T-Renault, 97T/4)
5th, E. de Angelis (97T-Renault, 97T/3), 1 lap in arrears

**South African Grand Prix, Kyalami, 19 October,
191 miles**
Retired, E. de Angelis (97T-Renault, 97T/3), engine
Retired, A. Senna (97T-Renault, 97T/4), engine

**Australian Grand Prix, Adelaide, 3 November,
192 miles**
Retired, A. Senna (97T-Renault, 97T/4), engine
Disqualified, E. de Angelis (97T-Renault, 97T/3), joining grid
position after delay on warming-up lap

| Drivers' World Championship: | 4th, A. Senna, 38 points |
| | 5th, E. de Angelis, 33 points |
| Constructors' Cup: | 4th, Lotus, 71 points |

## 1986

**Brazilian Grand Prix, Jacarepagua, 23 March, 191 miles**
2nd, A. Senna (98T-Renault, 98T/3)
9th, J. Dumfries (98T-Renault, 98T/2), 3 laps in arrears

**Spanish Grand Prix, Jerez, 13 April, 189 miles**
1st, A. Senna (98T-Renault, 98T/3), 104.07 mph
Retired, J. Dumfries (98T-Renault, 98T/2), gearbox

**San Marino Grand Prix, Imola, 27 April, 188 miles**
Retired, A. Senna (98T-Renault, 98T/3), wheel bearing
Retired, J. Dumfries (98T-Renault, 98T/2), wheel bearing

**Monaco Grand Prix, Monte Carlo, 11 May, 161 miles**
3rd, A. Senna (98T-Renault, 98T/3)
Did Not Start, J. Dumfries (98T-Renault, 98T/2), failed to qualify

**Belgian Grand Prix, Spa-Francorchamps, 25 May, 185 miles**
2nd, A. Senna (98T-Renault, 98T/3)
Retired, J. Dumfries (98T-Renault, 98T/2), spun off, holed radiator

**Canadian Grand Prix, Circuit Gilles Villeneuve, 15 June, 189 miles**
5th, A. Senna (98T-Renault, 98T/3), 1 lap in arrears
Retired, J. Dumfries (98T-Renault, 98T/l), accident

**United States Grand Prix (Detroit), 22 June, 158 miles**
1st, A. Senna (98T-Renault, 98T/3), 84.97 mph
7th, J. Dumfries (98T-Renault, 98T/2), 2 laps in arrears

**French Grand Prix, Paul Ricard, 6 July, 190 miles**
Retired, J. Dumfries (98T-Renault, 98T/2), engine
Retired, A. Senna (98T-Renault, 98T/3), accident

**British Grand Prix, Brands Hatch, 13 July, 196 miles**
7th, J. Dumfries (98T-Renault, 98T/2), 3 laps in arrears
Retired, A. Senna (98T-Renault, 98T/1), gearbox

**German Grand Prix, Hockenheim, 27 July, 186 miles**
2nd, A. Senna (98T-Renault, 98T/4)
Retired, J. Dumfries (98T-Renault, 98T/2), water radiator

**Hungarian Grand Prix, Hungaroring, 10 August, 190 miles**
2nd, A. Senna (98T-Renault, 98T/4)
5th, J. Dumfries (98T-Renault, 98T/2), 2 laps in arrears

**Austrian Grand Prix, Österreichring, 17 August, 192 miles**
Retired, A. Senna (98T-Renault, 98T/4), engine
Retired, J. Dumfries (98T-Renault, 98T/2), engine

**Italian Grand Prix, Monza, 7 September, 184 miles**
Retired, J. Dumfries (98T-Renault, 98T/2), gearbox
Retired, A. Senna (98T-Renault, 98T/4), transmission

**Portuguese Grand Prix, Estoril, 21 October, 189 miles**
4th, A. Senna (98T-Renault, 98T/4), 1 lap in arrears
9th, J. Dumfries (98T-Renault, 98T/2), 2 laps in arrears

**Mexican Grand Prix, Autodromo Hermanos Rodriguez, 12 October, 187 miles**
3rd, A. Senna (98T-Renault, 98T/4)
Retired, J. Dumfries (98T-Renault, 98T/2), electrics

**Australian Grand Prix, Adelaide, 26 October, 192 miles**
6th, J. Dumfries (98T-Renault, 98T/2), 2 laps in arrears
Retired, A. Senna (98T-Renault, 98T/4), engine

Drivers' World Championship: 4th, A. Senna, 55 points
13th=, J. Dumfries, 3 points

Constructors' Cup: 3rd, Lotus, 58 points

## 1987

**Brazilian Grand Prix, Jacarepagua, 12 April, 191 miles**
7th, S. Nakajima (99T-Honda, 99T/l), 2 laps in arrears
Retired, A. Senna (99T-Honda, 99T/4), engine

**San Marino Grand Prix, Imola, 3 May, 185 miles**
2nd, A. Senna (99T-Honda, 99T/4)
6th, S. Nakajima (99T-Honda, 99T/3), 2 laps in arrears

**Belgian Grand Prix, Spa-Francorchamps, 17 May, 185 miles**
5th, S. Nakajima (99T-Honda, 99T/l), 1 lap in arrears
Retired, A. Senna (99T-Honda, 99T/4), accident

**Monaco Grand Prix, Monte Carlo, 31 May, 161 miles**
1st, A. Senna (99T-Honda, 99T/4), 82.08 mph
10th, S. Nakajima (99T-Honda, 99T/l), 3 laps in arrears

**United States Grand Prix (Detroit), 21 June, 158 miles**
1st, A. Senna (99T-Honda, 99T/4), 85.70 mph
Retired, S. Nakajima (99T-Honda, 99T/l), accident

**French Grand Prix, Paul Ricard, 5 July, 190 miles**
4th, A. Senna (99T-Honda, 99T/4), 1 lap in arrears
Not classified, S. Nakajima (99T-Honda, 99T/l), 9 laps in arrears

**British Grand Prix, Silverstone, 12 July, 193 miles**
3rd, A. Senna (99T-Honda, 99T/4), 1 lap in arrears
4th, S. Nakajima (99T-Honda, 99T/5), 2 laps in arrears

**German Grand Prix, Hockenheim, 26 July, 186 miles**
3rd, A. Senna (99T-Honda, 99T/4), 1 lap in arrears
Retired, S. Nakajima (99T-Honda, 99T/3), turbocharger

**Hungarian Grand Prix, Hungaroring, 9 August, 190 miles**
2nd, A. Senna (99T-Honda, 99T/4)
Retired, S. Nakajima (99T-Honda, 99T/3), drive-shaft

**Austrian Grand Prix, Österreichring, 16 August, 192 miles**
5th, A. Senna (99T-Honda, 99T/6), 2 laps in arrears
13th, S. Nakajima (99T-Honda, 99T/3), 3 laps in arrears

**Italian Grand Prix, Monza, 6 September, 180 miles**
2nd, A. Senna (99T-Honda, 99T/4)
11th, S. Nakajima (99T-Honda, 99T/3), 3 laps in arrears

**Portuguese Grand Prix, Estoril, 21 September, 189 miles**
7th, A. Senna (99T-Honda, 99T/4), 2 laps in arrears
8th, S. Nakajima (99T-Honda, 99T/3), 2 laps in arrears

**Spanish Grand Prix, Jerez, 27 September, 189 miles**
5th, A. Senna (99T-Honda, 99T/4)
9th, S. Nakajima (99T-Honda, 99T/3), 2 laps in arrears

**Mexican Grand Prix, Autodromo Hermanos Rodriguez, 18 October, 173 miles**
Retired, A. Senna (99T-Honda, 99T/6), clutch, spun off
Retired, S. Nakajima (99T-Honda, 99T/3), accident

**Japanese Grand Prix, Suzuka, 1 November, 186 miles**
2nd, A. Senna (99T-Honda, 99T/6)
6th, S. Nakajima (99T-Honda, 99T/3)

**Australian Grand Prix, Adelaide, 15 November, 192 miles**
Retired, S. Nakajima (99T-Honda, 99T/3), hydraulics leak
Disqualified, A. Senna (99T-Honda, 99T/4), finished second, but disqualified because of over-size brake ducts

Drivers' World Championship:     3rd, A. Senna, 57 points
                                            11th=, S. Nakajima, 7 points

Constructors' Cup:     3rd, Lotus-Honda, 64 points

# 1988

**Brazilian Grand Prix, Jacarepagua, 3 April, 188 miles**
3rd, N. Piquet (100T-Honda, 100T/2)
6th, S. Nakajima (100T-Honda, 100T/1), 1 lap in arrears

**San Marino Grand Prix, Imola, 1 May, 188 miles**
3rd, N. Piquet (100T-Honda, 100T/2), 1 lap in arrears
8th, S. Nakajima (100T-Honda, 100T/l), 1 lap in arrears

**Monaco Grand Prix, Monte Carlo, 15 May, 161 miles**
Retired, N. Piquet (100T-Honda, 100T/2), damaged nose wing
Did Not Start, S. Nakajima (100T-Honda, 100T/1), failed to qualify

**Mexican Grand Prix, Autodromo Hermanos Rodriguez, 29 May, 184 miles**
Retired, N. Piquet (100T-Honda, 100T/2), engine
Retired, S. Nakajima (100T-Honda, 100T/4), turbocharger

**Canadian Grand Prix, Circuit Gilles Villeneuve, 12 June, 188 miles**
4th, N. Piquet (100T-Honda, 100T/2), 1 lap in arrears
11th, S. Nakajima (100T-Honda, 100T/4), 3 laps in arrears

**United States Grand Prix (Detroit), 19 June, 158 miles**
Retired, N. Piquet (100T-Honda, 100T/2), accident
Did Not Start, S. Nakajima (100T/4), failed to qualify

**French Grand Prix, Paul Ricard, 3 July, 190 miles**
5th, N. Piquet (100T-Honda, 100T/3), 1 lap in arrears
7th, S. Nakajima (100T-Honda, 100T/1), 1 lap in arrears

**British Grand Prix, Silverstone, 10 July, 193 miles**
5th, N. Piquet (100T-Honda, 100T/3)
10th, S. Nakajima (100T-Honda, 100T/1), 1 lap in arrears

**German Grand Prix, Hockenheim, 24 July, 186 miles**
9th, S. Nakajima (100T-Honda, 100T/1), 1 lap in arrears
Retired, N. Piquet (100T-Honda, 100T/2), spun off

**Hungarian Grand Prix, Hungaroring, 7 August, 190 miles**
7th, S. Nakajima (100T-Honda, 100T/2), 3 laps in arrears
8th, N. Piquet (100T-Honda, 100T/1), 3 laps in arrears

**Belgian Grand Prix, Spa-Francorchamps, 28 August, 185 miles**
6th, N. Piquet (100T-Honda, 100T/2)
Retired, S. Nakajima (100T-Honda, 100T/1), engine

**Italian Grand Prix, Monza, 11 September, 184 miles**
Retired, S. Nakajima (100T-Honda, 100T/1), engine
Retired, N. Piquet (100T-Honda, 100T/2), clutch, spun off

**Portuguese Grand Prix, Estoril, 25 September, 189 miles**
Retired, N. Piquet (100T-Honda, 100T/2), clutch
Retired, S. Nakajima (100T-Honda, 100T/1), spun off

**Spanish Grand Prix, Jerez, 2 October, 189 miles**
8th, N. Piquet (100T-Honda, 100T/2)
Retired, S. Nakajima (100T-Honda, 100T/1), spun off

**Japanese Grand Prix, Suzuka, 30 October, 186 miles**
7th, S. Nakajima (100T-Honda, 100T/1), 1 lap in arrears
Retired, N. Piquet (100T-Honda, 100T/2), driver unwell

**Australian Grand Prix, Adelaide, 13 November, 192 miles**
3rd, N. Piquet (100T-Honda, 100T/2)
Retired, S. Nakajima (100T-Honda, 100T/1), accident

Drivers' World Championship:     6th, N. Piquet, 20 points
                                            16th=, S. Nakajima, 1 point

Constructors' Cup:     4th, Lotus, 21 points

# 1989

**Brazilian Grand Prix, Jacarepagua, 26 March, 191 miles**
8th, S. Nakajima (101-Judd, 101/1), 1 lap in arrears
Retired, N. Piquet (101-Judd, 101/2), fuel pump

**San Marino Grand Prix, Imola, 23 April, 191 miles**
Not classified, S. Nakajima (101-Judd, 101/1), 12 laps in arrears
Retired, N. Piquet (101-Judd, 101/3), engine

**Monaco Grand Prix, Monte Carlo, 7 May, 159 miles**
Retired, N. Piquet (101-Judd, 101/2), accident
Did Not Start, S. Nakajima (101-Judd, 101/3), failed to qualify

**Mexican Grand Prix, Autodromo Hermanos Rodriguez, 28 May, 190 miles**
11th, N. Piquet (101-Judd, 101/2), 1 lap in arrears
Retired, S. Nakajima (101-Judd, 101/3), gearbox

**United States Grand Prix, Phoenix, 4 June, 177 miles**
Retired, N. Piquet (101-Judd, 101/2), accident
Retired, S. Nakajima (101-Judd, 101/3), throttle cable

**Canadian Grand Prix, Circuit Gilles Villeneuve, Montreal, 18 June, 188 miles**
4th, N. Piquet (101-Judd, 101/2)
Did Not Start, S. Nakajima (101-Judd, 101/3), failed to qualify

**French Grand Prix, Paul Ricard, 9 July, 190 miles**
8th, N. Piquet (101-Judd, 101/4), 2 laps in arrears
Retired, S. Nakajima (101-Judd, 101/2), engine cut out

**British Grand Prix, Silverstone, 16 July, 190 miles**
4th, N. Piquet (101-Judd, 101/4)
8th, S. Nakajima (101-Judd, 101/2), 1 lap in arrears

**German Grand Prix, Hockenheim, 30 July, 190 miles**
5th, N. Piquet (101-Judd, 101/4), 1 lap in arrears
Retired, S. Nakajima (101-Judd, 101/3), spun off

**Hungarian Grand Prix, Hungaroring, 13 August, 190 miles**
6th, N. Piquet (101-Judd, 101/4)
Retired, S. Nakajima (101-Judd, 101/3), accident

**Belgian Grand Prix, Spa-Francorchamps, 27 August, 190 miles**
Did Not Start, N. Piquet (101-Judd, 101/4), failed to qualify
Did Not Start, S. Nakajima (101-Judd, 101/3), failed to qualify

**Italian Grand Prix, Monza, 10 September, 191 miles**
10th, S. Nakajima (101-Judd, 101/3), 2 laps in arrears
Retired, N. Piquet (101-Judd, 101/4), spun off

**Portuguese Grand Prix, Estoril, 24 September, 192 miles**
7th, S. Nakajima (101-Judd, 101/3), 1 lap in arrears
Retired, N. Piquet (101-Judd, 101/4), accident

**Spanish Grand Prix, Jerez, 1 October, 191 miles**
8th, N. Piquet (101-Judd, 101/4), 2 laps in arrears
Retired, S. Nakajima (101-Judd, 101/3), accident

**Japanese Grand Prix, Suzuka, 22 October, 193 miles**
4th, N. Piquet (101-Judd, 101/4)
Retired, S. Nakajima (101-Judd, 101/3), engine

**Australian Grand Prix, Adelaide, 5 November, 164 miles**
4th, S. Nakajima (101-Judd, 101/3)
Retired, N. Piquet (101-Judd, 101/4), accident

| | |
|---|---|
| Drivers' World Championship: | 8th, N. Piquet, 12 points |
| | 21st=, S. Nakajima, 3 points |
| Constructors' Cup: | 6th, Lotus, 15 points |

# Bibliography

*Autosport Lotus File* (Temple Press, Twickenham, 1988)

*Classic & Sportscar Lotus File: Seven, Elite, Elan, Europa* by Mark Hughes (Temple Press, Twickenham, 1986)

*Colin Chapman's Lotus* by Robin Read (Foulis, Yeovil, 1989)
Former Sales Manager's personal story of the early days of Lotus at Cheshunt

*Colin Chapman: The Man and His Cars* by Gérard Crombac (Patrick Stephens Ltd, Wellingborough, 1986)
The only real biography of Chapman, very bland and highlighting his qualities, whilst ignoring his shortcomings.

*Illustrated Lotus Buyer's Guide* by Graham Arnold (Motorbooks, Osceola, 1986)

*The Legend of the Lotus Seven* by Dennis Ortenburger (The Newport Press, Costa Mesa, Osprey Publishing, London, 1981)
A clear and well-written sort-out of these confusing cars.

*Lotus* by Andrew Ferguson (Grand Prix Guides No 15, Kimberley, London, 1983)

*Lotus: The Complete Story* by Chris Harvey (Foulis, Yeovil, 1983)
In fact, a very brief résumé.

*The Lotus & Caterham Sevens* by Jeremy Coulter (Motor Racing Publications, London, 1985)
All the books in MRP's Collectors' Guides are excellent surveys of their subject.

*Lotus & Caterham Seven Gold Portfolio* (Brooklands Books, Surrey, 1988)

*Lotus Elan Auto History* by Ian Ward (Osprey, London, 1984)

*Lotus Elan, 1962–1973* (Brooklands Books Surrey, 1986)

*Lotus Elan 1962–74, Collection No. 1* (Brooklands Books, Surrey, 1986)

*Lotus Elan 1963–72, Collection No. 2* (Brooklands Books, Surrey, 1986)

*Lotus Elan Gold Portfolio* (Brooklands Books, Surrey 1988)
The Brooklands books are excellent collections of road test reprints.

*Lotus Elan, Super Profile* by Graham Arnold (Haynes Publishing Group, Yeovil, 1987)

*Lotus: The Elan, Cortina & Europa* by Richard Newton and Raymond Psulkowski (TAB Books, Blue RidgeSummit, 1986)

*The Lotus Elan and Europa* by John Bolster (Motor Racing Publications, London, Reprinted, 1985)

*The Lotus Eleven* by Dennis Ortenburger (Patrick Stephens, Wellingborough, 1988)
Not very well produced, but a comprehensive book on an important subject.

*The Lotus Elite* by Dennis Ortenburger (Patrick Stephens, Wellingborough, 1990)

*Lotus, The Elite, Elan & Europa* by Chris Harvey (Oxford Illustrated Press, Yeovil, 1982)
A beautifully illustrated and detailed account of these early models

*Lotus Elite, 1957–64* (Brooklands Books, Surrey, 1985)

*Lotus Elite and Eclat, 1974–81* (Brooklands Books, Surrey, 1986)

*Lotus Seven, 1957–80* (Brooklands Books, Surrey, 1985)

*Lotus Esprit Turbo* by J. Simister (Salamander Books, London, 1989)
Beautifully illustrated book on current production car.

*Lotus, The Sports, GT and Touring Cars* by Chris Harvey (Osprey, London, 1982)
Nicely illustrated, but rather superficial.

*Lotus: The Sports-Racing Cars* by Anthony Pritchard (Patrick Stephens, Wellingborough, 1987)
Not the author's best, but the only book devoted to the sports-racing cars.

*The Original 1962–1973 Lotus Elan* by Paul Robinson and Christopher Ross (Motor Racing Publications, Croydon, 1989)
Described on the cover as 'Essential Data and Guidance for Owners, Restorers and Competitors', this is a very accurate representation, fully endorsed.

*The Original Lotus Elite* by Dennis Ortenburger (The Newport Press, Costa Mesa, California, 1977)
A well researched and well illustrated book on the first – and perhaps the finest – Lotus road cars.

*The Sporting Fords, Volume 1: Cortinas* by Graham Robson (Motor Racing Publications, London, Second Edition, 1989)
Full run-down of the Lotus-Cortina included.

*The Story of Lotus 1947–1960. Growth of a Legend* by Ian H. Smith (Motor Racing Publications Ltd, London, 1970)
Revised edition of the enthusiastic and very readable *Lotus – The Story of the Marque.*

*The Story of Lotus, 1961–1967 Growth of a legend* by Doug Nye (Motor Racing Publications Ltd, London, 1972)
Comprehensive successor volume to the above.

*The Story of the Marque Lotus* by Ian H. Smith with additions by Michael Henderson (Motor Racing Publications, London, Second Edition, 1961)
The original, very personal Lotus Story.

*Theme Lotus* by Doug Nye (Motor Racing Publications, London, Second Edition, 1986)
The standard book on Formula 1 and Indianapolis Lotus cars by the standard Formula 1 marque historian.

*The Third Generation Lotuses* by Graham Robson (Motor Racing Publications, 1983)
The Collector's guide to the new Elite, Eclat, Esprit and Excel, but now needs updating.

The author recognizes that there may be omissions in this list and would welcome details of any omitted or new titles c/o Aston Publications.